ALL ROADS HOME

ALL ROADS HOME

A LIFE ON AND OFF THE ICE

BRYAN TROTTIER
WITH STEPHEN BRUNT

McClelland & Stewart

Paperback edition published 2024
Hardcover edition published 2022

Library and Archives Canada Cataloguing in Publication
Title: All roads home : a life on and off the ice / Bryan Trottier, Stephen Brunt.
Names: Trottier, Bryan, 1956- author. | Brunt, Stephen, author.
Identifiers: Canadiana 2022019324X | ISBN 9780771084492 (softcover)
Subjects: LCSH: Trottier, Bryan, 1956- | LCSH: Hockey players—Canada—Biography. |
CSH: First Nations hockey players—Canada—Biography. | LCGFT: Autobiographies.
Classification: LCC GV848.5.T76 A3 2023 | DDC 796.962092—dc23

All photographs are courtesy of the author unless otherwise specified.

Book design by Andrew Roberts
Cover art: front cover image © Bruce Bennett / Getty Images
Typeset in Dante by Sean Tai, Toronto

Printed in the United States of America

McClelland & Stewart,
a division of Penguin Random House Canada Limited,
a Penguin Random House Company

www.penguinrandomhouse.ca

1st Printing

For Buzz and Mary. I love you, I miss you

CONTENTS

HOCKEY ACCOMPLISHMENTS

First Hockey Goal—1964

Climax-Val Marie Weyburn Peewee Champions—1967, 1968

Climax Yorkton Bantam Champions—1970

Climax Provincial Midget Champions—1971, 1972

Swift Current Wrigley Midget Champions—1972

WCHL All-Star—1975

WCHL Player of the Year—1975

World Junior Team Canada MVP—1975

9 NHL All-Star Games—1976, 1978, 1980, 1981, 1982, 1983, 1985, 1986, 1992

Calder Memorial Trophy as NHL's Rookie of the Year—1975-76

2 1st Team All-Star Selections—1978, 1979

Hart Memorial Trophy as NHL's Most Valuable Player (Regular Season)—1978-79

Art Ross Trophy as NHL's Regular-Season Point Leader—1978-79

Conn Smythe Trophy as NHL's Most Valuable Player (Playoffs)—1979-80

6 Stanley Cups as Player—1980, 1981, 1982, 1983, 1991, 1992

2 2nd Team All-Star Selection—1982, 1984

Budweiser NHL Man of the Year—1988-89

King Clancy Memorial Trophy as Player Who Exemplifies Leadership—1988-89

Inducted into Saskatchewan Sports Hall of Fame—1997

Inducted into Hockey Hall of Fame—1997

National Aboriginal Achievement Award—1998

National Aboriginal Achievement Award—1998

1 Stanley Cup as Assistant Coach—2001

Inducted into Saskatchewan Hockey Hall of Fame—2012

Eagle Feather Recipient—2014

Inducted into Canada's Sports Hall of Fame—2016

NHL Top 100 Player Selection—2017

FOREWORD

THE DREAM OF A VAL MARIE FARM BOY

by Jesse Thistle

Growing up in Canada in the early '80s meant one thing for boys—playing street hockey as the Stanley Cup–winning dynasty of the New York Islanders. My buddy Aaron was always scoring ace and right-winger Mike Bossy. I, on centre, was Mr. MVP, Mr. Art Ross, Mr. Bryan Trottier himself. My buddy Leeroy was Clarke Gillies to complete the deadly Trio Grande line. Our street hockey team was the Hockley Hawks—we lived on Hockley Path—but we weren't very good. We had none of the magic of the famed Islanders. We never won one trophy in any of the street hockey leagues we entered, even the imaginary kind.

My love of the Islanders started when my grandpa Cyril once said, while watching their famed '82 playoff run, "That kid there with the moustache, Trottier; he's Native and from Saskatchewan like you boys. Isn't that something?" My grandpa was referring to me and my two brothers, ourselves half Métis-Cree from Saskatchewan, who'd been taken in by our paternal grandparents in Brampton, Ontario, after my mom and dad couldn't be around for us. From the day my grandpa told me about Trottier's background, I played Trottier on our street, and did so even as the dynasty started to fall apart. There were so few known Indigenous players back then; it really meant something to see one in the NHL. And the fact he was one of the best players of his era, well, that made me—and I'm sure many other Native kids back then—very proud. It gave us a hero to emulate; a dream to aspire to; a positive role model to follow. Beyond that, it also gave us some wicked Trottier O-Pee-Chee Hockey cards—none for trade ups or trade aways, only accruing. I'd still trade away a Gretzky for a Trottier any day.

Just how decorated an athlete Bryan Trottier became, however, even I did not know until I read this memoir. He stands as *the most decorated Indigenous athlete of all time in all of professional sports*. And I'll tell you why most people do not know that Trottier stands as the G.O.A.T Indigenous athlete—it's because he is humble. As you read this book remember this concept of humility; this is the mark of a true warrior for his people. Being humble is one of the seven grandfather teachings of Algonquian peoples in North America—Bryan is Michif (Métis), Cree, Chippewa (all three are Algonquian in culture), French, and Irish. The teaching of humility honours individual achievements as part of the complexity of Creation. Those who live by humility, the teaching states, instill great joy for one's people and their welfare without personal boasts or acts of pride. Indeed, those who live by humility let their actions speak for themselves; they lead by example. Bryan's humble leadership stood out to me time and again as he recounted when he hugged the Stanley Cup like his boyhood hero Jean Béliveau. Then the play-by-play in his other Cup wins, like the whole of this wonderful book, felt humble and powerful, like I was there skating alongside Bryan as it happened and he opened his heart and told you matter-of-factly what happened. I especially saw the kind of humble person Bryan was when he honoured his friend Tiger Williams for being there for him one very vulnerable and fateful night—a night where literally everything could've been different. I saw his humility again when he talked of his mother telling him to stay out of his teammate's crease, how he had to listen to his mom, and when she put the tape around his first goal puck (no matter how tough you are, you'll cry when you get to this part for sure—aren't we all just trying to make our moms proud?). And when he talked of ranching with his father Buzz, and the lessons of "bare down" and "don't do a job to get it done, do it to get it done right," and the time spent practicing his wrist shot on the frozen creek of their Val Marie farm.

I'd like to believe that Bryan's rise to be one of the greatest NHL players who ever lived was because of where he was raised and who his people are. The Trottiers are one of the most illustrious Métis-Cree bison hunting clans. I know this because I am an historian. The ranch Bryan grew up on in Val Marie now sits at the foot of the Grassland National Park, one of the most dramatic landscapes in all of Canada, if not the world. And there is a reason why Saskatchewan is called the land of the living sky. The terrain is comprised of rolling flats of domestic grasses as far as the eye can see, crowned with high-altitude flares of clouds like God's brush strokes over top of a canvas of infinite blue. The sunset photos can never capture just how special and immense and powerful it all is. You need but one look to know the Grasslands around Val Marie are sacred lands; this, the ancient home to the now returning bison. Trottier's bison-hunting ancestors would've ranged after the bison through the area of Val Marie, over the Cypress Hills, and down to Montana near Rocky Boy reservation, and over to the Missouri River, just as mine did. His ancestors even hunted with my own across the Montana ranges. Before colonization, the Trottiers were among the most wealthy and powerful Michif-Nehayaw clans, and when Canadian settlement took root out west after 1870, Bryan's family successfully secured a homestead acreage and passed it down through the generations to Bryan's time. For me, as a Métis-Cree historian and author, this was the strongest and most hopeful part of his story. I say this, because so many of us didn't secure land and were marginalized onto Crown land as squatters as Canada formed—this was what happened with my mother's Michif-Cree family, the Arcand-Morrissette clan, for their part in the Northwest Resistance under Louis Riel where Métis and Cree stood up to defend their lands against settler encroachment. Bryan's story in many ways represents the prospects of what Indigenous Peoples can offer if they have access to land and are given a shot. Like everyone else, they can benefit from the resources and wealth of the land, becoming successful farmers, landowners, hunters, ranchers, and athletes. And they can even produce legendary hockey players, the likes of which can go on to win seven Stanley Cups, instill great pride in Indigenous Peoples, and inspire generations of our youth to dream, much like I did when I played number 19 alongside my buddies years ago in that Brampton suburb. Trottier's career mirrors the epic land he grew up in and the storied people he came from—both are sacred and both represent the best of us Michif-Cree. Really, I don't think any other person could've been the G.O.A.T. Indigenous athlete of all time other than the dreaming farm boy, Trottier, from Val Marie.

Jesse Thistle

PROLOGUE

It was the spring of 1965. The game was back east, and we were at home on the ranch in Val Marie, Saskatchewan. I was eight years old. It is my first vivid memory of the National Hockey League.

I remember sitting on the floor, on a little blanket, watching TV with Mom and Dad. Even in black and white, you could tell the Stanley Cup was shiny. Funny, but somehow it seemed more shiny then than it does now. They handed the Cup to Jean Béliveau, but he didn't pump it up over his head the way players do now. Instead, he kind of grabbed it and hugged it.

I looked over at my dad, Buzz, sitting in his rocking chair, and he had a big smile on his face. He wasn't the biggest Montreal fan—the Toronto Maple Leafs were our team—but he loved Jean Béliveau. He loved all of the great players and he would praise them, even though in life Dad wasn't a guy who was inclined to offer a lot of praise. But Gordie Howe, Béliveau, the best of the best, those players he revered. And so I loved those players, too. I remember when I realized that Howe, the best player in hockey, grew up in Saskatchewan, just like I did. That was awesome.

"Dad," I said to him, "someday, I want to hold the Stanley Cup just like that."

"Well," Dad said, "you had better practice, then."

For every kid, it's a crazy dream, but for me, living on a ranch not far from the Montana border, I had never even played organized hockey.

We didn't have a minor league yet in Val Marie. I had just barely started to skate. My first pair were men's skates—hand-me-downs. They were so big that when I laced them up, the eyelets would be touching. I had to pack the sides with cardboard to make them stiffer, and I had to fill up the toes with Kleenex. I got my own first pair of skates for Christmas in 1963. Mom and Dad got them down at Jim Sharpe's store. I think they cost three bucks, and I remember reading that lettering on the blade: ST. LAWRENCE MANUFACTURING.

There was a twisted, winding creek that ran through our land, Frenchman Creek, with a beaver dam that created a larger pool. It would freeze over in winter and we would skate around all the stuff that was frozen into the ice—sticks and pieces of wood, everything that blew off the trees, even the odd dead cow. We would walk from the house down to the river, crawl down the riverbank, skate, skate, skate, then crawl back up to the house to warm up.

Dad just seemed to know when the ice needed to be flooded. After supper he would go down to the creek and say, "Watch this." The beaver dam had created a walkable bridge across the creek, a natural two-foot drop in the water level. Dad looked massive in the twilight evening dusk. Straddling the beaver dam, snow and ice sparkling, he swung the axe with ease and might, one swing right on target, breaking through the ice and twigs, and the water just flew out of there like it was coming out of a fire hydrant. It would flow over the old ice, and in the morning you'd have a fresh surface. It was just as if a Zamboni had gone over it. It was incredible.

I didn't know how to practise. I barely knew how to skate, let alone shoot and stickhandle a puck. My dad was a right-handed shot, and he showed me how to hold a stick, how to stickhandle, how to shoot. He put up a board that was my first makeshift net.

I would be down on this little creek, doing everything righty like my dad, trying to hit that board. If I tried to turn the stick over where it felt more comfortable, Dad would bark at me: "Hey! Left hand on top!"

Push, snap, weight—front foot to back foot, snap wrist, top one under, bottom wrist over. Point stick to target.

Dad hit it every time. He did it, and then he would smile, as if excited. I wanted that feeling.

It wasn't until I started playing street hockey with my friends, and then minor hockey when it finally came to town, that I realized I was actually a left-handed shot, but still, when Dad was around I'd kind of switch back and forth to keep him happy.

I thought every kid in Canada lived the way I did. I thought that everyone lived on a ranch and had an outhouse and did chores every morning and rode horses and went to rodeos and gymkhanas and could only get one channel on television and played music with their family and skated on a frozen creek. It felt so far away from the NHL.

MAY 24, 1980. NASSAU COLISEUM, UNIONDALE, NEW YORK.

This is that crazy dream.

When Bobby Nystrom scored the overtime goal against Philadelphia in Game Six that won the first Stanley Cup for the New York Islanders, the celebration started down in the corner of the rink, and everybody piled on top of him. But I never made it there. When I leaped off the bench, my back foot caught on the top of the boards and I went flying.

I can remember feeling so tired in that moment, completely exhausted—and I had never felt tired at all through the playoffs. The adrenalin just keeps you going, but the moment it's over, the moment you win and you know you're a champion, the adrenalin stops. I picked myself up off the ice, and the first guy I saw was Ken Morrow. He grabbed me and I hugged him. "Are you tired?" I asked him.

"Yeah, I'm tired," he said. "But we won the Cup!"

It's weird how your senses peak at certain times. I have a vivid memory of the horrible smell of Kenny's sweaty jersey as I hugged him. Your vision, your hearing, your sense of touch, your sense of smell, all your senses are just totally magnified as you try to grasp the moment.

Kenny let me go, and then Duane Sutter grabbed me, and we kind of did a jig on the ice, holding each other. We started towards the pack in the corner, and we were grabbing everyone along the way. I never quite made it to the pack, but I especially remember Gordie Lane and Clark Gillies in the middle of it, a pair of giants with those big, black playoff beards.

Now, all of a sudden, they were bringing the Cup out of the corner doors in the boards. Denis Potvin and I went over there, and I remember wanting to hug it, just like Jean Béliveau. I wanted to put my arms around it—so that's what I did. Denis grabbed one side and I grabbed the other and we both hugged it and stared at each other with crazy smiles on our faces. We both had tears in our eyes.

I'd sat next to Denis in the dressing room since my rookie year. Through all those years, this is what we had talked about. Now here we were—he was the captain and I was the alternate captain of the Stanley Cup champion New York Islanders. We'd done it.

As the captain, he got to be the first to grab the Cup and pump it up over his head. I was standing right next to him, and I reached up and grabbed hold of his hand and wouldn't let go.

"You want this?" Denis asked.

Of course I said yes.

When you hold the Cup for the first time, you notice how cool it is to the touch. You can feel the names that are engraved on it, and you start looking for your favourite players. I wanted to see Jean Béliveau's name, I wanted to see Gordie Howe's name, I wanted to see Stan Mikita's name. You could find them really fast if you knew what years to look for.

Immediately, there were guys trying to grab the Cup out of my hands. *Don't steal that away from me so fast!* I wanted to hold on to it for as long as I could.

Then Clarkie grabbed it and dashed out of the group of guys. He was so big, but he looked even more massive in that moment. He went to centre ice and kept pumping it up and down.

I just couldn't help myself. I went right behind him because I wanted to hold that thing again.

The crowd at the Coliseum was going crazy. The noise in that building was deafening. I can remember Gordie Lane talking to me and I couldn't hear a thing he said, even though he was a foot from my face. I was lip-reading—I think we all were, it was so bloody loud.

I looked up into the crowd and I picked out one face. There were fifteen thousand people screaming at us, and for some reason I locked on to this one lady, twenty-five rows up. I didn't know who she was, but somehow I could hear her voice over everyone else.

"We love you guys!" she screamed.

"I love you, too!" I screamed back at her.

There was something special about those fans on Long Island. When I first came to New York, I was really scared. I felt completely out of my element when I left our little town to play junior hockey in Swift Current, never mind going across the continent to one of the biggest cities in the world. I was petrified. I didn't want to fail. I felt like I was so young in a man's world. But it became my home. I was born in Saskatchewan, but I was raised on Long Island, I grew up on Long Island, I moved from childhood to manhood on Long Island. I felt like Long Island had adopted me, and of course I embraced it. I felt like part of the community, part of their family. It never felt like player and fan. It felt like we were all part of the same thing. Long Islanders.

We were their only professional sports team. We weren't New York. We weren't Manhattan. We were *the Islanders*. The Rangers got most of the press. We were the expansion team, the up-and-comers . . . and maybe if you were looking over from Manhattan, we were the stepchild, the country cousin. That's why we had such a great rivalry with the Rangers for all those years.

We were a young team. Maybe young and dumb, maybe young and naive. But that core group of guys were special, and tremendously talented. We had great management with Bill Torrey, great coaching with Al Arbour. And we got all of that support from the fans. We just loved being able to win for those people.

It was magical. In a lot of ways, indescribable—the sense of satisfaction, the dedication, the feeling of being appreciated. All of that goes through your mind in those seconds when you win it all. Everything comes together in that moment. You think about your family, about the sacrifices that were made, about your teammates and coaches throughout the years—all the people who got you there. I wanted to share it with them all. The guys I grew up with in Val Marie: Jeanson, Syrenne, Olson, Bellefeuille, Reid. My buddies in Climax: Desjardins, Kirk, and Goodall. Laidlaw, Mything, Jarman, and Gryde. My junior coaches, Stan Dunn and Earl Ingarfield. And of course my family, all of my family. I wanted them to feel that same sense of happiness and joy. It was complete satisfaction. And somewhere, I knew Tiger was smiling for me.

When you start out, you think, "If I could play one shift of one game in the NHL, I'd be happy." Then you get that one shift and you're so hungry for more. Then you score your first goal.

But from the beginning, I dreamed of winning the Stanley Cup. I wanted that feeling of being the best. And that memory of Jean Béliveau being handed the Cup, the shiniest of trophies, the symbol of hockey history, stayed with me. If you have your name engraved on it, it's going to be there forever.

And then, once that happens, once you're a champion, once the party is over, all you can think is: *How am I going to do that again?*

CHAPTER 1

VALLEY OF MARY

I love my hometown. I'm from Val Marie, a Saskatchewan prairie town, and it was a great place to grow up. The population was maybe five hundred then. It was vibrant, surrounded by farmers and ranchers. Main Street had three gas stations, a bunch of general stores—Labelle's, Syrenne's, Sharpe's, and Lizzie's. We also had a convent, the hospital, a church, and a school, all at the south end of town. The curling rink and skating rink were across from the school. And, like all of the towns on the prairies, it had a Beaver Lumber, a grain elevator, a hotel—a beer parlour, really—and a Chinese café.

Grampa Trottier lived three doors down from the town's blacksmith, and I remember always seeing piles of metal around. The rear alley separated the back door of the beer parlour from Grampa's outhouse. Everybody in town had an outhouse. *Oh glory!*

Val Marie was the last stop on the main railway line that connected it to little towns like Orkney, Bracken, Climax, and Shaunavon. These days, a lot of the kids have moved away and those little towns are just hanging on. All of the grain elevators are abandoned.

At nine o'clock every night, a siren went off, and that was the signal for all of the kids to get home. The siren was at the fire hall, where they kept the town's one fire truck. It was an old-fashioned truck with a big old drum on the back that required a lot of priming and pumping. A true beauty, a classic, vintage, painted in bright firehouse-red. If you were a kid and you heard the siren while you were walking back from the hockey rink or the curling rink, you knew you'd better get home fast—or else.

Mom and Dad met at a community dance in the early '50s. Dad's real name is Eldon, but he goes by Buzz Trottier. Where he got the nickname, nobody knows. His dad, John, was Cree-Métis, and his mom, Annie, was Chippewa, from Montana. Mom is from Climax, which is about forty miles down the road from Val Marie. Her maiden name is Gardner—Mary Gardner. I always loved when I heard someone call her name. Her ancestry is Irish, and her family had come to Saskatchewan to farm.

They were married in '54. Dad went to work on one of the big cattle ranches in the area because there wasn't enough money to support two families working the Trottier farm in Val Marie. Mom made a few extra dollars as the cook, too. Dad didn't work there very long; he took off to work on the oil and gas rigs because there was more money to be made. He did that for a couple of years, and that's what brought us to Redvers, Saskatchewan, near Weyburn, where I was born. From there, it was on to Rouleau and Moose Jaw.

After Dad passed away, at the visitation, a young man around my age came up and introduced himself to me and Mom. He told us the story of how a fella named Buzz Trottier saved his dad's life. They'd been working together on the rigs and my dad had pulled him out of a collapsing ditch. It was amazing to hear this. That's all he knew, yet he was still compelled to come. The young man had heard of Dad's passing and driven seven hours to pay his respects. I remember saying to my mom how impressed I was that this stranger had come all of that way to honour Dad and his memory. Of course, Dad had never said a word to any of us about this, but that was the kind of guy he was. He wasn't boastful about these things.

Some of my earliest childhood memories are of Buffalo, Wyoming. It was a real cowboy town in the foothills of the Rockies. Beautiful country. We lived in a cabin on the edge of town. My older sister Carol started school there, and that's where my brother Monty was born.

I can still remember the time when I was running to get away from Mom, who was angry with me for some reason or another. I looked back to see how far behind me she was and *wham*, I rammed into the nub of a low-hanging branch. I spent the next two hours having first aid performed on me by a less-angry Mom. I still have the scar on my forehead. I guess you could say that Buffalo, Wyoming, left its mark on me.

By 1960, my dad was working in road construction, so we left Buffalo and were living in a trailer that he could haul around to follow the crews. For a while we were in Malta, Montana, then to Colorado, and then to Hermosa, South Dakota, where we lived in a trailer court. That's where I started school. Dad's oldest sister, Laura, had married Emile de Montigny, who was from Whitefish, Montana. Uncle Emile and Dad were best friends. My uncle was the mechanic and Dad operated all of the machines, from road graders to push-cats. They took what used to be narrow little gravel roads and turned them into major interstate highways. They built a lot of Route 25 and Route 70 through the western US.

We moved around with the crews for a good couple of years. I learned to ride a bike down in Strasburg, Colorado. I remember Dad bought me my first baseball glove in Denver when I was five years old.

In the winter of 1962, we were in Fort Collins, Colorado. When I was in Grade 1, we moved back to Val Marie from the States. Grampa Trottier was getting older, so Dad came home to help out on the ranch and eventually took it over. We left Fort Collins in December and it was freezing cold when we got to Val Marie. Holy cow, was it cold! We moved into Grampa and Gramma's house for the winter while Dad worked at fixing up the ranch, because it was in need of some repair and updating.

Our family ranch was three and a half miles south of Val Marie. We lived in the farthest southeast corner of what was termed "the flat." The government had built some irrigation land just west and south of the town, and we were on the edge of one of the greatest natural landmarks, Seventy Mile Butte. You could see the butte out our picture window—it's part of Grasslands National Park now. It's beautiful country, wispy clouds against the blue sky, badlands, lots of coulees with all kinds of wildlife—white-tailed deer, mule deer, antelope, rattlesnakes, coyotes. My dad used to say, "People take this country for granted. I don't want you to ever take it for granted." And we never did. We loved it and still do.

We always had a small herd of cattle on the ranch, a bull or two, and lots of horses to ride. We had at least a couple of pigs and sometimes as many as twenty or thirty. Chickens were everywhere and we had one milk cow, Ana-May.

Our ranch house was small—maybe a thousand square feet—pretty small for our family at that time. At this point, there were my folks, me, my sisters, Carol and Kathy, and my brother Monty. Dad eventually added a lean-to kitchen to the front of the house. It wasn't big, but it was functional. There were two bedrooms in the back, a small hallway, a living room—and an outhouse in the backyard. We had a fuel-oil stove that kept the house nice and toasty.

My sister Carol got her own bed, and the rest of us had bunk beds. My brother Monty and I slept in the top bunk, and Kathy usually slept in the bottom bunk. After my younger brother Rocky was born, he had his crib in Mom and Dad's room. When I was about nine, I moved from the bunk bed to the couch in the living room.

We kept ranchers' hours. Mom and Dad were always up early, before the crack of dawn. It didn't matter if it was summer or winter. Mom would be cooking or making coffee, and Dad would be strumming the guitar or playing the accordion. That became our alarm clock. As soon as it was dark, everybody shut 'er down. But I was always the last one to go to bed. I would stay up, doing homework or drawing or playing sock hockey with Rowdy, the cow dog. It was nice and quiet with everyone else asleep.

On some weekends, when Dad would be playing late with his band, I'd stay up with Mom, who would be waiting for him to come home. I always had trouble sleeping as a kid, and Mom never fought it. I think she enjoyed the company as she did her crosswords and had a last cup of tea, which she called her "toddy"—tea with a splash of Irish whiskey. Maybe that's why I still enjoy a toddy and doing a crossword at night.

When I was seven years old, my baby sister Beverly was born. I can remember everything about her. I can remember her face. I can remember how adorably chubby she was. I can remember her soft little baby smile. And I can remember her funeral. Beverly died when she was six months old. A crib death.

We were in Malta, Montana, staying with my uncle George and aunt Shirley. Mom went in to check on Bev in the bedroom and came out saying that Bev wasn't breathing. Although I was young at the time, I could sense the panic in Mom's voice.

It was my first memory of death. Grandpa and Grandma Gardner came to town, and both families were together at Grampa Trottier's house. It was one of the only times I can recall them coming to Val Marie. We still have a picture of both families together from that time. You can see the sadness in everyone's eyes. And Mom looked completely drained. To this day, my heart aches for her and every mother who has had to endure such a loss.

When my brother Rocky came along in 1964, Mom was super protective. Rocky doesn't remember it now, but when he was a baby, there wasn't a second when she let him out of her sight.

Mom never spoke about Beverly after that. Never, ever, ever. We would ask her, "Mom, tell us about Beverly."

"No," she would reply, almost unemotionally.

So we just stopped asking. I think it was just too painful for her to relive the whole thing. And I never wanted my Mom sad, ever!

When Mom died, we found out that the burial plot below Beverly's grave was available. the five of us kids agreed that she was going to be buried right at the foot of Beverly's grave. We wanted Mom near her daughter. It felt good to have them so close to one another. I believe with my whole heart that they are resting peacefully in each other's presence.

CHAPTER 2
THE RANCH

Breeding, raising, and selling cattle was a big part of ranch life. We took in feeders, yearlings that my dad took to market in either the spring or fall, depending on what kind of price he could get for them. We fed them grain or hay all winter long to fatten them up. Dad took great pride in his livestock—good horses and good cattle. We didn't have a big herd, but he managed it well. Forty to eighty cows and usually four to twelve horses. Price swings on cattle made it a bit of a gamble, but we did it for quite a few winters when I was young.

Dad did a lot of bartering back then. A horse trader by nature, he loved to wheel and deal. Sometimes he'd trade horses for food, or sometimes for machinery. Pigs, cows, horses—something was always coming and going. Sometimes, a deal was made to make a couple of bucks; sometimes it was done to upgrade. And sometimes it was done just to help folks out. One time, Dad sold one of our best horses, L'il Bear, for a few bucks and three knot heads (Dad's term for the ugliest, stupidest, mulish horses in the country). They weren't good working horses, so my brother Monty and I thought it was a pretty bad trade. But Dad had a knack and was able to flip the knot heads into another deal or upgrade—a few piglets, a young bull, or a cow ready to be butchered.

We did a lot of haying, mostly in the riverbeds. We didn't have any farmland for grain, but the riverbeds would flood in the spring, and their rich, sandy soil produced really good alfalfa hay, which Dad also bartered and sold. We'd put up between 1,500 to 3,000 bales a year. There was a lot of baling to be done and a lot of bale picking. Dad tried to do a little grain farming in the riverbeds as well. He'd grow oats for the horses and some barley for the pigs. We did a little bit of seeding, a little bit of combining.

There was always a lot of work to do. It wasn't fun carrying five-gallon grain pails twice a day to those hundred or so head of yearlings every winter, but I think it helped work my upper body a bit. Dad called it "muscle development." *Okay, I got it.* He was trying to motivate me.

Throwing bales to feed the herd was a hoot because I got to steer the truck while Dad got in the back, busting bales and tossing them off in a long windrow. In the winter, if the snow got too deep, it was by horse and sled.

There were times when it was just so cold that Dad would tell me I couldn't come out in the morning, and I should just get ready for school instead. I wanted to help him so bad.

I was milking cows by the time I was seven or eight years old. I started out doing one side of the cow while Dad did the other, but eventually I took over the whole cow. When the cow had a calf, I would milk one side and the calf would get the other. Just for fun while milking, I would aim a squeeze and squirt the barn cats in the face as they sat waiting for their treat of warm milk. Once in a while, I'd pick off a chicken or two if they passed by me.

The scariest moment I had while milking was when I saw a hairy devil hand come out of nowhere, grab a chicken by the throat and drag it behind the wall of boxes where the hens laid their eggs. I dropped everything and ran for the house. Try to explain that to your mom and dad!

Later that day, Dad and Grampa jacked the corner of the barn up about eighteen inches. Rowdy, our star goalie dog, ran after the rats that scattered for new darkness. Grampa had the shotgun with him and blasted a weasel and a muskrat. "Won't be getting any more chickens," he said. They lowered the barn and that was that. Life on the ranch.

It was busy in the mornings, busy in the evenings—chores twice a day. I always had a lot of work to do. There were horses in the corral to train and look after, pigs to feed, and there were always jobs that needed to be done around the corrals, mending fences, fixing gates, spreading barnyard poop to the fields and gardens—Mom loved her natural fertilizer—before and after school.

We also did a lot of custom baling and bale picking for other people and made some money that way. We had good equipment, and Dad taught me how to drive a tractor and operate the thirty-six-bale New Holland picker. I had to be up some mornings by 4:30 and work all day. Mom would clean out an empty plastic jug, fill it with water, and stick it in the deep freeze for the night. We'd take it with us and leave it in the haystack, and that would give us cold drinking water for the day. Sometimes Mom would bring lunch, and sometimes she'd just send us off with a sandwich and an apple. I'd usually try to bring a friend to help me, and sometimes my sister or a cousin would help out. That made it easier because I needed somebody to move, turn, or push a bale and keep things moving. We picked five to ten thousand bales a summer. At five cents a bale, it added up after a while.

There was a rodeo or gymkhana happening almost every week during the summer in places like Mankota, Cadillac, and Val Marie. Most people know about the rodeo—bronc riding, bull riding, calf roping, steer wrestling, and all of that. While rodeos mainly had men participating, gymkhanas are a little different. They're kind of like a cowboy/cowgirl sporting event where both men and women compete. You can have a silver-haired cowgirl entered in the barrel racing, and you may have older cowboys and kids racing, too. Fathers and sons would compete together; fathers and daughters; husbands and wives. Gymkhanas were wonderfully inclusive.

I started doing rodeo stuff when I was about eight years old. Dad was a real good cowboy, and I think he wanted to expose me to anything athletic—and cowboying is definitely athletic. Dad was good at breaking horses—getting them used to the saddle and the bridle. He would break two or three yearlings every spring. We learned a lot by watching him, and we went riding almost every day.

The only rodeo event I really did as a young kid, from nine years old to thirteen, was a bit of steer riding. It's designed for young kids. You climb on the back of a yearling or two-year-old steer that's young and green. This kind of steer riding is pretty tame compared to what you see in bull or bronc riding, but when I was on the back of that young steer, I felt like I was a real rodeo cowboy. It was great fun!

My brother Monty and I would practise on the milk cow's calf or some bum calf (an orphan whose mother died giving birth) that we were bottle-feeding in the corral. I thought it was quite ingenious to see some kids wear their hockey gear when they were riding a steer so they wouldn't get hurt. It was a pretty funny sight.

Then the rodeos started getting very competitive. When I was younger, the participants were usually all local cowboys. But more professionals started showing up. They were better trained and very focused. We were in awe of their skills and they cleaned up on the prize money.

My brother Monty was a terrific cowboy. He loved horses and still does. Monty would ride bareback around the yard and raced the afternoon school bus when he was around five years old. He and old Putt Putt were quite the pair.

Monty tried saddle bronc riding for a few years. He did well, because he's alive to talk about it! Dad entered calf roping for five or six years, and he and I took a stab at team roping, but we never finished in the money, so we stopped rodeoing.

But we did well at the gymkhanas. They had events like pole bending (weaving in and out of poles while riding a horse at full gallop), barrel racing (a cloverleaf around three barrels at full gallop), and the ring race, where you'd ride, full gallop, around an oval course spearing six, eight, or ten rings hanging in different places. There's also the hide race, which can be pretty tough but was great fun. Each team consists of two people, and they race around a track marked off by a barrel. The one riding the horse has to pull a stiffened dry cowhide that is flying and swinging around like crazy. Waiting by the turn is the hide rider, who jumps on the cowhide and holds on for dear life. It can get a little messy for the hide rider, as dust and shit fly up and get everywhere—it was always best to keep your chin tucked and your eyes closed until the race was over. Dad was the horse rider and I would be the hide rider until I got too big and heavy, so eventually my brother Monty, who was much lighter, took my place and I became the horse rider. Boy, he was a tough bugger! I loved being either rider, but being the horse rider was a lot less grimy.

Monty's old buddy Putt Putt's registered name was Motor McCue, but Dad gave her a nickname. She was a golden buckskin mare with a strawberry wine–coloured pinstripe along her back, from her mane to her tail, and a perfect white star-blaze on her forehead. She was a gorgeous horse with a perfect gait, stride, and gallop for all of the gymkhana events. She was an athlete.

At the gymkhanas, everybody would put in a few bucks to participate and then the winner would take home the pot. On a good day, we'd go home with four or five hundred dollars. Even on a bad day, we would usually make enough to pay for the gas and a couple of beers for Dad and a hot dog for us. We really loved the competition.

We had our struggles as a family, but you tend to remember only the good. Looking back, I think I had a great childhood. My parents loved me unconditionally and I loved them just as much. My dad was true grit and no-nonsense. He was tough, and he made us tough because of that. I never wanted for much. If I needed something, I would kind of sheepishly ask for it, but it always seemed like my parents were one step ahead of me. "We know you need new running shoes. We know you need new skates." Next thing you knew, I'd have them. They always found the money.

We always had three meals a day, fresh eggs, fresh meat, and a lot of potatoes. And I mean *a lot* of potatoes. I didn't always like doing the chores, but I liked the fresh milk we had, and I liked the great meat. I remember friends would come out from town and be amazed that we had fresh milk every day, and we had all of this delicious food. We didn't have to get store-bought. I used to tease my town friends and tell them they were eating coyote or rattlesnake when it was really chicken or deer.

When we first moved to the ranch, we didn't have a telephone, but by the time I was ten or twelve we had phone lines put in. It was called a party line—just like on *Green Acres*. We could pick up the receiver, and if someone else was talking, we could listen to their conversation—and they could do the same to us. Our ring was three long and two short—that's how we knew a call was for us. We knew everyone's ring on the party line, and who was calling who.

My parents listened to a lot of radio. We almost always had it on, tuned to CKCK or CKRM from Regina. They'd get the news of the day and music—always country and western music. After Dad's first song of the day on the accordion or guitar, the radio was turned on.

Our house was heated in the winter by one big, giant oil stove right in the middle of the living room, and we had to heat a five-gallon bucket of oil and dump that in the tank before we went to bed at night. Again, that was life on the ranch. I thought everyone went through the same thing.

CHAPTER 3

FAMILY, MUSIC, AND BOUILLON

My grandfather John Trottier was born in Swift Current, Saskatchewan, on the back of a wagon back in the late 1800s. He was the oldest of ten kids. His father, my great-grandfather Patrice, was one of the last buffalo hunters of his generation. He wasn't a big man, I never met him, but they say he was tough. Patrice was Métis—he had that Louis Riel look about him. He married a girl from Fort Qu'Appelle, a full-blooded Cree lady, whom I only knew as *kookum* (which is the Cree word for grandma, though I think her real name was Tilly). I've seen pictures of her, and she was a very beautiful lady. She was also an educated woman, and quite brilliant financially. My great-grandparents were land-rich. They had the homestead in Val Marie, some land around Qu'Appelle Lake, another home in North Battleford during the summer months, and a great big house in Ponteix.

My grampa was taken away from his family as a young child and put in a residential school. He left there in Grade 3 and went home. We don't know a whole lot about what happened, and he never talked about it. As the oldest child, it's possible he ran away to help his father hunt and work the ranch. And Grampa loved to hunt. He hunted twelve months out of the year—deer, pheasant, ducks, and geese. Beavers and weasels were trapped—no animal was safe around Grampa. All animals were used for meat and pelts, and Gramma even put snakes and rabbit in the stews. His generation didn't know the word *poaching*—all they knew was that they had to feed the family.

Even though he only had a Grade 3 education, Grampa Trottier spoke several languages—Cree, Chippewa, French, and English. How amazing, I thought. Here I was, struggling with one language, and there was Grampa, with no education, talking away with anybody and everybody as fluently and comfortable as all hell. Grampa was ten years older than Gramma when they married. They spoke in Native tongue most of the time. And although my dad didn't speak the language, he would still understand what they were saying when they spoke to him, and he would answer back in English.

Grampa was a big, powerful Native man. He was at least six feet tall and probably weighed 220 pounds. Gramma was an attractive lady. Her family name was Gladeau and they were part of the "Landless Indians" who had to fight for decades to get the land that was rightfully theirs in Montana. She came from a wonderful family, but they had a very rough life when she was growing up.

Listening to my grandparents converse was quite entertaining, even more so when Gramma's sister Mary-Rose came over. They would sit there and cackle away with each other in two different languages, Plains Cree and Chippewa. We never really knew how much they understood each other, but they would laugh at the same time, and sometimes they would be arguing and it would get quite heated. They would raise their voices and throw their hands in the air. Then one would try to explain something in their tongue and throw *their* arms in the air, and away they'd go again.

There's so much humour in Native cultures. When we couldn't understand what she was saying, Gramma would hold her arms out to us and say, "*Astum meyochis.*" I thought she was saying, "Come here, my little loved one." But what it really meant was "Come here, shitty ass."

We joined Gramma and Grampa at the occasional powwow, and Dad would be there with his guitar and join the bands and play songs around the campfires. There was great music, and I loved the dancing. I would always try to mimic how the men danced as Dad played. These were some of my most vivid memories of that time in my life.

Grampa built a small house in town for his family. They now had a footprint in town during the cold winter months as well as place where they could go when the roads to the ranch got impassable. Gramma always had a large pot of something brewing on the stove in that house. You could find a chicken head floating in there, or something else looking back at you. Gramma called it *bouillon*. We'd eat some of it, but the pot would stay on the stove, and the next day she'd throw more stuff into it—beef, pork, chicken. We had some interesting things to eat at my grandparents' house. Pig's feet. Tongue. Mealtimes were always a bit of an adventure.

It felt like there was always something fun going on in that house. Grampa was into working with leather and Gramma was always making or mending something for the grandkids with her foot-pedal sewing machine. Grampa had gun racks for his rifles, and my cousins and I would go hunting with Grampa and chase the geese and ducks and partridges out of the bush and the reeds. Grampa would stand on the bank and blast away. How he never shot one of us grandkids is still sort of amazing.

Music was always a big part of life at the Trottier house. My grandparents had a piano in the front room and Grampa loved to play the fiddle. Gramma would chord the piano, Grampa on the fiddle, and us kids would be the audience. Gramma would purposefully play the wrong chords from time to time, and Grampa would give her a little playful smack. We laughed every time. Grampa played Métis music—old-time waltzes, jigs, stuff like that—and if Dad was there, he'd sing a song.

The way I remember it, my aunt Ruth, who was a year or two older than Dad, had a guitar, and she taught him a couple of chords and he just took off.

Dad had a gift when it came to music and singing. He wanted all of us kids to carry on that love of music. I don't remember a time when Dad didn't have a band. He played to us all the time. He even taught me how to play bass by ear so I could be part of his band. He'd say, "Just listen, you'll hear the rhythm. Don't get frustrated. Just follow my fingers." And that's all I did.

His older sister Joanie played terrific piano—again, all by ear. Nobody read music—everyone in the family was self-taught. Listening to Aunt Joanie play the piano was like listening to old ragtime saloon-type music. She would just bounce on the piano and her hands were dancing. She'd look at you while she was singing and still hit all the right keys.

I always felt accepted and comfortable in the Native communities. I felt mostly like I was accepted because of my grandparents. I was John and Annie Trottier's grandson, and that was all that mattered.

We had many big gatherings: family reunions, funerals, weddings, celebrations. When something brought the Trottier family together, there were lots of us—fifty, sixty, seventy people or more. I remember the small things. The kids running around and playing—there were so many of us. We played something that at the time was called "squaw wrestling." Two people would lie on their backs, side by side, facing opposite directions, then raise their inside leg in the air three times—and on the third time, they would lock legs and try and flip the other person over. It was great fun until my cousins Jerry and Brock started flipping us with such force that we would do a couple of somersaults in the air. It was fun to see someone else tumbling, but it wasn't much fun when it happened to me.

Booze was always a part of every gathering. There would be some homemade wine and definitely beer. My brother Rocky and cousin Kenny loved to finish the last swig in every bottle before they were placed back in the case for refund. A cigarette butt inside a can or bottle caught them by surprise a few times.

And there was music. So much music. Piano, accordion, fiddles, lots of guitars, and singers galore. All of my aunts loved to sing, and Dad would harmonize with them. I still love all those old songs, especially "That Silver-Haired Daddy of Mine."

I guess you could say my dad's side of the family all had First Nations features. Every aunt was beautiful and all the men handsome. So Mom being Irish stuck out a bit. Uncle Lloyd and Uncle Jerry, my dad's brothers, had also married non-Native ladies, so Mom wasn't alone.

Mom fit in with the Trottiers very well. She was embraced and therefore very engaged in our little Indian world. She learned how to make bannock, a delicious kind of fried bread, and she liked learning how to do things that were associated with the Cree and Chippewa cultures. Gramma and Dad's sisters were great to her. Mom cooked all of the Native stews and meats as if she had been doing it her whole life.

I never felt out of place at our family reunions or the few powwows I went to. And I never felt out of place with my Irish grandparents and my mom's family. On both sides, I always felt like I was with my people.

My mom's family, the Gardners, lived about a mile north of Climax when she grew up. It was a town roughly the same size as Val Marie, but it felt bigger and busier. It too had an ice rink and curling rink—they always seemed to be the centre of small Saskatchewan communities, along with the hotel, with its beer parlour. That's where you'd find everybody. Those little towns had lots of energy, even though folks didn't have much in the way of money.

My grandpa, Andy Gardner, came to Canada from Ireland with his parents, and my grandmother's family, the Alexanders, became local farmers too. Grandpa Gardner had scoliosis when he was young, and I think he had a hard life growing up. He was always bent over and never complained. He never missed a hockey game when I came to Climax to play. My grandma was a frail, tiny, beautiful Irish lady who was always excited whenever Mom and the grandkids came to visit. She always had cookies for us, and a box full of balls that we could play with outside. When I got older and was playing hockey in Climax, I would stop by to see Grandma. She was always so happy to see me. I left with a baked treat, Grandma's gentle hug, and her warm Gardner smile. I loved that my mom had her mom's smile. Both of my Gardner grandparents had a little bit of an Irish accent in their voice. When they'd say my name, it was as though there was just one syllable in it. It sounded like "Brine." And I really liked it.

Grandpa Gardner was quite resourceful. People who had lived through the terrible Depression in the '30s were mindful not to waste anything, saving wherever they could. Although he was a farmer, he also drove a road grader that was pulled by a team of horses so he could make a little extra money. There was no pavement in those days—everything was gravel and grid roads, so there was lots of grading to do. My siblings and I used to think my grandparents were much richer than us because at Christmastime they would always send us a pair of pants or a shirt or something like that, and I'd think, "God, Mom's family must be so rich because they can send us clothes." Looking back, I don't think they were rich at all. Now I know they just wanted Christmas to be special.

There were six kids in Mom's family—Jean was the oldest, then Mom, John, Margaret, Donny, and Linda. I always felt like the Gardners were highly respected in Climax, and that added to my Gardner pride. My uncles John and Donny were great athletes, in baseball and hockey, and I felt like everybody in town looked up to them. Dad and Uncle John were about the same age, and they played some hockey together in their youth, so there was always that little bond as brothers-in-law. I enjoyed the friendship Grandpa Gardner and Dad had, because there was always laughter between them. Dad had tremendous respect for Grandpa Gardner. It was nice to see that he would look up to him, even though Grandpa was physically hunched over with scoliosis. There was a real sense of family when the Gardners and Trottiers got together.

My mom was the most beautiful woman I have ever known—not just because she was pretty, but because of how she treated people and how she was loved by her friends. Mom had the perfect smile. When you talk about the auburn Irish hair, that was Mom—she was Irish to the bone, sort of like Maureen O'Hara, only prettier. When Mom was young, she was a little bit of an Irish sprite. She found ways to sneak out at night and go with her friends to parties and dances when she shouldn't have. There'd be times when she and her older sister Jean would think back and talk about that and laugh, just the two of them. Me, I was just a wallflower, listening unintentionally.

Mom was a terrific teacher. She wanted her children to be good at a little bit of everything. When Dad was playing music, we'd go up to Mom and ask, "Can you teach us how to polka?" and she would drop everything and teach us all to dance—we got to have one or two dances with Mom every time, and we learned how to polka and waltz. Those are some of my favourite memories. She taught us life skills every day, like how to bake, darn a sock, pluck chickens, care for a garden. Mom was ready to help us learn anything, especially when it came to taking care of ourselves, and she made us feel proud about who we were.

Mom was always protective of us kids, but as she aged, she became more protective of her grandkids. Don't ever say anything negative about her grandkids unless you wanted to get both barrels. Somewhere along the way, she lost her filter. Like the time she was at the ball field, watching one of Kathy's kids play softball. When Mom would go to watch her grandkids, she'd park next to the field and sit in her car. It didn't matter which team, but if one of the kids made a good play, she'd honk her horn.

This one game, she went with her friend Mildred and parked her Toyota pickup right behind the opposition team's bench. She was honking away until one of the kids from the opposition—they were eleven or twelve years old—left the bench and walked over to my mother and said, "Hey lady, stop honking your horn in our ear."

"Fuck you!" she said. Her language could get a little rough sometimes. When she told me the story later, I couldn't stop laughing. "What's so funny?" she asked. She was really angry at that kid. I said, "Mom, you said 'fuck you' to a little boy." Mildred said she was so embarrassed, she couldn't shrink low enough in the cab of Mom's truck. My mom got hot all over again. "Well, don't tell me not to honk my horn, I'll honk my horn whenever I damn well please!"

That was so my mom. She told me another story, about the time she was standing outside the café, having a cigarette. She probably had a little fire in her that day. A patron leaving the café said something about "these smokers" and their "disgusting smoke." Mom heard what she said and just let her have it. "Fuck off! This goddam government is making us stand out here, freezing our ass off to have a fucking smoke." When she told me the story later, she was fired up all over again.

I laughed so hard, I was crying.

Dad was tough, but Mom was probably just as tough. She didn't take any crap from anyone, including Dad. If they got to arguing or squabbling, she would stand up to him—and they would have some real brouhahas. I hated to hear them argue, but I knew she wasn't going to back down. Mom had a long fuse, but when she'd had enough, she'd had enough.

Dad was the disciplinarian in the family, for sure. But Mom could just give me a look with her eyes, and I would know that she was hurt. I never wanted to make my mom sad. I couldn't bear to hurt her or make her feel like I'd let her down. That was worse than getting kicked in the ass by Dad. I'd take a thousand kicks in the ass rather than see my mom look disappointed in me. It was so wonderful to see the other side of it, when I made her proud. It's all I ever wanted to do.

Every once in a while, Mom would bark at me to get me to do something—and I didn't like to be barked at, period. I felt like she was bossing me around. "Go weed the garden." "Time to feed the chickens." "Look after the cows." One thing after another.

When I was twelve or thirteen, I finally said to her, "Mom, if you want something or need something, just please ask me.

Don't order me around. I hate that. If you want something done, just ask."

Well, that pretty much changed everything. I remember her saying, "Okay." And she just changed. She started asking me to do everything, instead of telling me. "Bryan, can you help me with this," or "Can you haul some water up for the washing machine?" I wasn't being barked at anymore, but I had created a new monster—it felt like now she was asking me to do more and more. I told her all she had to do is ask, and she asked. And asked. And asked.

It kind of changed our relationship in a good way. I was growing and I was gaining a sense of independence. But I was also going to protect my mom to death. We were not a hugging, "I love you" kind of family when I was growing up. But I became extremely protective of her. I didn't want Mom to have to be the heavy. I'd be the heavy for her. If my brothers and sisters didn't mind Mom, I did the barking at them—maybe too much at times, but at least Mom didn't have to.

CHAPTER 4

THE GOOD, THE BAD, AND THE RAGGEDY ANDYS

Most folks in Val Marie spoke French. Not surprising, really, considering that families with names like Legault, Dumonceaux, Lemire, Duquette, Lebel, Cornette, Perrault, Vermette, Leblanc, and Syrenne made up most of the town. Dad understood some of it, but he didn't speak the language, so if someone asked him a question in French, he'd always answer in English.

Our school was run by nuns, and they spoke French to me all day long. I didn't understand a thing they said. My last name sounds French, so they must have assumed I knew what they were saying. It eventually got to the point where I could make out some of what was being said to me, but I was really guessing most of the time. I knew *va* meant "go" and *viens* meant "come." I'd watch the other kids to see what they would do and how they would respond. I had friends like Claude Jeanson, who would help me fake my way through the day. Claude didn't speak a lick of English and he was a year older than me, so he must have been held back to repeat a grade. We just hit it off right away. Claude taught me some French and I taught him some English. He was always in trouble at school, but boy, was he fun to hang out with.

Grade 3 was the first year I didn't have to go to "French-French" class. Mom helped when she said to the sisters, "You know Bryan doesn't speak French, right?" We were in a blended class where they spoke both languages. Instead of being taught by one of the nuns, my teacher was Sister DeMass. She was bilingual and

I really loved that year because I could finally understand everything that was being said during our lessons.

I was a shy kid. I was Dad's right-hand man when we were on the ranch, but I was a homesick mama's boy at heart. When people would talk to me, I would just look at my shoes. My face would turn beet red when people would compliment me. In those days, a lot of kids were like that. It wasn't just Native kids, but I know that Native kids really relate to that feeling of being homesick, shy, and self-conscious. I was most comfortable at home, where I knew I was safe. Mom knew what I liked to eat, and I'd help Dad with odd jobs and chores. "Hand me a Phillips screwdriver," he'd say to me, or "Go fetch me a half-inch wrench."

I didn't like public speaking. But I was a really good storyteller and I liked writing stories. I think I've always had a good imagination, and back then I could easily make stuff up for my writing assignments. I hated doing oral reports in class, but if I had to, I would read a funny story so that everyone would laugh. I really liked it when I made the girls laugh, for some reason.

I'd get good grades in math, spelling, and reading. History was okay. French was a push and so was science. But I gave my best effort in all of my subjects. Dad praised the grade for effort. I liked everything about school: I enjoyed learning and writing and being able to see my friends every day.

Because of who he was, Dad and his generation dealt with a lot of discrimination growing up. He said his whole family had their share of fist fights and scraps because they were taunted and teased a lot.

When I was a kid, I honestly didn't experience a lot of discrimination. Maybe that's because we really didn't understand what it was when we ran into it. We'd come home crying from school sometimes because other kids would call us names—usually "half-breed." Mom would say, "Well, you *are* a half-breed. You are half Indian and half Irish. But most people are half-breeds. They're half something and half something else." After that, I'd go to school and somebody would call me a half-breed and I'd think, "Well you're a half-breed, too—you're half French and half Norwegian." Pretty much everybody I knew had some form of mixed blood.

The kids who said those things couldn't understand why they didn't affect me. But it was because of how I was raised by my parents. They taught all of us kids that discrimination was a form of jealousy! I didn't really understand that until I got older. I felt, and still feel, a lot of pride about my roots. And I hope other kids feel the same way about their families. One of the many gifts that my parents gave me was a perfect blend of blood—my mixed Native and Irish heritage. There is an incredible amount of resilience, stamina, and strength in our people.

When I was about six years old, my cousin Larry and I were inseparable. Even though he was six months older, Larry was a little smaller than I was and we didn't look like we could be related because he was slender and I was stocky. We were both kind of Raggedy Andys—shirts untucked and hand-me-down jeans. We weren't exactly poor, but we looked a little bit like street urchins, I guess, even though both of our moms really cared about our appearance. They were always reminding us to wash our face and hands, comb our hair, brush our teeth. They took a lot of pride in how we looked, but we were just kids, so we probably didn't care as much as we should have.

Larry was fun to hang around with, but he kind of had a chip on his shoulder. He wasn't big, but he didn't take any crap from anyone. He was a lot more brash and brave than I was, and when I was with him, I always felt like I was with a guy who was more mature than me. I was very naive and I wasn't the bravest soul. Larry was the opposite. He was right out there, front and centre, and he didn't give two hoots what anyone thought of him. If you had something bad to say about Larry, he'd come right back at you. Larry wasn't big, but he was tough, just like his dad, my uncle PeeWee.

There were schoolyard fights all the time in those days, but nothing serious. Whether Larry was jumping in to protect me in a scrap, or vice versa, we started to get a bit of a reputation. Larry was (and still is) good family. We've always trusted each other and care about each other a lot. Back in the day, we got reamed out by the teachers every once in a while for fighting, and we probably missed a few recesses because we'd have to visit the principal's office.

One time when we were about eleven years old, Larry and I were down in Malta, Montana, a cowboy town. It was a regular trip for us. We had family there, and Dad had a lot of friends. We were playing bumper pool next door to the bar. We had started our game, and then this big kid came up to me and Larry, thinking he was going to intimidate us into giving up the table.

Larry wasn't fazed a bit. And when the monster kid grabbed the cue ball and basically told us to leave, Larry, who was probably a foot shorter, got right in his face and said, "Give me that back."

The guy wouldn't, so Larry hit him over the head with his pool cue. Needless to say, the fight was on. It was a hell of a brawl. I couldn't see where Larry went, and I wound up on top of this guy, throwing bombs. Finally, I felt my Dad's hand on my shoulder, pulling me off of the big kid.

"Okay, he's had enough," Dad said.

I know I found myself in more scraps than I wanted to be in because of Larry, but I wasn't going to let that bully intimidate my little cousin.

I remember Larry asking me afterwards, "Why'd you beat that kid up? I wasn't gonna fight him."

"Why'd you hit him over the head with the cue?" I asked him. "And where the hell did you go, dammit?"

"I went to get your dad, idiot! That guy was huge!" Larry retorted.

I loved Larry's fearlessness. It was good for me to be around him then—and it still is, all these years later. I need those kinds of people in my life. He helped me come out of my shell. I guess I had some of that feistiness in me, but I just needed someone to help me bring it out.

I love all my cousins, but Larry's the best cousin a guy could ask for. I love him and I'm proud of our kinship.

CHAPTER 5

A FIRST FOR EVERYTHING

I was eight years old when I started minor hockey in Val Marie. Before that, I played mostly on the little creek by my house. We skated on the outdoor rink in town once in a while, and it was great fun, too.

There was a men's team in town that would play on the outdoor rink. Dad would gear up and play against teams from Climax and Cadillac. It was a huge event in the town. It seemed like everyone would be shovelling snow off the ice before a game. There wasn't a Zamboni; instead, a hand-pulled barrel of hot water flooded the ice. All the snow got dumped over the boards—literally wooden boards, not what you see in rinks today. A lot of us would stand on those snowbanks to watch the game. There was nothing to protect us other than netting on either end of the rink. Thank God for heavy parkas and thick scarves to absorb errant flying pucks!

Dad was a terrific all-around athlete and an excellent hockey player with a really good shot. He was my first coach, and I remember that when we'd practise together, he'd tell me to pick a spot on the boards and try to hit it with my shot. And then he'd show me how to do it—he'd hit the spot just like that, and then he'd wink at me. He had one of those old-time wristers—*bang*! He'd always shoot quick and catch the goalie off guard. He'd just rip it. Watching Dad snipe a goal or two really lifted my sense of fatherly pride. My two uncles on the Climax team, Donny and

John Gardner, excelled at hockey as well. I'd watch and study them, just like I'd watch the stars on *Hockey Night in Canada*. I'd go out and practise everything I saw—pump fake, backhand top shelf—trying to emulate my early hockey idols.

Dad bought me my first stick at Art Labelle's general store. It was a five-and-dime store that sold everything from candy to household goods to clothing. It wasn't an expensive stick, but it had Gordie Howe's name written in dark black ink on the top part of the shaft. *Awesome!*

The outdoor rink was enclosed in '64. It was spectacular! Plus, we didn't have to shovel snow any more. My first minor hockey team only had about four or five kids my age who played, so we had to get together with some of the younger and older kids just to have enough players for a team. Sometimes I got to play on the forward line with the older guys. It was a little scary playing against kids who were two or three years older than me. They looked like giants. But it was exciting.

We would play against teams from the surrounding towns: Mankota and Ponteix were decent; Cadillac was always feisty; Shaunavon was the big-city team, because it was the main railway hub and had a much bigger population; Frontier had good teams. But it was Climax, which seemed to have its indoor rink before anyone else, that was the powerhouse. They had a bunch of kids my age who were really good hockey players and I remember wondering, *How did these guys get so good so fast?*

We didn't win many games in that first year, but we sure liked to play. I was usually on defence, but I'd sneak up and play forward and score a goal once in a blue moon, and then go back on defence. Dad told me I should play defence because I'd learn how to skate backwards and I'd also get a lot more ice time. I could skate pretty well by now—more quick than super fast—and I could skate backwards okay, which not all of the kids could do.

We still only had ten or eleven players, total, on our team, and some of them were really young—Bernie Syrenne's brother was three years younger than us; Danny Kane, Ray Lebel, and the Jobagy and Ronceray kids were two years younger. In most games, I'd play a shift at forward and then go back and play defence, then a quick rest, and I'd go back and do the same thing again. I played a lot, and when I did get off the ice for a few seconds, Dad, who was coaching, would say, "Rest fast," and then *boom*, I'd go back out.

I'll never forget my first goal. We were playing a game in Bracken. My buddy Claude Jeanson was on my team and he was a pretty good stickhandler. The only problem was that he'd stop skating when he stickhandled, and Dad would be yelling, "Move, Jeanson, move!" Being one of the better players on the team, Jeanson was a good little leader. He just forgot to pass the puck and move his feet when he was stickhandling. My other buddy Bernie Syrenne was probably our best player. He was a terrific skater and he could shoot. He was so smooth. I remember thinking, *I want to skate like Bernie and stickhandle like Jeanson.*

But back to my first goal. I was playing defence that day. Bernie dug the puck out of the corner and passed it to Jeanson in the slot. Jeanson gobbled up the pass and, like usual, was stickhandling like crazy in one spot. Everybody on the Bracken team was trying to get the puck away from him. He was stickhandling so fast, he just lost his balance and fell over, but still managed to keep control of the puck. I came up on his left and hollered, "Jeanson!" And from his butt, he whipped the puck over to me. It was a perfect pass.

It all felt automatic from here. I'd practised thousands of times shooting at the board right-handed, but instinctively, I switched to lefty and somehow shovelled that puck into the upper part of the net over the goalie's glove and shoulder. It must have been little-kid adrenalin. I'd never shot a puck left-handed before. That goal ended up being the game winner. I didn't know Dad kept the puck, but he gave it to me on the ride home. I stared at it the whole way, and heard Dad say, "I think you're a natural lefty."

We kept that old Viceroy puck. Mom put white tape around it and wrote "Bryan's first goal" on it. She placed it on the windowsill and it sat there until she passed away in 2011.

I still have a picture of our first team. Even in black and white, you can see what a bunch of misfits we were, some guys wearing Maple Leafs jerseys, some guys wearing red or white Montreal Canadiens sweaters. I'm wearing a generic maroon jersey, and two or three kids are just wearing parkas. Darryl Gard sold me his old quilted hockey pants for a dollar, and his shin pads that were way too big for me for another fifty cents. They didn't feel comfortable, but Mom said it didn't matter, that I'd grow into them.

We played half a dozen games that first year. We didn't get our matching team sweaters until the next season.

The next few years were more of the same. We didn't win many games, but I felt like I was getting better. I really started to get the hockey bug when I was about ten years old. Even more so when Dad got a call from Paul Desjardins, who was the father of future NHL coach Willie Desjardins. Paul asked him if I'd like to come over to Climax and play with them in a peewee tournament in Weyburn, which was a pretty big tournament at the time.

There were three of us that went from Val Marie: Bernie, Marcel Bellefeuille, and myself. Jeanson was too old, and we were maybe three of the better players in Val Marie, but I never thought I was good enough to play for Climax. They had matching jerseys in the Boston Bruins' colours. To us misfits in Val Marie, that was very intimidating. But they were good guys, and they turned out to be good teammates. I loved playing with them—I felt welcomed. Mom always said that her hometown, Climax, had the most unselfish hockey players. "Watch how they pass the puck. An assist is as important as a goal." Climax gave me a team jersey, number 11.

Willie Desjardins was our scoring machine. What a player he was—strong stickhandler, great shot, tricky, and deceptive. We all wanted Willie on our line. We never lost a game on our way to winning the tournament. And Willie was our leading scorer.

The next year, Dad took our Val Marie team to the same tournament, and we won it again. Go figure!

It was at the Weyburn tournament where I first encountered some racism in hockey. There was an all-Native team from Lebret. That was the same area of Qu'Appelle that my great-grandparents were from, so I was thinking, *Are these my roots?* I sat with Mom and Dad and watched one of their games. My parents praised them for how they skated, how quick they were and how unselfishly they played. Their stickhandling was spectacular. They fought hard but lost to the team from Milestone, who we ended up playing, and they were by far our toughest match. Willie scored with fifteen seconds to go for a 2–1 win. Eddie Magee was amazing in net. Dad had told him before the game, "Eddie, you're a cat. You're quick like a cat. You're going to be spectacular today." And he was.

But watching that Lebret game, we could hear whispers from some people in the crowd saying negative things about them: "Oh, they're probably thieves." "Their parents are probably drunks." I felt horrible hearing these things. I said to Mom, "These are good kids, they're good players and their parents seem so nice. Why are people saying these bad things about them?"

"They're just jealous," my mom said matter-of-factly.

Dad was very proud of the Native players who made the NHL. I wore number 10 all through junior hockey because of George Armstrong. He was one of Dad's favourites. Dad would tell me, "You're going to wear number 10." He didn't give me a choice, but I knew why. I loved George Armstrong, too, and the way he played. I knew Jim Neilson, who played for the New York Rangers, was First Nations. I never saw Freddy Sasakamoose play, but I knew so much about him because Dad had watched him play in Moose Jaw. He wasn't a big man, but he was a giant in our world, and Dad called him one of the fastest skaters he had ever seen. Freddy broke the barrier for Indigenous hockey players in the National Hockey League and gave us all inspiration. It made me think, *If Freddy can do it, if Jimmy can do it, and if George can do it, why can't I?*

In 1968, I went to my first hockey camp: the Gordie Howe Hockey Camp in Saskatoon. Bernie Syrenne, Carl Olson, and Marcel Bellefeuille went as well. I think it cost eighty bucks for the week, and I remember wondering how Dad could afford it. I won the award as the most accurate shooter at camp. I had to shoot the puck into a little square, and I can't remember how I did it, but I put four out of five into that little hole. Even the guys from Climax were impressed. Those hours shooting pucks with Dad must have paid off.

We never did meet Gordie Howe that week. Gerry and Herb Pinder were the main instructors at the camp. Both of them played for the Canadian Olympic team, and Gerry went on to play in the NHL and the WHA, while Herb became a player agent. They were just fantastic skaters, and really good to all of us kids.

In the spring of '69, Climax and Val Marie joined forces again to compete at the Yorktown invitational tournament. Climax grabbed four of us from Val Marie, and this time, Carl Olson joined Bernie, Marcel, and me to wear the black and gold. We won the tournament, of course, and Willie again was our scoring leader. That's three championships in three years. Our team never loses!

In the summer of 1970, I was fourteen and went to Stan Dunn's hockey school in Swift Current. I first met Stan, the coach of the Swift Current Broncos, the spring before. We had just won the provincial bantam tournament and they made a big deal of it in town. We ended up getting special championship jackets with the team logo on it, along with our names and numbers. That was really cool, and it was the first time I ever owned a team jacket. They held a banquet for us where Stan was the guest speaker. He was a celebrity—the coach of the Broncos! We all felt like big shots that day.

Stan had a gravelly, booming baritone voice, but when he spoke, he said something nice about all of us kids. Stan looked down at me. "Now this little guy down here . . ." I turned beet red and was so embarrassed when Stan singled me out. I can't even remember what he said. After his speech, we were presented with our jackets and plaques.

Stan spent a lot of time in our neck of the woods. We didn't know it then, but he would come down to scout local players. Everyone in our area apparently was considered Swift Current property. I guess that's how junior hockey worked then.

The camp was a two-week program, but after the first one, Stan gave Dad half of his money back. "Your son's ready to be an instructor," he told Dad. For the rest of the camp, I became an assistant to the main on-ice instructors.

And that's how I first met Dave "Tiger" Williams. He became my boss.

Tiger was one of the instructors. He had just finished his first season with the Broncos, so he was older than I was. I got to spend a lot of time with him that week, tagging along. Tiger wasn't super friendly to me the first week. He was an instructor, one of the big boys; I was just a peon player. But by the end of that second week, he warmed up and I became his little buddy.

I knew of Tiger's reputation. I knew he was a scrappy guy. He was also one of the hardest workers I'd ever seen. During the hockey school, the two of us would go to the rink early and stay late, just so we could work on our skills. But I wasn't part of the Bronco family, and Tiger didn't treat me like I was—yet.

After the hockey school, Stan invited me to attend the Broncos' training camp. I was excited. Heck, I was only fourteen years old and it was the first time I'd be competing with guys who had full beards and moustaches. I barely had any whiskers!

I felt I did pretty well at the camp. I scored some goals and it was a lot of fun to scrimmage with those guys. But they were so big, so strong, and so fast. I couldn't win any battles for the puck.

The experience was a wonderful gauge. Stan said some very nice things about the way I played, and that was important to me. It allowed me to test myself against grown men. I started to feel like I had the right stuff. And Stan said, "You just keep growing. I'll see you next summer at the hockey school."

The training camp for the Moose Jaw Canucks of the Saskatchewan Junior Hockey League opened right after the Broncos camp. Willie Desjardins's dad, Paul, and my dad decided to take us there to keep exposing us to a higher level of hockey. For the first two weeks, Willie and I were in town on our own—two fourteen-years-olds living in a motel by ourselves.

The SJHL was one step below the Western Hockey League. We were playing against eighteen-, nineteen-year-olds, and some were monsters. We played a few exhibition games, and Willie and I were taking some heavy hits from some of the older guys. But Willie was feistier and had more talent than me. He just wouldn't back down from anybody. We both did well, and Willie stayed and played for the Canucks that season. But Dad told me I was coming home. I was kind of relieved, because I wasn't sure I could compete against the biggest bruisers in that league. And Dad told me later that the team wasn't going to pay for my sticks, skates, or equipment.

"I want you to get on the bus at the end of the week and I'll pick you up in Swift Current," he said.

So I got on the Greyhound bus, carrying my hockey bag, my suitcase, and my two hockey sticks. We stopped in every town between Moose Jaw and Swift Current. It was a long trip. When Dad wasn't at the bus stop, I grabbed all of my stuff and walked down to the Imperial Hotel, thinking he'd be waiting for me in the bar, but when I got there, I didn't see his car in the parking lot. So I knew he wasn't there.

Then I thought he might be at our family friends', Gordon and Devona, the Nelsons, who lived in town. I grabbed my crap and walked over to their house. Nope, not there, either. They called my folks and, to save Dad a seventy-mile drive, arranged for me to get a lift back to Val Marie.

When I got to the ranch, the first thing Dad said to me was, "What took you so long?" *Ha.*

Mom asked if I was hungry. I said yes, and then I asked her, "Was Dad serious? Is he upset?"

"Does it matter?" Mom asked. "You're home!" Man, I liked the way she said *home*.

I thought I was coming home for good, but fate had another idea. I went to play for the Swift Current Legionnaires. Harry Barrett was the coach—he was in the farm equipment business, and he and Dad were friends. The Legionnaires were a midget team, made up of fifteen- and sixteen-year-olds, but they were part of what was really a Junior B league. The Legionnaires, the Saskatoon Blazers, and the Regina Pat Canadians were the only true midget teams. The rest of the teams in the league, like the Notre Dame Hounds and Weyburn Red Wings, were Junior B teams with guys seventeen, eighteen, and nineteen years old. Even though we were younger, we competed hard.

That spring, Val Marie and Climax teamed up again to go after the midget championship. We surprised ourselves and the whole province by winning it all for the second time! It was one more bullet in the gun belt to build our hockey confidence. What a great team we had! We had won five championships in four years. Now we were really wondering if the scouts were starting to pay attention to us.

At the same time, I continued playing games for the senior team back in Val Marie, and that spring I played midget hockey for Climax in the Saskatchewan Amateur Hockey Association provincials with Willie Desjardins. That year, I probably played the most hockey I ever played in a season—something like 120 games, playing sometimes five or six nights a week. When did I practise? I didn't have any time. I remember Dad looking back at it and saying that that was my best development year because I was playing a lot of games.

The original plan was for me to move to Swift Current for the season, but there was one small problem: in order to enrol in high school in town, I had to be a resident.

Mom and Dad wanted me to live with the Nelsons. They had grown up together—the Nelsons were from the Orkney and Bracken area. They had kids around my age; their son Byron and I were exactly the same age.

After a Legionnaires game, Mom, Dad and I went over to the Nelsons'. That's when Dad explained everything to me. "Gordon and Devona are going to adopt you so that you can go to school and play hockey here in Swift Current." So the Nelsons signed the papers to "adopt" me and make me an official resident of Swift Current. (To this day, I'm not sure if they ever did the necessary paperwork to "unadopt" me.)

Mom started crying as Dad talked to me. Just before they left to go home, Mom gave me a big hug and whispered in my ear, "You know this doesn't mean we don't love you." I knew that. I saw some tears in Dad's eyes, too. I guess it's scary to let go of a teenage son.

I really did understand: it was all about playing hockey; it was no big deal. I think my mom and dad knew I was homesick all of the time. They tried to see as many games as possible, so it was great to see them as often as I did.

I had some fun while living with the Nelsons. They owned a little trucking company, Western Delivery, and Gordon was great to invite me to help deliver some of the "big stuff," like a washer/dryer or a sofa. And once in a while, he would let me drive these big one-ton and two-ton delivery trucks that he had. I was fifteen years old, and I didn't have a driver's licence—not even a learner's permit yet! But I knew how from driving the pickups and operating the big machinery on the ranch. Now here I was, a farm kid driving all over the big city.

That arrangement lasted for only two or three months. Before Christmas, Dad had quite an accident. A horse fell on him and busted his foot and ankle up pretty good. He needed me back home to help. I moved back to the ranch. I jumped back into school in Val Marie and the rhythm of winter chores, but I continued to play for the Legionnaires.

Dad became my chauffeur for the rest of that season, driving me to games all over the province. I remember being on the road a lot, sleeping in the truck. I probably shouldn't say this, but sometimes after a game, Dad would have a beer or two and he'd say, "Okay, you drive for a while."

I was still without a licence. On the long trips, I would do the bulk of the driving—anywhere from 100 to 150 miles at a time. Dad would start the drive and get us clear of the city limits, and then I'd take over. Then he'd jump back behind the wheel for the home stretch.

During our drives, Dad would offer constructive criticism of my game, which I liked if it was positive but didn't like if it was negative. But I always welcomed that feedback. It was incredibly useful and also made the time pass in the car.

The next summer, Stan Dunn hired me back to work at his hockey camp. I bunked in with Stan and his wife, Sheila, and that fall, I came back to Swift Current for my second training camp with the Broncos, hoping to make the team.

CHAPTER 6

TIGER AND THE BRONCOS

As a coach, Stan was rough and gruff, but he was all business and he was always really good to me. I probably frustrated the hell out of him at times because I'm stubborn, shy, and maybe not the toughest kid. But Stan was like a commander, and from the start, he made me feel like I belonged.

And it wasn't just Stan; it was the whole family. His wife, Sheila, is a saint. She always made me feel welcome in their home. Their oldest daughter, Susan, and I are the same age, and we went to school together for a little while. She's a beautiful girl, just like her mom, and she was like another sister to me. Susan married the captain of my Legionnaire team, Greg Woods. That connection with the Dunns is a treasured friendship.

Years later, when I was inducted into the Hockey Hall of Fame, Stan and Sheila sent a congratulatory note along with a picture of me in my Broncos uniform with the inscription, "Keep taking good care of him." I loved the message.

Stan was also really close to Dad. What I didn't realize until later—really, until I made the Broncos—was that Dad and Stan were pretty friendly. Dad always called him "Stan the Man." I believe now that they had always been talking about me, from the time I was young, They were buddies and they spoke the same language. Dad trusted Stan, and Stan never broke that trust. Their shared bond was incredibly motivating for me, and made me work harder. I knew they always had my best interest at heart, and I never wanted to let either of them down.

Sometimes I'd hustle out of the dressing room after a game just so I could see Dad before he drove back to the ranch. And I'd find him wearing his cowboy hat, sitting with Stan in his office. It was Buzz and Stan time—sharing and finishing a six-pack of beer—and they would be talking and laughing, just like good friends do. I liked it and never interrupted.

Because of Stan and because of Tiger, I didn't feel like an outcast when I showed up at training camp. I didn't realize it at the start, but most of us were "imports." A handful of kids were actually from Swift Current, but the rest were from all over the west—Manitoba, Saskatchewan, Alberta, and British Columbia. Growing up, we were playing for our hometown teams, and now here we were, competing for a spot on the Broncos roster.

As camp went on, guys were being sent home one after another as the team was whittled down. Finally, I was one of the last rookies standing. Doing the math, I realized I was one of the twelve remaining forwards. Was it possible I was going to be playing with the big boys? I was nervous about asking Stan, so I walked by his office.

I took a deep breath.

"Stan, have I made—?"

Before I could finish asking, Stan got up from his desk and he shared some good news, and right behind it, he hit me with some bad news. I didn't understand it at the time.

"Bryan, we're going to keep you here." *Good news!*

"You're not going to play very much." *Ooo, bad news.* "I don't want you to get frustrated. Be patient. Understand you're going to play a lot before you're done junior."

And he was right. I didn't play a lot that first year. I was trying not to get discouraged. But when you're only playing eight minutes a game on the fourth line, with no power-play time and getting rag-dolled by guys twice your size, it isn't much fun. Stan was great, though. He just kept talking to me and giving me a lot of encouragement.

As much as Stan would bawl us out in between periods, he seldom picked on me in front of the other players. Stan had good structure and we loved how demanding he was.

There was the time in my rookie season when we lost a game in Calgary, 8–0. What made the loss even more painful was that, in addition to getting the shutout, the toughest guy on the ice during the line brawl in that game was the goalie: John Davidson. (Years later, Davidson would backstop the New York Rangers to the 1979 Stanley Cup finals, defeating what many believed was our heavily favoured Islanders team along the way.)

The whole trip back from Calgary to Swift Current, we drove in a blizzard, so it took forever. Stan must have been steaming the whole way.

It was about four o'clock in the morning before we got to a spot on the highway about a mile outside of town. Of course, most of the guys were sleeping. We stopped, Stan woke us all up, and told us to get off the bus, grab our equipment from underneath, and carry it back to the rink. That's what we did—carrying our bags for a mile through a blizzard. And when we finally got to the rink, Stan bag-skated us. *Really? A bag skate? At four in the morning?*

The next day at practice, Stan told us, "We don't ever lose like that again." And we never did.

When I called home and told Mom and Dad the story, Dad said, "I would have walked you guys the last *two* miles." When Mom came on the phone, the only thing she said to me was "I hope that you had your toque on."

No sympathy whatsoever. Lesson learned.

I had great respect for Stan. He was a strong leader. From the time I left home, Stan and Sheila always seemed to be there for me. I wasn't just a hockey player; I was part of a hockey family. I hold that close to my heart.

During Stan's summer hockey schools, I really got to know Tiger Williams. I gravitated towards him pretty quickly, and Tiger was quick to embrace me. Off the ice, he was always helpful, always prideful. He had street smarts—he was savvy and keen. For some reason, he really trusted me. He is friendly, loyal, all those things. To have Tiger as a mentor and to remain best friends to this day is something I will cherish forever.

After Swift Current, Tiger was drafted by the Toronto Maple Leafs and went on to have an amazing NHL career, playing nearly a thousand regular-season games. But what everyone probably remembers most about Tiger is that he still holds the NHL career record for penalty minutes by any player. He was a warrior.

Tiger was good for me. He treated me like a brother. And that's exactly how I felt about him. In fact, my whole family really liked Tiger and enjoyed when he would come to visit the ranch. He fit right in. He liked to hunt, ride horses, and chip in with chores. He loved Mom's cooking and all of the music that Dad played. It was like he was part of the family. He adored Mom, and Dad especially liked him.

Tiger is really sharp. For instance, he always found ways for us to make extra money. We'd help a guy build a shed or put a new roof on a barn, and make fifty dollars for the day. I always had extra pocket money because of Tiger.

Over time, I really got to know Tiger, the real Tiger. He was always himself around me, and I loved it.

Years later, I asked him about why he was so good to me. Just to shut me up, he said, "Because I'm afraid of your old man. He's going to kick me in the ass." A typical Tiger response that always makes me laugh when I think about it.

You may not believe this, but Tiger married the prettiest girl in Swift Current, his wife, Brenda. She fell in love with the real Tiger—the guy that I know—the warm, gentle Tiger who is so different from the player on the ice. They're two of my favourite people in the whole wide world.

Tiger isn't a really big man for the kind of game he played. He was maybe five foot eleven and 185 pounds. But he played like he was six foot six and bulletproof. He was our toughest player—and we had some rough fellas on that Swift Current team, including our captain Terry Ruskowski, Kelly Pratt, and Brian Back. But Tiger had a presence about him. He was the big man in the room.

He was also a student of the game—not just fighting—and he used to talk about hockey all of the time. "I'm going to try this." "I'm going to do this." "I want to do this." Tiger wanted to improve his game every day in practice, and he had purpose the whole time he was at the arena.

Tiger made himself into an NHL hockey player. He could play forward. He could play defence. He could scrap. And he could score goals—people forget that he scored a lot of goals. He scored because he practised to improve his shot and his skills. And maybe because he made a little more room and time for himself. Some weren't so willing to get within ten feet of him.

And luckily for me, the other message Tiger sent out was, "Don't touch this little kid over there or I'll beat the shit out of you."

The WHL, or the Dub, was a pretty vicious league in those days. Spearing, high-sticking, cross-checking, elbowing, leaving your feet to finish a check, and head hunting. Blood and guts. It had some scary characters.

I was five foot six and 160 pounds, so I had my head on a swivel all the time. I felt like a boy playing against men. I got into some fights I should have never gotten into against bigger, stronger guys than me, and generally got beat up. Not fun going to the penalty box thinking, "Oh man, I took another shitkicking."

But Tiger would encourage me. "That was a good punch," he'd say. "Keep throwing them."

"Fuck, Tiger. I only threw one punch."

"Yeah, but it was a good one."

After a while, Tiger told me that he didn't really want me fighting anymore. "Stick up for yourself, but be careful not to bust up your hands," he said. It's the same thing Clark Gillies told me a few years later when I got to the Islanders. "Number one, you're an ugly fighter," Clark said. "And number two, stick up for yourself and don't get hurt."

I never said this to Clark or Tiger, but I was thinking, *When I'm mad, I don't care.*

Thank God Tiger taught me how to protect myself. Every day after practice, we'd wrestle on the ice. He would come over and just start mauling me—not beating me up, but just controlling me. It was exhausting. I could barely hold my arms up afterwards. He never hit, but he would grab me, and he taught me how to grapple.

"Look, you've got good balance," he'd say. "Stay low, and use your strength. You're a farm kid. You just tie them and twist them and throw them on the ice and then hold them down. Neutralize them."

He added: "Most of the guys are not as tough as they think they are. Seventy-five per cent of the league is chicken shit. Twenty per cent are bluffers. But watch out for that other five per cent."

Eventually, I got to the point where if we got into a fight or a bench-clearing brawl and I paired off against one of those super thugs, I wasn't afraid anymore. Tiger had built my confidence. I figured if I could handle myself with Tiger Williams, if I could survive against the toughest guy in the league, I had nothing to worry about anymore. I got really good at grappling. Thanks, Tiger.

Still, every once in a while he would come to my rescue. A guy would bump me and Tiger would come in and thump him. I almost resented it a little bit.

"What the hell was that all about?" I'd say to him.

"He knows."

"He knows what?"

"To leave you the fuck alone. And I owed him one anyway."

But I did need him sometimes. His presence was welcome.

Early in that first season, prior to Tiger's training, I took some lickings. So bad that I was ready to quit.

Hockey wasn't fun. Not only was I not playing very much, but there were line brawls, bench-clearing brawls, and some mismatched fights I should have never been in. I had black eyes, lost teeth, fat lips, stitches—things that'd never happened to me before. I had my nose broken several times. It wasn't fun going to school looking like that.

At the same time, I was so homesick, even though I was only seventy miles from Val Marie. I think at some point every kid feels like that, but it's especially true for Native kids because we feel so isolated sometimes because of discrimination. You want to be around your own people. I remember when Ron Delorme joined the team. He's from Cochin, Saskatchewan, which is a Native community, and he's just a little younger than I am. When he joined the Broncos, he came up to me and said, "Bryan, I'm so glad you're on this team. I don't know if I'd play junior hockey if you weren't on this team."

He was good enough, tough enough, and hungry enough. I told him I was sure he would have found a way, but I knew exactly what he was talking about. When I first got to Swift Current, I wished there had been somebody else with Native blood on the team. And maybe there was, I don't know, but in those days nobody mentioned that they had Native blood unless they had to, or if it was obvious. Maybe not every family was like ours, where we were always taught to be proud of it. But I still felt that sense of being on my own.

When I went home for Christmas, I decided that I was finished playing junior hockey for good. Dad picked me up and that whole ride home was a fog. I couldn't wait to get back to the ranch. It was going to be a great Christmas, we'd have a nice Christmas dinner, and then I'd start high school in Val Marie again and maybe play a little senior hockey and just get back into the old rhythm. I was talking to myself the whole way.

It was the twenty-third of December, and the next two days were going to be awesome. And then came Boxing Day. We had a game scheduled on the twenty-sixth and I had to be back in Swift Current by noon.

Christmas with the family was great, and that made me even more homesick at the thought of going back. Everything had been perfect the past few days.

Now it was the twenty-sixth. I didn't say anything to anybody about how I was feeling. But in my head, I just had a little bit of a quiet rebellious moment. *I'm not going to go back. And once I don't turn up, Stan will realize that I'm not coming.* That's how I played it out in my head.

It was getting close to ten o'clock. Dad looked at me and said, "We'd better get on the road pretty quick. I think the bus is leaving at noon."

I mumbled something—"Yeah, maybe noon . . ."—just trying to kill time. If I delayed and delayed and delayed . . .

The clock kept moving—10:30. 10:45. It was an hour's drive door to door.

All of a sudden, the phone rang. I must have jumped ten feet in the air. Dad answered it.

"Hi Stan," he said. "Bryan? Yeah he's right here."

I remember thinking, *Shit* . . .

"Are you coming?" Stan asked me. "We'll hold the bus for you . . ."

"I don't know," I said. "I don't know."

"We'll hold the bus."

"I'm not sure, Stan. I don't know if I'm going to make it."

"You don't feel good?"

"I don't know," I said over and over again. "I just don't know."

I think Stan guessed what was going on. But he never let on.

"Okay," he said. "Well, practice is tomorrow morning, ten o'clock."

"Okay," I said. "Maybe . . ."

I wasn't telling him yes and I wasn't telling him no. But when I got off the phone, I felt so much better. *I think he knows I'm not coming to the game today. I think he knows I'm not coming to practice tomorrow—so I'm off the hook now.*

Not so fast.

As soon as I got off the phone, Dad looked at me.

"You're going back," he said.

"I don't know, Dad."

"Oh, you're going back."

I don't think I ever said out loud to Dad that I was staying home and going back to school in Val Marie. I didn't give him my whole plan. And he didn't say another word to me the rest of the day.

The next morning, there was a friggin' blizzard. But somehow, at seven o'clock, Tiger pulled up, driving his GTO, mag tires and all. He made it to the ranch on shitty, icy roads. I don't know what time he left Swift Current.

Boom. Boom. Boom. I heard the knock on the door, and Mom answered it.

"Oh, hi Tiger," she said.

"Hi Mary. What's for breakfast?"

"I'll make you some eggs. Want some bacon?"

Tiger sat down for breakfast as if he were a trucker in a diner. When I saw him, I asked him, "What in the hell are you doing here?"

"I'm bringing you back to Swift Current," he said, between bites. "Whether you want to come back or not. I'll hog-tie you and throw you in the car if I have to, but you're coming back."

"I don't know, Tiger," I said. "I don't think so."

Tiger, Mom, and Dad sat there having breakfast as if everything were normal, as if I wasn't even around. My stomach was in knots. I was thinking, *I'm not going back, there's no way I'm going back . . .* But I didn't say it out loud.

Then Tiger finished his breakfast.

"Well, you ready to go?" he asked me. "It's eight o'clock. We've got to get on the road. It's going to take us a while to get back because the roads aren't that good."

"Ah, I think I'm good, Tiger," I said. "I think I'm going to stay here."

"Oh no, you're coming back. Stan Dunn sent me down here to get you. You're coming back."

"I'm not sure. I don't think so."

And then Dad looked at me and said some of the most important words I've ever heard.

"You know, you can always come home."

I think every kid should hear those words. I realized that Dad was saying, "Go back. This way, you'll have no regrets." Somehow, those words just made me relax. Somewhere in my brain, I heard, *Don't quit, don't give up. You can always come home. Give it another shot.*

Looking back, I think the most interesting part is how both Mom and Dad finessed me. Mom usually softened a situation, and she had to because Dad could be pretty rough. He could have gotten up that day and said, "Get your ass in that car." And I probably would have resisted that. When I got stubborn, I got really stubborn.

But instead, he said just the right words at the right time: "You can always come home." It made leaving the house and getting in the car easier.

The next thing I knew, I was in the car with Tiger, heading north in the snowstorm. The roads were awful driving back. I spent the whole ride looking out the passenger-side window, trying to see the shoulder so we didn't go into the ditch. There were people stuck everywhere, but we didn't dare stop for anything, because Tiger figured that the minute we stopped, we'd get stuck. That's how bad the roads were.

When we got north of Cadillac, the roads got a little better. Tiger broke the silence.

"Look, I'm going to play left wing on your line, and no one's going to touch you anymore."

When we got back to Swift Current, Stan never said a word. And my teammates didn't say anything, either. I don't know if Stan said anything to them or not.

But over the years, Tiger would remind me of the story.

"Remember that time I dragged your ass back to Swift Current?" he'd say, and I'd answer, "Yeah, I do, you bastard," and we'd both laugh about it.

The first game back, I started with Tiger on my left wing. He looked at me, and all of a sudden, he became Tiger the Hockey Player. The first time somebody challenged me, he beat the shit out of them. "Nobody's touching this kid," he said.

Hockey became fun for me again. I could play without the worry of someone taking my head off. My head was still on a swivel, but I felt I was playing hockey, and nobody was going to hurt me anymore. The headhunters seemed to dwindle, and Tiger and I started lighting it up on the score sheet.

It was really important to have a teammate, and a friend, like Tiger Williams. As I said, he was really good for me.

During my junior year in Swift Current, after home games, Dad would say, "Okay, hustle up and we'll see you right after the game."

He needed me for the family band.

By now, my younger sister Kathy was doing most of the lead singing. I was the band's bass player, and Dad usually picked up a drummer or lead guitarist. The first time I played in the band, I was fourteen years old. We were just north of Val Marie, and I was pretty nervous. Thank God, it was all local farmers and ranchers we all knew. I was shaking when he plugged my bass guitar into the amp, but what I didn't know is that he didn't turn the amp on. I focused as hard as I could and thought I was playing all night long!

"That was a good session," Dad said to me afterwards. "I didn't hear one mistake. Next time, I'll turn the amp on."

The next time, he did—I watched the red power light come on. So again I focused, trying not to miss a change on any chord.

"I didn't hear any mistakes again. Next time I'll turn the volume up." He was building up my confidence, I guess.

I said, "C'mon Dad, can I turn it up so I can hear myself a little bit?" He smiled, and slowly, he started turning me up louder and louder.

Besides adding either a drummer and lead guitarist to the family band, once in a while, he'd invite Billy Howell or Gail Sylvester from Mankota, who both played great accordion music. There was good polka music those night. But most nights, there was just me and my sister. A true family band. Dad had created a good sound, consisting of traditional country songs of the '60s and '70s.

Back in Swift Current, Dad would watch the first period of my game, then take off and set up for a gig. My game would be over at 10:00 or 10:15 p.m., and by then, Dad and Kathy were generally an hour into the music. I'd get there as quickly as I could, my head still wet from the shower, and just hop on stage and start playing. Every time, Dad would say the same thing: "What took you so long?" The next thing you know, in would come Tiger and a few of my other Bronco teammates. The drinking age then was eighteen, so they'd come and enjoy the music, too.

After I made the Broncos, I had to find a new place to live in Swift Current. I was ready to go back with Gordon and Devona, but the high school said it had its own arrangement with a wonderful woman named Mrs. Ross. She was terrific and lived only a few blocks from the comprehensive high school (also known as "The Comp").

For the first few weeks, I'm not sure if Mrs. Ross even knew I played for the hockey team. She didn't know that when I left the house in the mornings, I wasn't going to school—I was going to practice. Then I'd go directly to school from the rink, and return home around 3:30. On game nights, I'd tell her I was heading out to the hockey game. I guess maybe she thought I was going to watch. Some nights, I wouldn't get home until eleven or twelve o'clock.

When I got home late, Mrs. Ross would worry about me.

"You have school tomorrow," she'd say.

"Don't worry," I'd tell her. "I'll get to school, no problem."

I wasn't lying, or even trying to lie. What I really meant was that I would get up, head to practice, and then get to school afterwards.

Mrs. Ross worried and cared, and was a little bit tough on me at times. She had a great laugh and was a superb cook. Her breaded pork chops and chicken-fried steak were my personal favourites.

When I dropped out of school after Christmas, Mrs. Ross said I'd have to leave because she was operating a boarding house for the school, not the hockey team. Mom and Mrs. Ross worked it out somehow, and I remained there for the rest of the season. Mrs. Ross became my biggest fan. It wasn't home, but she made sure that I was always well fed, well rested, and prepared to play my best hockey. A late-night snack was always waiting for me if I came home after eleven.

My decision to drop out of school was hard to explain to people. It makes it sound like you're a failure. But I was missing so much school, it was getting difficult to keep up with all of my classwork. It was impossible for me to study and do homework on the bus. I would get so carsick when I tried to read, and the smell of the old bus didn't help. I learned that standing up front and looking out the big window, staring at the road, really helped.

Practice was at ten every morning, so I was missing all of my morning classes. I went to school in the afternoon for two subjects, math and comprehensive writing, in the first semester. Most games were on the weekend, with the odd game midweek. But when we'd go on a road trip through Manitoba, to Brandon, Winnipeg, and Flin Flon, we'd be gone all week. The West Coast swing to Vancouver, Victoria, and New Westminster was a week-long trip, too, so by the end of the semester, I'd missed weeks of school.

As I've said before, I liked school. I loved everything about it. I liked seeing my friends and I liked the energy of the classroom. And one of the most influential people in my student life was my comprehensive writing teacher and guidance counsellor. We all knew her in Swift Current as Mrs. Uher, but you probably know her as Lorna Crozier, one of Canada's most respected poets. She had a big smile and great energy and she was always positive. Her enthusiasm was contagious, and being in her class was great fun for me. And Mrs. Uher liked my writing. She would always circle a particular word or phrase with a comment like "That was well used."

I think Mrs. Uher had a great impact on a lot of students. I'd walk into her classroom and she made it a point to greet me. "Bryan, we are going to get you through high school," she'd tell me. "I know you like hockey, but we are going to get you to graduate." I vividly remember sitting down with her at least a dozen times because I was missing so much school. After each road trip, she'd be waiting with my assignments. "I've got your homework," Mrs. Uher would tell me. "Here's what you have to get done, and here's your homework for the next road trip." Lorna was terrific—always prepared, always encouraging.

But by Christmas, at the end of my first semester of Grade 11, I figured I had to do something different. During one of Mom's visits, I explained to her my thinking. "I can only be a junior hockey player for a certain amount of time. And I can always go back to school. Hockey is kind of getting in the way of school, and school is kind of getting in the way of hockey. I can only get four subjects a year, and I want to give all my attention to hockey. If I don't make it in hockey, then I'll go back to school. I can always go back to school."

I knew as Mom's eyes filled with tears that I was breaking her heart. It hurt to make her cry, but Mom rallied like moms do. She grabbed my hand and said, "I know you will." And we didn't speak of it again.

But Dad had a different reaction. When he found out, he was furious. He didn't speak to me for at least two months.

Dad had always told me how much he loved school, but had to leave after Grade 6. His oldest brother Lloyd went to fight in World War II, and Dad was now Grampa's only son to help on the ranch. He had been doing chores like a man since he was six years old. So before his teenage years, schooling was done for him. He had it tough, and I'm sure that's why he wanted all of his kids to finish school, go to college, and have the opportunities that he didn't have.

Our report cards were extremely important to Dad. He didn't focus on the grades in arithmetic, spelling, or composition—it was the grade that you got for effort that he looked at right away. He loved seeing the A for effort. The message I took from that was that if you did your very best, the rest would take care of itself. Whatever the task, I'm always going to give it my best effort and focus.

He still came to my games, though. I know this because he wore a cowboy hat pretty much every day of his life. I'd always look up to see if there was a cowboy hat in the stands, and I was always excited to see it, but he wouldn't stick around afterwards to say "hello." That was tough.

When he finally started talking to me again, neither of us brought up the subject of school.

Although my Dad and Grampa never received their diploma, each of us graduated with a different kind of education. I feel as though hockey has given me a wonderful education, the kind no institution could.

CHAPTER 7

SECRET DRAFT

It was my second year with the Broncos when things really took off. We made the playoffs. We beat out the Flin Flon Bombers in the first round. And then we took on the Regina Pats, who had a great junior player named Dennis Sobchuk on their team, as well as my future left winger Clark Gillies. We lost to them in six games, a tough, hard-fought series. They went on to win the Memorial Cup—good for them. We felt that if we won that series, we would have won it all.

In addition to our great coach, Stan Dunn, we had a really good team. We had Tiger. Terry Ruskowski, our captain, was a dynamic player and a great playmaker. I really admired his game because I played a little like him, only he was a lot scrappier than I was. And tough as nails.

We had Brian Back from Biggar, Saskatchewan—where they have a sign saying, NEW YORK IS BIG . . . BUT THIS IS BIGGAR. He was short and stocky and never lost a fight. In goal, we had Lorne Molleken, who played terrific and went on to become a very successful coach.

I definitely wasn't the star of the team. We had older and stronger leadership with Terry and Tiger, but I really liked the fact that they relied on me.

Back home in Val Marie, folks were happy because I was a local kid playing for the Broncos. I can't lie, I liked the small-town fuss. And I received the best compliment when a good family friend,

Rene Cornett, told Dad, "Nobody outworks your boy." I tried to play hard for my teammates, and I was glad it showed.

The city of Swift Current really embraced us that year. I think the fans realized that even though we were going to make some mistakes, we were playing our hearts out every shift. We reflected the work ethic of the area. All of the hard-working farmers and ranchers. We wanted them to get their money's worth.

Our home, the Civic Centre, was unique because it had a tractor that pulled the Zamboni on a three-point hitch, leaving a trail of blue fumes that mixed with the cigarette smoke, creating a constant bluish haze in the building.

Frank Matovich was our radio announcer, and he loved our Bronco team. He oozed favouritism—a true homer. Win or lose, according to Frank, we always outplayed the opposition. His broadcasts were filled with energy and excitement, and he was extremely popular with his listeners. The Bronco superfan that he was, I think he got so caught up in the play, he'd forget he was announcing the game sometimes. Like this one time, he got so excited describing a play involving Tiger: "Williams over the blue line, he has a good head of steam, winds up for a slapshot, he shoots . . . *ohhhh*! He hit the fucking post!" Whoops. An errant F-bomb. The call became infamous.

My hockey life seemed pretty simple then; I had just enough money to cover room and board, and a couple of extra bucks for gas and entertainment. For four to five hours every day, as a team, we were all connected. Practice became our bonding time. It was just great to be on the ice, with all kinds of drills, and then line rushes and scrimmages.

After practice, I'd either head off to school or go to someone's house—usually Tiger's—to play cards or board games. I wasn't that good at cards, but I enjoyed learning. Losing a buck or two was like losing a million dollars when you're playing junior hockey. But looking back, it was worth it for the pure enjoyment of hanging out with the guys.

On road trips, the cards came with us. Euchre and hearts were the games of choice. We had a lot of laughs teasing and poking fun at one another. Whoever won a game would claim an imaginary championship belt. It would change hands multiple times during the course of the bus ride. It was a big deal to win the last game of the road trip, because you carried the belt until the next road trip. Those were big bragging rights!

Also during my second season with the Broncos, Mom and Dad moved into a little house in Swift Current. For a change, Dad had no winter chores. He usually had feeder calves to look after, but that winter he got a job with the Métis Association. At that point in his life, he became quite active in Métis and First Nations affairs and felt he could make a difference in the socio-political challenges. He became consumed, and he cared deeply and started going to more meetings and powwows.

It was fun having the family in the city, and it was especially great to have Mom's cooking full time.

My sister Carol became a loyal fan—and still is. She became a billet to out-of-town Broncos players, was a season-ticket holder, and went to all the games. During the games, Carol spent most of her time screaming at the referees. Coincidentally, years later, I was on a flight with Kerry Fraser, who was an NHL referee for years, but before that he worked in the Western League. We started talking about the old days in the Dub.

"I hated Swift Current," Kerry said. "There was this one person in the crowd that just screamed at me the whole game."

"Yeah," I said. "That was my sister Carol."

——

I didn't know it at the time, but Earl Ingarfield and Gary Kirk, who were both scouting for the New York Islanders, spent a lot of time watching me those first two seasons in Swift Current. But they sure enjoyed sharing the stories with me later of how they had driven through snowstorms to scout our team when we played in the Hat, or in Calgary or Swift Current.

They told me later that, even though they were scouting nineteen-year-olds, every game they scouted, I did something that made them notice me. I'd either hit somebody, or score a goal, or make a play that seemed to make a difference on the ice. I wasn't that big, but I threw my body around. I didn't spend a ton of time in the penalty box. I wasn't a dirty player. I didn't go headhunting. I didn't try to maim anybody. I was kind of a payback guy. If somebody hit me, I hit him back. I'd thump the guys who thumped me. I took that attitude with me right into the NHL. I took my penalties, but I didn't have a whole bunch of misconducts or fighting majors.

I still felt small that season. I was five foot eight, 170 pounds, and I looked like I was twelve years old. I definitely didn't look like I was ready to play in the NHL.

To me, strength, skill, and speed meant everything. I'd try to gauge myself against the best in the league. Players like Dennis Sobchuk, Lanny McDonald, Tom Lysiak, and Ron Chipperfield in Brandon. I didn't know if I was as good as those guys. I know I didn't feel strong—I had farm boy strength, but not man strength. I thought, *Oh my God, these guys are so strong. They're so fast. I need to keep getting better.*

Towards the end of that season, I got a very exciting call from the Cincinnati Stingers of the World Hockey Association.

It was an interesting time in hockey. The WHA had started in 1972 as a rival league. Its teams were paying NHL veterans big money to jump leagues, starting with Bobby Hull. Star players were getting incredibly large contracts. But they also started signing eighteen-year-olds to pre-empt the NHL, which wasn't drafting players till they were twenty. It was risky, but the WHA had to get to the players before the NHL did. For example, the Stingers signed Sobchuk, who was playing for the Regina Pats, to a million-dollar contract—$100,000 per season for ten years. Fans and reporters were calling him a "Million-Dollar Baby," but I had great respect for him because he was such a tremendous player.

To complicate things further, in 1974, the WHA actually held two drafts—a "secret" two-round draft in February, and then a regular one in June after they reached a deal with the Canadian Amateur Hockey Association that allowed them to draft underage players, so long as they only did so in the first two rounds. The NHL adopted the same rule later that year. It turned out that, because my eighteenth birthday was in July, I fell just inside the cut-off for underage players.

I didn't know any of this at the time. Heck, unlike today, where the draft is on TV and the players' profiles are everywhere, I didn't even know I was being scouted, let alone that I had been drafted by the Stingers in the second round, eighteenth overall. The phone call told me they had selected me and wanted to sign me right away.

Then the team offered me $50,000 a year for ten years—$500,000 in total. "Bryan, this is guaranteed money," they said. "Even if you get hurt, even if you break a leg and you never play hockey again, this money's going into your bank account. The first year, the first practice, this money is guaranteed. You get it, no matter what."

Cool, I thought. *I better let Dad know.*

But there was a catch. They said that if I didn't sign the contract, and I made myself available for the NHL draft, the team would pull the offer.

The Stingers's offer was more money than my parents would probably see in their lifetimes. But to Dad's credit, he wanted to make sure I had proper representation. First, he talked to his local attorney, who suggested the names of several highly regarded agents, including Tiger's agent, Herb Pinder, whom I had met at the Gordie Howe hockey camp; Alan Eagleson; and the team of David Schatia and Larry Sazant out of Montreal. Dad then did most of the calling and interviewing. I really didn't know what to say or ask about anything. We liked David and Larry a lot and decided to go with them. Dad really liked that they explained how the Stingers' offer could be used as leverage in bargaining with an NHL team if I were drafted.

I wasn't stressing over any of it. I was a seventeen-year-old kid. I don't know if I was naive or stupid, but my thinking was that, worst-case scenario, I could decide to try my luck with the NHL draft and Cincinnati would pull its offer. If, for some reason, I didn't get drafted by an NHL team in 1974, I'd just go back and play junior hockey for another year.

Cincinnati's manager called me the day before the NHL draft. He was very kind and very polite, and he made one last pitch on behalf of the Stingers.

"I'm sorry," I told him. "The advice I'm getting is that I should go into the draft. And if you pull your offer, you pull your offer. And if you don't, we can talk after the draft."

The manager said, "Bryan, we're pulling our offer right now."

Dad left the final decision to me. He didn't want to sway me. In my mind, I wasn't anti-WHA, but the Stanley Cup was in the NHL.

So it all came down to the first two rounds of the NHL draft. Would I get picked?

I knew later that Earl and Gary had promoted me hard within the Islanders organization. I probably wasn't high on anyone's draft charts. I was still smallish, but managed to be in the top ten in scoring in the WHL. I'm sure the other scouts who worked for the team, including Jim Devellano, were pushing other players. But Earl and Gary must have fought for me. They told everyone that this kid may be small, but he's got some jam, he's got some moxie. He's tricky. He's deceptive. They did their best to sell me to general manager Bill Torrey and coach Al Arbour.

The NHL draft was held by conference call that year, in secret. I guess they didn't want the WHA to know what they were doing, so they couldn't tamper with any of the players. But once the call took place, nothing was a secret for very long.

Greg Joly of the Regina Pats was the first-overall pick, by the Washington Capitals. The Islanders used their first pick, fourth overall, to take Clark Gillies, another member of the Memorial Cup champion Pats. My teammate in Swift Current, Don Larway, went eighteenth overall—the last pick of the first round—to Boston.

The Islanders' turn came up again at number twenty-two, the fourth pick of the second round. They had all of their hockey people gathered together in a room: Bill and Al, Aut Erickson, Henry Saraceno, Devellano, Earl and Gary, and I don't know who else. Supposedly, there was a big debate in the room, and it was coming right down to the wire. Jimmy D was promoting his Ontario players, Saraceno was pushing his Quebec players, and Bill had his own ideas. The Western League scouts, Earl and Gary, were there, pushing me as hard as they could. When NHL president Clarence Campbell said, "New York Islanders, you're on the clock," they still hadn't made a decision who they were going to pick.

Aut Erickson was holding the phone, and the seconds were ticking down.

They had a list of names. "Tell me, who's the best *hockey player* out of that group?" Al asked.

Earl and Gary both piped up: "Bryan Trottier." Guys who were in the room told me it was almost like they said it in stereo.

Mr. Campbell came back over the phone, telling the Islanders they had to make their pick now.

And Aut Erickson said, "Islanders select Bryan Trottier, Swift Current Broncos."

To this day, I don't know what would have happened if the Islanders didn't pick me there. I'm not sure any other NHL team would have even taken me in the second round, and because I was underage, no one could have picked me after that.

My best guess is that when the league announced that the New York Islanders had selected Bryan Trottier, the other teams were going, "Who the hell is that?"

Just as promised, when the Stingers found out I had gone into the NHL draft, they pulled their contract. But to me, it didn't matter. I was going to the Islanders and the NHL. It was one of many defining moments for me—sort of like the day when Tiger Williams dragged me back to Swift Current.

If the draft hadn't worked out—no NHL and no WHA—I would have finished school, like I promised Mom, and then played college hockey, hopefully for the Saskatoon Huskies, and received an education. But now I knew that I was at least going to have a chance to play in the NHL.

As soon as the Islanders drafted me, I got a call from Aut Erickson. Over the phone, he introduced me to Bill Torrey, Al Arbour, and everyone else in the room. All of them sounded so excited, and of course, I was, too. Bill told me I'd be getting a call from his secretary, Jeannie Boyle, to arrange my flight to Montreal, where we would meet and negotiate, and I'd be presented with my first NHL contract.

The Islanders flew us to Montreal first class—me, Mom, and Dad. Because I was only seventeen and still a minor, my parents would have to sign any contract for me. Here we were, sitting in first, and on the same flight Clark Gillies, who had been a first-round pick, was sitting in economy next to Earl Ingarfield. I was jealous of Clark because he got to sit next to Earl, and he was jealous of me because I was in first class.

First class had free booze. And before Mom and Dad knew it, they were bombed.

At some point on the flight, Dad explained our negotiating strategy. "Whatever they offer us," he said, "we're going to say that we're going home to think about it. Because their second offer is always going to be better than their first."

"All right," I said. "We've got a plan."

When we landed in Montreal, Mom and Dad still had a buzz on. Their eyes were glazed. "Oh my God, I'm looped," Mom laughed. And Dad was three sheets to the wind. We got off the plane, got our suitcases, jumped into the limo that was waiting for us, and went straight to my agents' offices to meet Bill Torrey.

Mom and Dad were still trying to shake the cobwebs.

Bill had his trademark bow tie on. He was a very impressive person, and also very friendly and sincere. I liked him right away.

"Hello, Mr. and Mrs. Trottier. How are you?" he said, shaking their hands.

When I called him Mr. Torrey, he corrected me.

"Call me Bill," he said.

After greeting Mom and Dad, Bill focused completely on me for the next fifteen or twenty minutes as he laid out the Islanders' offer. It was a five-year deal. It started at $75,000 the first year, then went up to $80,000 the second year, $100,000 the third year, and $125,000 in the fourth and fifth years.

Salary-wise, it was way more money than Cincinnati had offered, and the Islanders had no clue the Cincinnati offer had been pulled. There was also a $250,000 signing bonus—plus, the team would buy me a car of my choice. (When I got that bonus, it was the first time I'd really had a lot of money in the bank in my life. It was kind of scary. We took half of that bonus and bought a lifetime annuity with it, and I'm still getting cheques from it to this day.) Bill started going through all of the details. But it was going in one ear and out the other. I wasn't absorbing any of it because all I could think of the whole time was what Dad had said to me on the plane: tell him we're going to go home and think about it.

Finally, Bill said, "So, what do you think?"

And Dad piped up.

"Where's the pen?"

So much for our strategy. I asked Dad about it afterwards. "Weren't we supposed to go home and think about it?"

"They're crazy to offer you that much money, and we're never going to get more than that," he said. "You got a big bonus. You got a car. We'd be stupid if we didn't take that and run."

After Dad signed the contract on my behalf, Bill pushed me to decide what car I wanted. The room went silent. I think they were worried I was going to ask for a Lamborghini or an expensive Mercedes-Benz, some kind of sports car.

They all stared at me, and I looked at Mom and Dad. I paused for a few moments. And I said, "Dad's a big-car man. He needs a big car. I want a Chrysler New Yorker."

And the whole room smiled, almost in relief.

When we got back home I went car shopping, and I ordered a 1974 Chrysler New Yorker Brougham. It felt like half the car was chrome, and it had a dark blue leather interior and a blue vinyl roof. It was state of the art, with all the bells and whistles. It was gorgeous.

It was a pretty exciting day when the car arrived in August. I was playing my last season of junior with the Broncos, who were now based in Lethbridge, and I drove it to an exhibition home game against Saskatoon. There's this big Chrysler sitting in the parking lot, and all of the Saskatoon Blades came out to look at it. I bet they were thinking, *This guy must be an idiot—he could have had a sports car or a pickup, and instead he's got this boat.*

When I left for New York to join the Islanders the following season, I handed Mom and Dad the keys and said thank you for everything. Dad didn't believe it at first.

I came home the following summer and the car was gone.

"What happened to the New Yorker?" I asked Dad

"I couldn't fit all of the musical instruments in the trunk," he told me. "So I traded it for a van."

And that's what he had done—he'd traded that beautiful New Yorker for a 1969 Ford van that he fixed up, complete with shag carpeting in the back.

Horse trading and upgrading. That was my Dad.

CHAPTER 8
A TASTE FOR A BLACK ACE

When I signed my contract with the Islanders, Bill Torrey told me that he was 99 per cent sure I would be going back to junior for another year. The team believed the extra season would give me a chance to mature physically and to develop good leadership skills.

My Broncos moved from Swift Current to Lethbridge the same summer I signed my pro contract. I don't know the whole story of why it happened. Bill Burton was majority owner, and it was his decision to move the franchise. I do know that Gary Kirk and Earl Ingarfield, who had scouted me for the Islanders, ended up being investors, and Earl became our coach.

I had heard that Burton wasn't very welcome in Swift Current for a long time after the team relocated. The decision he made was not popular at all.

In August of '74, the Islanders arranged a press conference in Lethbridge. Al Arbour came out to announce I would be staying in junior in Lethbridge, and that Earl Ingarfield would be my coach. Al and Earl tag-teamed me, reminding me that the final year of junior would be a great development opportunity for me and not to waste it. Al said he hoped I wasn't disappointed about not being invited to training camp with the Islanders. I was—but I knew I had to trust their decision.

Dad was there, too, nodding in agreement. The press conference and the time I spent with Al and Earl really juiced me up. I became ultra-focused and looked forward to the start of the season.

Afterward, Dad raved about Al Arbour. "He looked me in the eye and had a firm handshake. You pay attention to this guy," he said.

Life is funny. When I started to play for Al, he used the two phrases that Dad always used: "smarten up" and "bear down." I had heard those words a thousand times from Dad. He used to also say, "Don't do things to get them done—do them to get them done right." Coincidence? Maybe. But it made me pay attention.

Prior to the Broncos' training camp, I was selected to be part of a Western Hockey League all-star team that played eight exhibition games against the World Hockey Association All-Stars. They were preparing for a series against the Soviet Union. It was two years after the famous Summit Series, but the guys who were in the WHA—including Bobby Hull—hadn't been allowed to be part of the '72 team.

Calgary became our home base for the next two months. Scotty Munro was our head coach. He was tough, but I really liked him, and I think he liked me, too. The series ended up being another good way to gauge myself against professional hockey players. Being small—I was now five foot nine and 185 pounds—I couldn't get over how much bigger the WHA fellas looked than they did on TV.

Competing against guys like Serge Bernier and Marc Tardif—big, strong guys—and veteran defencemen Whitey Stapleton and J.C. Tremblay was both intimidating and exciting. I remember thinking how confident and poised they were when they controlled the puck. They never panicked. I also remember thinking, *Would the pros be friendly?* It's crazy what kind of questions

Mom and Dad—
love at first sight.

A favourite picture of
my parents.

Val Marie.

The ol' ranch, barn, and the corrals.

Grampa and Gramma Trottier playing for the grandkids.

Grandpa Gardner,
Gramma Trottier,
Grandma Gardner,
Grampa Trottier.

Dad's Family.

Val Marie, Main Street, circa 1962.

Kathy, Carol, and me, when I didn't even know what skating was!

Putt Putt—the greatest athlete in gymkhana history.

The Raggedy Andys

Learning to skate on
Frenchman's Creek.

My first hockey team, with buddies Syrenne, Jeanson, Labelle, Bellefeuille, Magee and others.

First goal ever—December ’64

Peewee champion for the 2nd time, with Willie and Bernie.

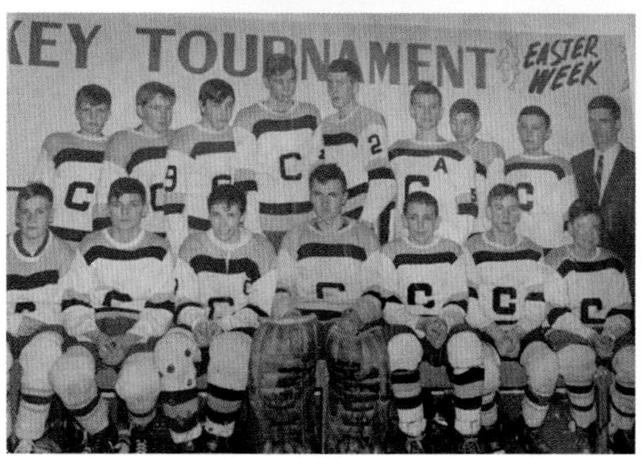

Our Climax team never lost! Peewee, Bantam, Midget—undefeated!

Terry, Leo, and Brent join Tiger and me visiting a little buddy.

My last year in junior with Earl.

go through your mind when you are nervous and adrenalin is pumping.

I had a good series. I played in seven of the eight games and posted seven points before I hurt my shoulder. Our best game was a 2–1 victory in Calgary. We were thrilled to win that one. The WHA All-Stars totally outplayed us, but we snuck away with a victory. We played as hard as we could, hoping to give them some good competition. We had Kim Clackson from Saskatoon on our team, and he was as tough as they come. Clacker was never intimidated, and I felt a little bigger and safer when he was on the ice.

But the bottom line is that we were just kids, seventeen, eighteen, and nineteen years old, and the WHA players were men. They were proud, they were going to represent Canada, so they didn't go easy on us. It wasn't chippy—there were no Gordie Howe flying elbows—it was just good, honest hockey. Gordie Howe had his two sons, Mark and Marty, with him. They weren't that much older than most of us, but they already had a year or two of pro hockey under their belts. I really enjoyed being on the ice against them.

Bobby Hull and Gordie Howe would often come to our rooms or our bus throughout the series, encouraging us—Bobby with his huge smile and gravelly voice. The two of them made a huge impression on us, Gordie especially. I'd heard all of these stories about Gordie and how you'd better watch out for him and his elbows if you went into the corner with him. But he was really good to us kids. He'd come over and talk to us in the locker room and on our bus, complimenting us in his quiet voice. I remember thinking, *Here's the greatest hockey player in the world, and he's an even better person.* Both were true ambassadors for the game—humble, impeccable, and confident. Like every kid, I wanted to be like them and treat people the way they treated people.

After that series, I was in great shape when I got to Lethbridge. I bunked in with Gary Kirk and his wife, Laureen, and their three boys for a couple of weeks and became part of their family. Dinnertime was lively; conversations were everywhere. The Kirks were normal, everyday Canadians, and we remain friends to this day.

I had put on a good ten pounds and grown an inch or two since the end of the previous season. And for some reason, I felt stronger and more confident after that WHA series. I was really looking forward to having Earl Ingarfield as my coach, and as Earl had promised, he pushed me and turned out to be the best mentor I could have had at that time.

I would stop by Earl's office once or twice a week, just to visit and pick his brain. I loved hearing his stories about the NHL—he'd played for the New York Rangers, Pittsburgh Penguins, and California Golden Seals—and he answered my questions with such patience. *Do you think I'll be fast enough? What was it like taking faceoffs against Béliveau and Mikita?* He was always willing to share his knowledge and make time for me.

Earl had played against some of the greatest players of his time, and most of them were my favourites. Being compared to the greats was very motivating for me. Earl was good at using them as examples.

"You were strong on the puck like Esposito."

"Keep protecting the puck like Mahovlich."

"Your backhand pass reminded me of Keon."

I would have been nuts not to enjoy this stuff.

But Earl had moments when he had to be the bad guy. He held me accountable. I didn't like it, but at least Earl was fair and accurate. A lost faceoff that resulted in a goal or opposition chance got a "Bear down, Bryan." A mediocre shift was "unacceptable."

He'd shake his head and say, "Your standard has to be so much higher at the NHL level."

Sometimes, Earl would say, "You're better than that." I'd get mad, but I knew he was right. I *was* better than that.

If I made a mistake, he'd call me aside or ask me to stop by his office after practice. He never embarrassed me in front of my teammates. Most times, even before he started to speak, I pretty much knew what I had done wrong and what was coming.

Earl made our tête-à-têtes quick and painless. "Hey," he would say, "bear down and don't do it again." It got to the point where, before he said anything, I'd say, "Earl, I know what you're going to say."

Eventually, it became just a look and a nod. His look said, "You know what I'm going to say," and my nod back said, "I get it. And I won't do it again." Any criticism he gave me was followed by "Now get out there."

My confidence soared under Earl. I'd play thirty to thirty-five minutes a game, with time on the power play and killing penalties, and I was double-shifted and took last-minute faceoffs. I did it all. It was all great developmental and situational time.

One night, the team had a hell of a brawl in Calgary. All six of us on the ice against all six of them. We were going at it pretty good. It felt like I was slugging it out with everybody out there. I ended up getting kicked out of the game and watched the third period from the stands with my cousins. We lost the game, and I was thinking, "Oh my God, I'm going to catch hell from Earl for going crazy out there."

As I was getting on the bus, Earl came up to me and said he "wanted a word." He didn't look happy. *Oh no, here it comes.* But instead, he said, "Bryan, I like that feistiness in you every once in a while. But don't make a habit of it, okay?" Then he smiled. Did he actually credit me for losing it out there? Yup! But not without the message "We need you on the ice and in the game."

Enough said.

I nodded.

Earl named me captain of our Broncos. Little did I realize at the time that it was going to be an education in leadership. And Earl was a spectacular teacher.

He told me that the first thing that I had to understand was that just because I was captain, I shouldn't take anything for granted. "Expectations will be high, and you can handle it," Earl told me. "Your execution and conduct both on and off the ice should be that of Béliveau and Howe." I only nodded, but my brain was thinking, "Well, all right."

"If you have trouble with any of it, come see me and we'll figure things out." I'll never forget these words. I loved the role and loved having Earl as a resource. He called it a natural next step for me, and he was right. I didn't want to let Earl down, nor did I want any reports going back to the Islanders that I was just getting by and not putting in the effort.

The first time Earl asked me to hold a locker-room meeting with the players was a jolt. I said, "Earl, I'm really not 100 per cent sure what I should say to the team."

"You'll figure it out," he said with a smile that told me, "You've got this."

Finding the right words and message the first time was uncomfortable, but it actually became less and less awkward each time afterward. Plus as anyone who wears a *C* on their jersey knows, there are plenty of good leaders on the team with you; some are wearing *A*s and some aren't, but everyone has leadership skills to contribute and the group rallies quickly. Ron Delorme was my rock that year. Our Bronco team jelled because of it.

Was Earl preparing me for the days ahead when I might become a quiet leader on a young Islanders team? Maybe.

Thanks, Earl.

On and off the ice, life in Lethbridge was wonderful. The city embraced the team and vice versa. The fans appreciated our hustle and grit. We were scrappy and we competed hard. Earl made sure we were prepared for battle, and I always left the rink exhausted.

Our home rink was brand-spanking new. "State of the art" was the term most used to describe the Sportsplex. It had the largest blue curtain I'd ever seen at the south end of the building. It was bigger than anything I had ever seen on the Ed Sullivan, Carol Burnett, or Red Skelton shows combined. It was a real showstopper! At least eighty feet tall from the ceiling to cement floor—the perfect backdrop for a sporting event or concert.

The Sportsplex stood on the outskirts of Lethbridge, surrounded by a treeless parking lot, which meant there was nothing to block the prairie winds that would carry the chinooks from the Rocky Mountains. These winds were usually warm, but in Lethbridge they always seemed to be constant.

We all enjoyed our time in this great little city. They welcomed all of us and we appreciated it.

I got a chance to reunite with my old teammate and buddy from Val Marie, Bernie Syrenne. He had moved to Lethbridge with his family a few years prior, so I got together with him quite a bit. He played Junior B hockey in Taber and later married his high school sweetheart, Joyce, and moved to Fort McMurray. Our dads had played hockey together years earlier and were long-time friends, so my parents usually stayed at their place when they came to town for a game.

Our team was solid. Ron Delorme, Greg Woods, and I were the team's centres. Lorne Molleken and Rollie Boutin were between the pipes. On defence we had John Lutz, Don Johnson, Doug Gillespie, and Darcy Regier. I liked our squad. I started the year on a line with Brian Sutter and Alex Tidey. Alex was a very good goal scorer with decent wheels. And Brian, well, let's start by saying he's a Sutter—intense and competitive to the bone. He could get as greasy and grimy as anyone and had a knack to score. Brian could scrum pucks as well as anyone, and against the biggest and toughest. He loved to score as much as he loved to drop the mitts. He was fearless and wouldn't back down from a challenge. Brian was a terrific teammate, a great person, and definitely a Sutter through and through.

We lost Brian late in the season when a bruised thigh muscle started to calcify. Losing him to an injury was probably one of the biggest reasons our little Bronco team didn't get past the first round of the playoffs. He personified grit.

Over the Christmas break in '74, Brian and I were selected to play in the World Junior Championship. It was only the second time the tournament had ever been held, and it wasn't quite like the world juniors we know now. Team Canada was made up of an all-star team picked only from the Western Hockey League. All our games would be played in Winnipeg and Brandon. There were six teams: Canada, the United States, the Soviet Union, Finland, Sweden, and Czechoslovakia. It was a single round-robin with no playoffs.

We had a terrific team. Jackie "Shakey" McLeod was the coach. We stayed at the old Viscount Gort Hotel in Winnipeg for two and half weeks. Sudsy (Brian Sutter) and I were roomies, and as usual, I was homesick. I wanted to be home for Christmas so bad. After the month in Calgary for the WHA series and two weeks in Winnipeg, it felt like I was never home.

It was an incredibly cold walk from the Viscount to the Winnipeg Arena. We would try to cut through the Polo Park Mall that separated the two buildings, but it was closed in the morning, and we nearly froze to death on that walk from the hotel to the rink.

The local fans packed the old Winnipeg Arena for every game. It was a phenomenal atmosphere. And the stands were full of NHL scouts—at least, they looked like scouts to us. We had no clue who they were, but we saw them sitting there, wearing fedoras, with their little pads and pens.

The hockey was fast-paced and incredibly skilled. What an experience! It was a chance to gauge myself against international competition at the highest junior level, against great players from all over the world.

We ended up winning the silver medal, after losing 4–3 to the Russians. We outshot them something like 50–20, but their goaltender, Vladimir Myshkin, stood on his head and had an incredible game.

I somehow ended up being named the most valuable player for Team Canada and won a Panasonic television—an old tube TV. We had lost the game and I didn't feel like celebrating, but I was happy to get it. It was an honour to be recognized in this way. They shipped the TV to the ranch in Val Marie, and when it arrived, I said, "Enjoy, Mom."

Mom treasured that TV. For forty years, it stayed in her room. It barely worked, but it was her son's trophy, so it was going nowhere.

The Broncos were eliminated from the '75 playoffs in the first round, and I immediately headed home to help Dad with spring chores. We were branding calves, and Tiger came down to help out. We had just put the branding irons away, and Tiger and I were walking back to the house, when Mom opened the door and said, "Bill Torrey is on the phone."

"Bryan, would you like to come to New York and watch some playoff games? We just beat the New York Rangers, so we're going up against Pittsburgh in the second round."

I wasn't saying no to that. I got a quick nod from Dad. "Yup, even though we have work to do here, you should go."

Teams are allowed to carry extra players during the playoffs in case of emergency. They're known as the Black Aces, and I became one of them for a couple of weeks. I was there to watch and learn—to "observe," as Bill called it. But the big surprise—and bonus—was being able to skate with the team in practice and actually do a few drills. I also got the chance to hang with them off the ice. I didn't know it, but as a junior, I was ineligible to play anyway. But Al would say to me, wryly, "Get ready, kid, you never know when you might get used."

It was only the Islanders' third season in the league, and they had made the playoffs for the first time. They had just beaten the Rangers, two games to one, in the preliminary round, and had started their best-of-seven quarter-final series against the Pittsburgh Penguins. I got there in time for Game Three at the Nassau Coliseum, after the Islanders had lost the first two games in Pittsburgh. They wound up losing that game, and then came all the way back to win the series in seven games—one of the greatest comebacks in NHL history.

My heart was pounding with excitement the first time I walked into the Islanders locker room. I got introduced to every player, one by one. The first player I met was Dave Fortier, then Garry Howatt, and Billy Smith. We went around the room: Billy Harris, Ed Westfall, Gerry Hart, J.P. Parisé, Jude Drouin, the Potvin brothers. Veteran Bert Marshall was in his stall, putting Tiger Balm on his legs to warm them up. Excitedly, I stuck out my hand to say hello, and instinctively, Bert grabbed my hand and shook it. Hot Tiger Balm slithered through my fingers and dripped to the floor. Bert tried to apologize, and the whole room was howling.

The last thing I wanted was to be the centre of attention or distraction. I wanted to be a wallflower. I didn't want any special attention. I wanted to watch, learn, and absorb—seen but not heard. It didn't quite happen that way, though.

The entire team pulled me in and welcomed me. Everybody made me feel comfortable. The team fitted me for skates and equipment, and I borrowed Bob Bourne's stick so that I could practise with the guys. I didn't know I was going to get the chance to be on the ice. Man, it was exciting.

I did watch, with big eyes. And I did listen, with big ears. I was a sponge. I was amazed by everything about a professional NHL team. I didn't want to miss anything, and I especially wanted to remember everything. And everything seemed first class. *Man, oh man!* And the players? They were powerful and smooth. Every play was executed with conviction. *Wow!*

One of my favourite memories from that spring was my first meal with an NHL pro. Bill Smith's first son was born during these playoffs, and he was handing out cigars on the bus. "Here's one for you, too, kid."

When he finished passing out the stinky stogies, he passed by me again and said, "We're going out for Chinese. Hey, you like movies?"

I nodded. I was surprised and excited. My first NHL meal and movie were with Billy Smith, and we've been best friends ever since.

I even got asked to drive some of the players' cars from the hotel to the Coliseum. (During the playoffs, everyone was locked up in a hotel during the home games.) One day, it was Eddie Westfall's Porsche Carrera; the next, it was Billy Harris's Cadillac Seville. Cruising the Long Island Expressway, creating our own Black Aces convoy.

There were five French-speaking players on the team, as I recollect: the Potvin brothers, Jean and Denis; J.P. Parisé, with his deep, booming voice; Jude Drouin, with his full, black playoff beard; and André St. Laurent, nicknamed "The Pinto" for the birthmark near his testicles. I guess because of my last name, they assumed I spoke French. I spoke very little then, but understood enough to know that I had been asked to dinner after Game Five in Pittsburgh. "All right," I thought to myself. "I can fake my way through this."

I laughed when they laughed and tried my best to follow, but they spoke so damn fast. One-word answers and shoulder shrugs could hide my ignorance for only so long.

All of the guys huddled around me and snuck me into a lounge. Jude, in French, told me to roll my collar up and look at the ground to hide my young face. The legal drinking age in the state was twenty-one, but voilà, this eighteen-year-old kid walked into his first Pennsylvania bar with *"les boys."*

It was André St. Laurent who finally figured out that I wasn't bilingual.

"You don't speak, French, do you?" he asked me in English.

"I speak a little," I said.

"Do you understand it?"

"A little," I responded. Busted. This got a good laugh from my French hosts.

The best part of the whole evening was that I was hanging with NHLers. They didn't treat me like a teenager. I sat in the bar and I wasn't a kid anymore. It was as if that very night, I grew whiskers!

I called home on the morning of Game Seven against Pittsburgh. "When are you coming home?" Dad asked—not "Are you having a great time?"

"We're going to Pittsburgh for Game Seven." I told him.

"Well, hurry home. We've got work to do."

The Islanders won Game Seven, and were set to face Philadelphia in the next round.

"Are you going to stick around?" Bill asked me.

"I'd love to," I told him, "but Dad wants me home."

Bill sort of smiled and said, "Okay, it was great you came in."

The trip proved to a great experience. I met the team, I got to skate with them, gauge myself against their speed and skill, and I wouldn't be coming to my next camp a stranger. All of this made me even more eager to get in the best shape I possibly could for the season coming up.

When I got home, the first thing Dad said to me was, "Okay, hop on the swather. We're cutting hay. What took you so long?"

Great to be home!

CHAPTER 9

MAKING THE TEAM

When I arrived at Islanders training camp in September, '75, I didn't feel like a stranger. Being with the team during their playoffs, I knew all the names and faces, and hopefully the guys remembered me.

I had a rancher's tan after spending the summer working—not a farmer's tan, where half of your arms are dark and then you are as white as a ghost where the T-shirt covers you up. Mine was different. I usually had my jeans and boots on and wore a cowboy hat. Seldom did I wear a shirt. Sunshine and ninety-degree days were plentiful, so I had a deep, red tan from my head to my waist. But from the waist down, I was lily white. My white legs seemed to shine during the dry-land workouts while wearing those thigh-high '70s gym shorts. Everyone else had legs that were bronzed and tanned. They were probably thinking, "Look at this strange country bumpkin." Secretly, I liked them teasing me because it made me feel included.

When we got down to work at Racquet and Rink in Farmingdale, which was the Islanders' practice arena, whatever experience I'd gained from the year before, whatever my draft position, didn't matter now. I was just another rookie trying to make the team. Forty other draft picks, free agents, and guys who had played in the minors the previous year were in the same situation. And Al made it clear to all of us from the start that we would have to earn every chance we got.

There were only twenty-one stalls in the main room, so the team had a separate dressing room to segregate the lowly rookies from the NHL vets. None of us in the rookie room knew each other very well. I had met Brad Anderson and Neil Nicholson the previous spring, when we were Black Aces together. Neil Smith, who much later became the Rangers' general manager and won a Stanley Cup with them in '94, was there. He had been drafted right out of college. It impressed me that Neil was a college kid coming to an NHL camp. He had a confidence about him and had a solid camp.

Defenceman Pat Price, who played junior in Saskatoon, was also a familiar face. Pat got headlines for being the first-overall pick in the 1974 WHA draft. He signed a huge contract with the Vancouver Blazers before that team folded, and now here he was, at his first NHL camp, because the Islanders had also drafted him in the first round. Expectations were high for Pat.

No headlines for me. I was a second-rounder, still smallish. I'd grown a bit—I was now five foot eleven, 195. I was just trying to get a grip on things, and somehow I was going to get myself noticed. I wasn't looking for headlines; I was looking to earn a spot on that roster. The young Islander team had had some success in the playoffs, so my thinking was that I wanted to get people's attention. It didn't matter who had the puck, I'd finish every check. My instinct was that I would hit everything that moved, bump him, sting him if I could—nothing dirty, keep it clean, but get noticed. I just wanted everyone to know I was there.

We played eleven exhibition games in fifteen days, and I played in all of them. But I didn't play one shift on the power play and I didn't kill any penalties. I was hoping to, but I never got the chance—and of course, I didn't dare complain. I didn't score a goal, I didn't pick up many assists and I don't remember talking to Al or Bill much during training camp, nor did they speak to me.

Every day, I would see one or two kids packing their bags. They were either heading home, back to college or junior, or for a little more seasoning in the minors. It was sad to see them leave. I kept wondering, *Am I next?*

Suddenly, I was the only guy left in that big, quiet room. I was the last man standing. With a couple of days to go before the start of the season, Al came in and sat down beside me.

"We think we're going to keep you for a while," he said. "We might not keep you here long. We'll get you out of the hotel. You're going to meet a family that you can board with for as long as you're here."

The Islanders could keep me for nine games and then make a decision on whether to keep or send me back to junior for the rest of the year. But for the moment, at least, I was in the NHL.

I met Warren and Pat Amendola after our last exhibition game. Warren ran the Koho hockey equipment company in the States, and he and Pat had three sons, Renny, Russ, and Rick. Warren was welcoming, sincere, but firm. He set down the rules of the house and I followed them. Pat was warm and friendly and had a beautiful smile. They immediately made me feel like part of the family. I ended up staying with them the whole year.

I was the only rookie to start with the Islanders that year. And as good as the veterans were to me, they did keep me in my place. On the first road trip we took, they said, "Okay, rook, you take care of the luggage . . ."

"Wha . . . ?" I had no idea how to take care of everyone's bags. We flew commercial in those days, so checked luggage was the norm. Ed Westfall, with the biggest smile on his face, quipped, "Rookies make sure that the luggage gets from the airport to their hotel rooms. And don't screw it up, kid."

I had to find a skycap at the airport to help me load the bags onto the bus, then I needed a bellhop at the hotel to help me get them off of the bus and up to everyone's room. I was so careful about doing the job right, even though my wallet was a little lighter after tipping everyone.

By the fourth or fifth road trip, I was deliberately sending bags to the wrong rooms. If a teammate complained, I would say, "Dammit! I tipped that friggin' bellhop really well, too. Sorry about that." The boys were getting pissed, and eventually, I lost the job. I'd never been happier to be fired in my life.

The other standard hazing ritual for rookies back in those days was shaving—not just your face, and not just your head. Any part of your body that had a speck of hair on it was fair game. Eyebrows, armpits, pubic hair. Every day, the guys would sing the Gillette jingle from the commercials, letting me know that it was coming, sooner or later. So I'd stay on the ice until I saw the last player leave. I'd just wait them out so I wouldn't get shaved. The trainers would come out and yell at me, telling me it was time to go home. I managed to dodge the ritual by feigning extra practice time on the ice.

I was still the low man on the totem pole when I started my second year. I remember the guys telling me, "We didn't get you last year, but we're going to get you this year."

Crap, I thought. *I'm going to have to wait them out again.*

Somehow, I slipped by again. But they did get Mike Kaszycki, who came up halfway through that season. The boys were eager to shave somebody, and poor Kaz was the victim.

But I did get pranked by the guys during my rookie year. Al's birthday set the stage.

Jude Drouin and Jean Potvin came to me and said that, every year on Al's birthday, there was a tradition that a rookie must hit him in the face with a cream pie.

So, I said okay. What did I know? It was tradition, right?

They handed me the pie. I waited with my back to the door. Al walked into the dressing room and was now right behind me. I turned quickly and hit him square in the face with the pie. Bull's eye! "Happy birthday, Al!"

Al always wore glasses, and when I hit him with the pie, I broke the frames right in half.

I was mortified, and the whole team scattered. I was alone, staring at my coach with thick coconut cream pie dripping off his face. Al didn't say a word. He turned and walked towards the training room next door. Immediately, I knew I had been set up.

The guys started giving it to me, saying I'd be out of there, that I'd be back in junior. I started to think he was calling my junior team to send me back, maybe calling the airlines to book my flight.

I don't think I slept a wink that night. I was freaking out.

The next day, Al came in and his glasses were taped together at the bridge of his nose. He looked like one of the Hanson brothers from *Slap Shot*.

He looked at me and said, "Well, kid, look what you did."

Al was making a joke of it, and I didn't dare laugh. I figured that he now had something on me. If I screwed up even a little bit, he could always bring up the pie in the face and the busted glasses.

But he never did. And I never did, either.

The guys goaded me into doing it again during my second season. I was a lot gentler with my throw. I even had a towel ready for him this time. It was all in good fun, and Al was a good sport.

In Gramma and Grampa Trottier's house, there was a large porcelain vat, probably twenty-five gallons, that they called the wine crock. It had a wooden lid on it, and there was a ladle that hung on the side. Each time Gramma and Grampa would walk by, they'd taste and sample it and say, "Oh, it's almost ready!" It seemed to me they were always throwing something in the crock—dandelions, chokecherries, Saskatoon berries. Each time the lid was lifted, you could see and smell the fumes. It was so thick. The wine crock was in the spare bedroom where all the grandkids slept when we stayed overnight. Some mornings, I'd wake up in a fog from smelling those fumes all night.

Everyone in town knew that Gramma and Grampa had some homemade wine brewing, and it became a popular spot to stop and have a taste. No one got turned away, regardless of the hour, and I got to know a lot of the people in Val Marie through these "tasting" visits.

I never liked the taste of alcohol. Personally, I hated the smell coming from the vat, so maybe that added to my distaste of alcohol and, as I grew up, influenced how I felt about drinking in general. I tried beer and didn't like the taste. I didn't like the taste or smell of whiskey or wine. It wasn't a conscious decision not to drink; I just didn't like any of it.

Looking back, there was some alcohol abuse in our family, but I think there was some alcohol abuse in a lot of families at that time. Dad struggled with alcohol, and it became a bigger issue for him later in life. It's a tough habit to break. In the 1980s, he joined Alcoholics Anonymous. Dad was alcohol-free for the last twenty years of his life. We all rallied and supported him, and it was just one more thing that made me proud of him.

There was no lack of drinking in hockey, and I can't say that I was never a part of it. I did celebrate a time or two with the team, but it always took me a few days to recover. That licorice taste and smell of sambuca still makes me feel sick to this day. (Damn you, Duane Sutter, for that.) At season-end parties, I'd have a few drinks with the guys, too, but the truth is, I just didn't like the taste of alcohol. It got to the point where I'd just go around with ice in a glass.

There's a story that got back to me from around the time I was drafted that always made me feel uneasy. When I was drafted by the Islanders, some people were speculating that, because of my First Nations heritage, if I weren't a drunk now I'd probably become one later. These types of stereotypes suck!

I was nineteen years old my first year in the league, and the legal drinking age on Long Island was twenty-one. And somehow, the guys would find a way to get me in the bar so that I could hang out with them. They'd hand me a glass of orange juice or a Coca-Cola, and I'd sip on it and enjoy their company.

The team had a two-beer limit after each game, and the two beers would be sitting in your stall, waiting for you. Because I didn't drink, I was the most popular guy in the room. Billy Smith usually got one of my beers, and Clark Gillies would walk by and I'd discreetly hand him the other.

Smoking was much the same story for me. I didn't like the taste or smell of tobacco. What really influenced me away from smoking was that both my parents told me "athletes don't smoke." They told me that I wouldn't be able to breathe as well if I smoked. And I wanted to be an athlete. I prided myself on my stamina, because when I was younger, we only had eight or nine kids on a team and I'd play forty or fifty minutes of a sixty-minute game. I loved being on the ice, so smoking was never going to be part of my life.

I saw both grandfathers die from smoking-related cancers. Grampa Trottier actually made his own pipe tobacco out of willow bark. He ended up with throat cancer. He missed smoking his pipe, so even after he got cancer, he put his pipe in his mouth "sans tobacco." Grandpa Gardner was what some folks refer to as a two-packer, and cancer got him, too. And although Mom smoked—she wasn't a heavy smoker—she was quite stern and direct when it came to the effects of cigarettes and tobacco. For these reasons, I never smoked, and my brothers and sisters never picked up the habit, either.

When I first got to the big leagues, it blew my mind to see NHL players smoking cigarettes. How could they play in the NHL and do that? In my first few years in the league, the guys smoked right in their stalls between periods and after games. That, too, was a little shocking as well.

A favourite memory of that 1975 camp is when Clark Gillies, from Moose Jaw, and Bobby Bourne, from Kindersley, invited me out to lunch after morning practice. We were all from Saskatchewan and we'd played against each other in junior. We went to a lounge called the Crow's Nest, and on the ride over, they kept talking about the importance of "hydration."

Clark walked away from the table, then came back and put a pitcher of beer on the table. I thought to myself, *Well, I guess I'm going to be having a beer with the Sask boys today*. I kind of laughed to myself and said to Clark and Bob, "I don't know if you realize, but I'm only nineteen years old, so I'm underage and I'm not supposed to be drinking. But sure, whatever."

And Clark said jokingly, "Hey kid, this is mine. Get your own."

Then Bob Bourne came back and sat down with *his* pitcher of beer and asked, "Do you want some?"

A pitcher of beer each, and a dry sandwich. That was their lunch that day. And we had two hours until we were supposed to be back on the ice. I choked down my ham sandwich and washed it down with a soft drink.

Lunch with these two was a laugh fest. It was one of the early times that I really felt included and part of a team. I made it a point to do the same for new kids at camp.

CHAPTER 10

ROOKIE

There's nothing like putting on an NHL jersey for the first time. It's a moment I always dreamed about. I had goosebumps. The New York Islanders crest on the front, the number 19 on the back. *This is my jersey; my NHL identity. People are going to recognize me as number 19.* I will remember that feeling forever.

Well, it was sort of my own jersey. It was really Craig Cameron's old one. He had worn number 19 until he was traded to Minnesota in January of '75. The jersey was way too big, but I didn't care. Craig was also six foot three and weighed, like, 230 pounds. I was five-eleven and 190.

If you can find my rookie card, you can see how enormous and oversized the jersey was. You can barely see my hockey pants! It was so large, the neckline exposed my shoulder pads. It Hung on me like an oversized muumuu dress.

And I loved it!

How did I end up with number 19? Well, Jim Pickard, the Islanders' equipment manager, sat with me and presented the available numbers. Nineteen was the lowest one available. And it sounded good. The number felt perfect. I was nineteen years old. Paul Henderson wore number 19 when he scored for Canada in the Summit Series in 1972. I was thinking about all of the other number 19s in the league. Johnny McKenzie wore number 19 for the Bruins. And Larry Robinson in Montreal. Maybe this number is going to have some mojo for me.

Jimmy loved it, too, and handed me the jersey that night. I wore that jersey all my first season, and didn't get one that fit me properly until the playoffs the following spring.

The Islanders' budget seemed to be pretty tight in 1975. Jimmy Pick handed me a pair of long underwear, the old-fashioned style with the button-up flap in the back. "Here you go, Trots, your game gear. The only pair you'll get all year." Again, I didn't care.

"Let's get your sticks ordered, Trots." It was the next item on Jimmy's to-do list for me. I thought to myself, *I get my own pattern? I get to order my own sticks?* Buzz Deschamps was the Koho stick rep. I handed him the Bob Bourne pattern I was using and he said, "We'll get you a dozen sticks to get you started and we can make any changes that you want right away. And we'll keep tweaking until it's perfect." Jimmy then said I was allowed five dozen sticks for the whole season, and I thought to myself, *Holy cow! That's sixty sticks!* I never in my whole life had sixty sticks. I probably hadn't used sixty sticks in total to that point. This NHL life was something else.

Everything was beyond first class that rookie year. Way better even than I thought it would be. I loved being in the NHL. In junior, we had to pack our own bag, haul it to the bus, haul it off the bus, and hang up our equipment to dry before we left for the hotel or home. And here, in the NHL, I would come to the rink and my stuff would be hanging up in my stall, and after the game, all I had to do was pack the bag and someone (usually one of the locker room boys) would grab it, put it on a trolley, and roll it to the bus. I wouldn't see it again until the next day, when it would be neatly hung in my stall all over again. Now, who wouldn't love that?

I played my first regular-season game in a place where they don't even have NHL hockey anymore: Kansas City, Missouri, home of the Scouts, who moved to Denver at the end of that season and, after a short stint as the Colorado Rockies, eventually became the New Jersey Devils. It was October 8, 1975.

The Kansas City Scouts' logo was pretty cool. It had a picture of a proud Native on the back of a horse. It impressed the hell out of me.

The game was a bit anticlimactic and ended in a 1–1 tie. Though the score made it sound uneventful, for me, every shift was more exciting than the last, and I probably ran around the ice like a chicken with my head cut off, not accomplishing much, but burning a lot a fuel. At the end of the game, the only thing Al said to us was "Let's get ready for the next one." I liked the message. We'd gained a point on the road, it wasn't a loss, we did nothing negative, we did nothing that deserved a compliment. Let's just get ready for the next game.

But it was still so friggin' exciting to be able to play my first NHL game.

The first NHL pass I received in that KC game was memorable for a whole bunch of reasons. It was from Denis Potvin. He was only in his third season in the league and was already a superstar. Powerful, smart, and confident, Denis was our best defenceman. He could be nasty if necessary, but he elevated everybody's game. I'll never forget the speed of the puck as it hit the blade of my stick—*bang!* Right on the tape. I cupped my blade and corralled it. It stuck like glue. It had the perfect pace. The perfect placement. Not too far in front of me, and not in my skates. Would every NHL pass be like this?

After the game, I got out of my gear and showered—it might have been the fastest I ever changed—and then found a pay phone so I could call my folks. In those days, you couldn't watch every NHL game on television, and there were no sports highlight shows, and no Internet, so Mom and Dad wouldn't even know the final score until they heard it on the radio.

That night, I wasn't calling to tell them I scored a goal, or that I'd made a big play, or that I'd had the crap kicked out of me again in a fight. It was just to share my excitement.

I called them collect, just like I did back in junior hockey. Mom had always insisted on that. Habits don't disappear right away, I guess. I think they had anticipated I would be calling, because Mom picked up on half a ring. I told her everything about that first game—the buzz of the locker room, the jersey, my number, the warm-up, the excitement of stepping on the ice. I said, "Mom, everything was great." Then she handed the phone to Dad, and I repeated it all over again. Dad said Mom leaned in to hear it all again, too.

Our next game was the home opener at the Coliseum on Long Island against the Los Angeles Kings. My first NHL home game. I can tell you, it's a whole different kind of feeling. Now I was playing in front of *our* fans. I had watched some playoff games at the Coliseum the previous spring, but it wasn't my building then and they weren't my fans yet. Tonight, I was going to step on the ice and the Coliseum was my building, and the folks cheering were my fans. It's a wow moment. I was eager, anxious, and pumped for my first shift and my first shot couldn't happen soon enough. Here we go!!

My first NHL shot was not a rocket . . . but guess what? It went in the net. *Yeah, baby!* A spectacular goal it was not. It wasn't an end-to-end, Gilbert Perreault-dekes-the-goalie-and-taps-the-puck-into-the-net type of goal. But in my mind, it was even more spectacular.

There was a scrum along the side boards, top of the circle, and Billy Harris kicked the puck to me. I was close by for support and no one was covering me. I corralled the puck and took one step towards the net. A defenceman between me and Kings goalie Rogie Vachon. I made a little move to my left and punched a quick snap shot that went between the defenceman's legs.

I think Rogie was a bit screened and couldn't see the puck quickly enough. The puck went through him at what I call the "Trottier hole"—the gap on the blocker side between the arm and the body. I managed to sneak a lot of pucks through that hole during my hockey career.

I actually didn't see the puck go in or hit the back of the net. But I saw the crowd behind the net stand up with their arms in the air. I saw the goal light go on. And I think I saw the goal judge smile, too. Even he was happy for me.

It's the only time I can recall doing the tippy-toe dance after scoring a goal. Teammates were chasing me down and trying to hug and congratulate me as I spun in tiny circles like a ballerina. Big Clarkie grabbed the puck and handed it to me. I skated to the bench and flipped the puck to Jimmy Pick. He wrapped white tape around it and wrote in a big black Sharpie, FIRST NHL GOAL. It reminded me of what Mom had done when I scored my very first goal. Later that night, I thanked Jimmy for his thoughtfulness and he seemed surprised. "It's the best part of my job," he said.

After this crazy excitement, it was back to business. We had two more periods of hockey to play. I didn't think it could get any better than scoring a goal in my first NHL home game. But it did.

During the second period, while we were on the power play, the hockey gods smiled on me again. Clarkie, Billy Harris (or as we all called him, Harry O), and I all drove to the net on a Denis Potvin point shot. There were three guys storming the crease and only two defencemen to hold us back. One of us was going to be left open. The D-men chose Clarkie and Harry, and I was left open to gobble a big juicy rebound. All I had to do was pull it away from Rogie a bit and flip it over him. My shot had just enough oomph and arc to lob itself over a fallen Rogie. Goal number two! I think the puck barely hit the back of the net.

Harry asked me later, with excitement and urgency, "Why didn't you roof it? Why didn't you go top shelf? You gotta bear down, dammit!"

"I didn't have to," I managed to say. "I just had to get it over Rogie."

I don't even remember my third goal of the game. I don't remember the two assists, either. Cloud nine got elevated to cloud ten.

Somehow, a kid from Nowhere, Saskatchewan, scores a hat trick in his first NHL home game. A five-point night in the same game? Who the hell wrote this script? We won, 7–0. This would probably be a longer call home to Mom and Dad tonight.

I liked that my new teammates didn't make a huge deal about it. Obviously everyone, especially Al and Bill, was happy for me. But we can't control the media's excitement about something like this. Reporters and the cameras crammed in a tight circle around my stall. They were all smiling and asking me to describe each goal. I tried, but I was a bit overwhelmed. All I wanted to do was call home. This media scrum was taking away valuable time I needed to share this incredible game with Mom and Dad.

As much as I tried to hurry the hoopla, it increased. Dealing with postgame media was part of life in the NHL and part of being a professional hockey player. I never became completely comfortable with it, but I accepted it as part of the game.

After the game, I was exhausted, but the adrenalin was still high on the drive back to the Amendolas'. I watched an episode of *The Honeymooners* and calmed down with a little laughter. Then I called Mom and Dad. They had heard the score by the time I called, so I gave them a blow-by-blow description of the goals, the postgame mayhem and every great moment of the game. I really took my time and wanted to convey the incredible atmosphere of playing in front of the Islanders fans at the Coliseum.

Mom and Dad kept passing the phone back and forth. I was recounting the first goal to Mom, and she cheered. In my mind, I could picture Dad sitting there, visualizing the puck going into the net. Mom told me later that Dad teared up.

I was replaying the entire thing in my mind. Every faceoff, every shift. In addition to the goals and assists I notched, I also remembered things that didn't go so well—a missed check or a lost puck battle in the corner or a pass I should have gobbled up. No matter how long I played, I never wanted to stop being a student of game. It became a good habit to think about ways to improve and what I could have done better. It was late into the night and I still couldn't sleep. Finally, I dozed off during a rerun of *I Love Lucy.* I went to sleep hearing Desi Arnaz saying, "Lucy . . . you've got some 'splaining to do!"

As a first-year player, I couldn't understand why Al would pull me off the ice when a faceoff was in our end. I didn't like it at the time. Ed Westfall would replace me each time, and Eddie was masterful in the faceoff circle. I didn't dare say anything, so I kept my mouth shut. I'm glad I did. As much as it angered me, it pushed me to study all of the centres in the league—their skate and stick positions prior to the puck drop. These were the pros, and they had strength and a whole bag of tricks that I still had to learn. They could probably chew me up and spit me out any time they wanted.

Even though I didn't take many defensive-zone faceoffs, my time on the power play increased, as did my scoring opportunities and offensive production. Our confidence was growing as a power-play unit, and our group was young and skilled. After the first week of the season, our power-play percentage was in the top ten, and I found myself in the top ten in points. It was heady stuff, but a voice in my head reminded me, "Mind your *Ps* and *Qs*. Don't let it go to your head." Which I didn't.

As I said, the line of Clarkie, Harry O, and me was sizzling right along. We had chemistry. The Islanders' PR department created a contest for the fans to name our line. The LILCO Line was the winner. It stood for Long Island Lightning Company—a play on the name of the local power company, the Long Island *Lighting* Company. Did we like it? It was okay by us.

Billy Harris became my roommate on the road and one of my best friends (he's the godfather to my oldest son, Bryan Jr.). And Clark Gillies became another wonderful big brother. I was lucky. I had Tiger as my big brother in junior hockey, and Clarkie in the NHL. The hockey gods smiled on me twice.

Two weeks into the season, the weekly *Hockey News* came out and there it was: my name just below Guy Lafleur's. I was tied with him for the league lead in scoring. I couldn't believe it. My buddies back home had some fun jabbing me about it.

Through luck, hard work, or both, good things were happening. The dreaded deadline to send underage players back to junior was approaching and I didn't want to think about it, but it kept gnawing at me. I wasn't going to ask my GM or coach, who weren't really giving me much feedback. Although both were very encouraging, I still couldn't muster up the courage to ask. Al was giving me plenty of ice time, and I thought that was a good sign.

Finally, a day before the deadline, after practice, Al asked me to stop by his office upstairs. It was a quick, matter-of-fact, sit-down.

I was nervous and anxious. I held my breath as he started to talk.

"You're staying here through Christmas," Al told me. "You're doing well, so keep bearing down." There were no formalities, just *here's what we're doing, and here's what you need to keep doing.*

It felt great. As I walked to my car to drive home to the Amendolas', I reminded myself that finishing checks had gotten me noticed. I was going to stay aggressive and keep bearing down. Oh, and sneaking in a few points, especially on the power play, wouldn't hurt, either.

I was still fighting homesickness, but I had to keep it in check. So many good things were happening. I was fortunate. I had a great place to stay with the Amendolas, and I had a lot of support in the locker room.

My family came to New York right after Christmas. It would be the first time they saw me play in the NHL. I cried all the way to the airport when I picked them up. I didn't want them to know how homesick I was. By the time I got there, I had no more tears to shed. Thank God.

It wasn't like there was anywhere closer to home they could have seen me play. Winnipeg, Edmonton, and Calgary weren't in the league yet. Minnesota was a hell of a drive. And with four kids at home and the work on the ranch, I actually figured it was a long shot that they would see me at all that season. But the whole gang (with the exception of my older sister Carol) made it!

In true Pat and Warren fashion, everyone was welcomed at the Amendola house. We celebrated my sister Kathy's birthday at a North Shore restaurant called Jimmy's Backyard (an Islanders fave). I took them to all the Islanders' hangouts of choice—places like Café Continental, Giulio Cesare, and the Wheatley Hills Tavern. Besides the delicious food, Mom and Dad were impressed that the owners and chefs made it a point to come out and greet their son.

A special memory of Mom and Dad's first New York trip was the evening we went to Manhattan to see a Broadway show: the musical *Annie*. As much as they were excited to see live theatre, I think they were a bit skeptical as well. Theatre tickets were not outlandishly expensive in January of 1976, but Mom and Dad thought fifty dollars was ridiculous, since a movie in Val Marie cost $1.50. *Ha!*

Annie was a red-hot ticket, and I was able to get ours through Gregg Raffa, who became a great friend during my New York years. He snagged some phenomenal seats for us in the first row, smack dab in the middle of the theatre. Mom and Dad sat next to me on one side, and my brothers and sister were on the other. Our seats gave us an excellent view of the orchestra pit, as well as the musicians who were preparing for the evening. Dad looked back at me, almost bewildered, and said, "I never saw a fella in a tuxedo tune a fiddle quite so elegantly." It's a violin, Dad. Welcome to New York!

During the orchestra's warm-ups, Mom turned and asked me (of all people), "Why are the trumpets, tubas, and clarinets all honking in different notes? This ain't gonna sound good." I think I heard her say, "I've heard high school bands that sound better than this."

Then the play opened, the music started and the lights hit the stage. The magic of New York theatre transformed the stage into something larger than life. I couldn't see my parents' faces, but I bet they were the same as mine. *Oh my God.*

I didn't know what Mom and Dad were going to think about the whole thing. But when intermission came and the house lights came up, my folks couldn't stop smiling. They were talking to each other about all of their favourite parts. It was fantastic. Their initial skepticism had turned into all-out amazement.

After the show, we walked through Times Square because Dad wanted to see the bright lights of Broadway. Our path to Penn Station, where we would grab the train back to Long Island, took us through Forty-second Street. Now, in 1975, Forty-second Street was pretty rough around the edges. It was known as the porn and triple-X district. As we walked down the street, Dad got to pointing to the various sex toys in some of the shop windows in order to make Mom blush.

A guy passed by Dad and pushed a little flyer in to his hands and said, "Hey buddy, if you want to have a good time . . ."

He showed it to Mom and they both giggled like two little kids.

He held the flyer up. "Hey, look what's going to happen to me!" Dad shouted and laughed.

Welcome to New York, Dad.

CHAPTER 11

LESSONS FROM THE VETS

The whole first season I felt like a kid. I was amazed to be in the big leagues and playing against men who were so strong, trying to succeed while, at the same time, trying not to get killed. I was competing against players who were bigger and stronger than me. It was trial by fire. Even though a lot of good things were happening for me on the ice, I knew I had to get stronger.

The first time I played against the Montreal Canadiens, Larry Robinson (thank God he's not a mean person) took me out in the corner and pinned me against the boards. My chest and face were pressed against the glass—it wasn't like he took me out and just rammed me into the boards, he just squeezed me in there like a vise. Then he lifted me in the air so my feet were off the ground. I was dangling. I had no leverage. I couldn't even push myself away because my arms, my chest, my face—everything—was pinned.

The fans who were sitting against the glass in that corner of the Montreal Forum must have been laughing their rear ends off, seeing me stuck there like a suction cup.

Then Larry let me down gently and politely, and said, "There you go, little guy."

I was furious and also embarrassed. I was thinking, *Damnit Robinson, you're so damn strong and I hate you. And why do you have to be so damn nice about it?* He's not just a great player, he was a gentle giant until he got mad, and I didn't want to make him mad.

I ended up playing with Larry in the Canada Cup, and I enjoyed his company a lot. I told Larry that story about the time he pressed me into the glass at the Forum. He didn't remember it, but I sure did. He probably did it to everyone; to him, it was just another day at the office.

Eddie Westfall was our captain, and he was terrific to all the young players on the team. Single players were invited to his house for pre-game meals anytime. He was a great captain—Steady Eddie. We called him "18." He had won two Stanley Cups in Boston with Bobby Orr in the early '70s.

Eddie was the ultimate utility man. He could play defence, right wing, or centre. He was a natural leader in the locker room and always knew the right thing to say, at the right time. We all listened to him. He spoke like a leader and was highly respected.

I was one of the young and single guys on the team, along with André St. Laurent and Billy Harris, and Eddie made it a point to make sure we ate proper meals. And 18 was a terrific cook.

I actually played a trick on Eddie at one of those pre-game dinners. I had two false teeth, and after we finished eating, I took them out, put them in a napkin and stuck them deftly in my pocket so no one would notice. When Eddie started cleaning up, I said to him, "You didn't throw my napkin out, did you?"

"Yeah, I threw everything out," Eddie said.

"Damn, my false teeth were in there!" I said, pointing to the gap in my mouth.

"Oh no," Eddie said. He felt so bad and he dove into the garbage. "I'm so sorry. I can't find them," he said.

He was rooting through the drippings and sauces and came up with crumbs on his hands. He searched so hard for that darn napkin. Then I popped my false teeth back in my mouth.

"Never mind," I said. "I found them." And I gave Eddie a big smile.

"You little bastard!" he laughed.

To this day, Eddie still tells me he owes me one, and we laugh about it. I guess I was feeling my oats that day—a young kid playing a joke on a veteran.

On the road, Eddie was always the first one in the lobby, showered and shaved, looking dapper as always. I was the opposite. Me with my pillow head, I would sleep as late as I possibly could, looking dishevelled and wrinkled.

I'd find Eddie sitting in the hotel lobby, doing a crossword puzzle. And seeing him sitting there reminded me of home, of Mom, with her crossword puzzle, and how much she loved doing them, and how she made me a bit of a crossword fan. Eddie, like Mom, was a crossword wizard, while I was a newbie in comparison. I'd often sit down next to him and say, "Can I help?" Sure, he'd say. "What's a four letter word for so-and-so?" And I'd come up with a word if I could.

I wasn't in his league, but it was a small thing that we shared. It was a memory of home and it brought me comfort.

J.P. Parisé was another veteran I respected because, as much as he teased me, he treated me like I belonged. He had the best one-liners and delivered them in his deep, thick French accent, which to me sounded even more humorous. We became fast friends, and J.P. made me laugh a lot. "C'mon guys, let's pressurize der defence." "Hey rook, did you comb your hair wit da brick?" "Why do you order da hamburger when you can order da big steak?" I went on a date once, and he gave me some J.P. advice: "Hey kid, don't get too much entouchment." I cracked up.

Gerry Hart, a stalwart on defence, took me on my first Long Island boat ride. We cruised Long Island Sound for about forty-five minutes, then spent the next three hours washing the salt water off the boat. And I loved every minute of it. I was his first mate.

Bert Marshall, another stay-at-home defenceman, invited me for Chinese food at his buddy's restaurant. I was not a big Chinese food guy at the time, but Bert was full of NHL stories, and I was a very good audience. "Dinner's on me," he added.

As we left the restaurant, I thanked him. Bert chuckled and told me, "I can't fib you. The guy owed me a free meal. So you're welcome, but I didn't buy you dinner." Savvy veteran move.

The Salty Dog Restaurant, right across the street from the Nassau Coliseum, was a favourite postgame watering hole for the team. Of course, I was still too young to drink, but Thunder Bay native Ralph Stewart handed me a twenty-dollar bill and said, "Here, kid. Keep this in case you need some extra money."

"Thanks, Ralph," I said, "but I'm okay."

But he insisted.

"You can pay me back tomorrow."

The next day at the rink, I pulled out the same twenty-dollar bill and tried to hand it to Ralph.

"I didn't lend you twenty," he said. "I lent you a hundred."

I stammered, "Oh, I'm pretty sure it was a twenty . . ."

It was a joke, and the whole team was in on it. I was thinking, *Shit, maybe he did lend me a hundred. It was dark in there.*

And then, after thirty-forty seconds of hell, second-guessing myself, the whole locker room broke out laughing. They must have pulled this trick on every rookie, and I fell for it, hook, line, and sinker.

I didn't say a lot those first two years. I usually tagged along if the guys went out. I was the kid who laughed at every joke and wanted to absorb every story about the NHL. But being underage could be a little bit awkward.

We were on a road trip to Chicago, and the team was heading out for dinner. The first thing I asked was, "Are we going to a bar?"

"Don't worry, kid," Eddie said. "We'll sneak you in."

They had had gotten me into bars a bunch of times in the past. But not this night.

The guy at the door asked, "How old are you?"

"Twenty-one," I lied.

"No, you're not."

The other guys looked at me, looked at the bar, waved to me, and walked inside.

"See you later, kid," they said.

There I was, stuck in the middle of Chicago, with no clue where I was. I had to get a cab and make my way back to the hotel.

The same thing happened in Newport Beach, California. We were going to Blackie's by the Sea for dinner. "It's great," they said. "You'll love it."

"But isn't that a bar?"

"Don't worry, kid, we'll look after you."

I was all excited. Then the doorman asked for ID, and the guys left me there, hanging. They were all howling with laughter as they entered, waving once again. I had to find my own way back to the hotel.

The only city where my age didn't matter was Montreal. There were four or five places the players liked to go, including the Sir Winston Churchill—Winnie's—on Crescent Street. As I walked in and pulled the collar of my trench coat up to kind of disguise myself, the guy at the door would say, "Hi Bryan, how are you? Come on in."

Montreal is such a hockey-crazed city. I usually fell in love with every French gal in the place. I couldn't talk to them, but I enjoyed dancing with them, while the other guys just ignored them.

The girls thought it was funny that I didn't speak French, even with the last name Trottier. They'd be talking away to me in French and I'd be nodding my head and loving it. I have great memories of Montreal. I didn't have one drink, but I had the most fun.

Going around the league for the first time, I was like a tourist walking into all of those famous arenas. The Forum, Maple Leaf Gardens, Boston Garden, Chicago Stadium, the Olympia in Detroit. I'd wander the halls, looking at all the photos, thinking of all the other players who had walked through these same corridors.

These Original Six buildings were very special, and that feeling never went away after all of the years I played in the NHL. Going into those arenas was magical. It's the stuff you dream about as a kid, and I truly loved the history.

That first year, I got to meet some of my heroes. I got to meet Jean Béliveau and Stan Mikita. They were both genuine and down to earth. Each time we'd meet after that, they'd always greet me the same way: "Hi Bryan." Being around them made me feel like a star-struck eight-year-old all over again. My boyhood idols were not only great players, but great people.

To have the chance to play against Mikita was just awesome. Here I was, taking the opening faceoff against him in Chicago Stadium. I was looking down at his big, hooked banana blade. I won the faceoff, and all of a sudden, my hero whipped that blade in front of my face like Zorro. I didn't win another faceoff the rest of the night—against Stan or anyone else. He had successfully backed me off the faceoff dot farther than I had ever been. No way was I going to take another high stick in the face from Stan.

I'm not sure if Stan did that to everybody—but the trick worked against me. You learn stuff like that from veterans. Stan had won a couple of Lady Byng Trophies for being the most gentlemanly player in the league. But I took a trick from his bag away with me after that game.

Years later, after both of us had retired, I had a chance to visit with Stan at a charity game. I finally got my chance to tell him how I'd watched him and how he always impressed me with his play and how excited I was to play against him. He was so nice. I remember him saying, "Thanks, Bryan. You had a terrific career yourself." Each visit after that, we greeted each other as friends.

My first game on *Hockey Night in Canada* was one of my greatest memories. We were playing the Leafs in Toronto on a Saturday night, "coast to coast like buttered toast," and there was a real buzz in the locker room before the game. Millions of people would be watching, just like the way I used to watch the game on that little black-and-white TV back on the ranch.

And then I got word that I was going to be the guest during the first intermission. It was early in the season, I was still quite shy and very raw at giving interviews, and up to then, I had become very good at one-word answers. I guess hanging around in the top ten scorers in the league had made everyone a little intrigued about just who the hell I was.

I was excited that Brian McFarlane was going to do the interview. I had seen him interview so many others over the years. He led me into the conversation really well, and I felt incredibly comfortable talking to him. Brian asked me questions about my hometown and if I got my athleticism from my parents. I said, "Yes, my dad's a terrific athlete. He's Native. I also inherited his love of music and nature."

"And from your Mom?" he asked

"Mom's whole family is very athletic. And Dad said I inherited her big butt and long toes."

What was I thinking? Mom doesn't have a big butt or long toes? I just blurted it out. So stupid.

That interview with Brian was the first time that anyone had mentioned my Native ancestry and put a really positive spin on it. He said I was making a lot of First Nations people proud and to keep it up.

At the end of the interview, he asked me, "Is there anybody you'd like to say hello to back home?"

Another faux pas. I stuck my foot in my mouth again. I blew it. I didn't say hi to Mom and Dad, but instead said I wanted to say hello to everyone back home, watching the game in the beer parlour. Why did I say that?

I took a fair bit of teasing about that interview afterwards, being on national television and saying hello to all of my friends back at the beer parlour. I was nineteen years old and had never actually been in that damn beer parlour! And besides, everybody would have been at home watching the game.

I apologized to Mom afterwards, but she wasn't at all embarrassed. She didn't bawl me out. Her son was on TV playing in the NHL. A mom's true pride.

There was a genuine connection between our Islander team and the community we played for.

The Nassau Coliseum was our home, and I thought it was the greatest building in the league. And our fans were the greatest fans in the league. More than fourteen thousand of them jammed into the Nassau Veterans Memorial Coliseum. As our team improved, ownership and the county agreed to add more seating. It was a well-designed building that allowed for this expansion.

But the biggest thing was the noise level. To me, there was no other building in the league that carried the sound from the fans to the arena floor the way the Coliseum did. It was deafening. All the time. And it seemed that when we scored a goal, the decibel level rose even higher. We had the fans cheering, and the vendors shouting, "Bee-ah hee-ah!" in that real thick Long Island accent.

We loved the fans, and the fans loved us. Everyone in the building wanted us to know that they were cheering us on, whether they were season-ticket holders, ticket takers, or ushers.

We also had a fantastic booster club and several player fan clubs. Garry Howatt and Bob Nystrom had fan clubs. Then a Bryan Trottier fan club sprung up. In time, Clark was added, and then Bryan and Clark and Billy, and finally Bryan and Clark and Mike Bossy. It was another way for the fans to get closer to the players. And we loved it. Events during the hockey season were few, but in the summer we'd have a barbecue and maybe a softball game, and afterwards, fans would get a chance to interact with the players.

Playing the Rangers raised the level of intensity for the teams and the fans. It was a classic rivalry—the big city versus the suburbs, the established team versus the upstarts. Fans, media, everyone bought into the hype. The emotions carried from the stands to the ice during those games. And as a result, the players did not back down and the rivalry produced some high-intensity hockey.

The hype and the rivalry didn't always continue off the ice. We did lots of charity events with the Ranger players and got to know them as regular people. We're hockey players; we're cut from the same cloth. We got along really well at all of these events. But the next time we were on the ice against them, it was all business again. "Okay, we've got to hate you now. Sorry."

Madison Square Garden was not a friendly environment for the Islanders. In the '70s, the glass around the rink was lower from blue line to blue line. During warm-ups, Ranger fans would hang over the glass and yell obscenities at us. Our veterans weren't rattled; they were always quick with a retort. I remember one time an MSG fan hollered at J.P. that so-and-so "is going to knock your teeth out tonight."

"Well, at least my teeth aren't green," J.P. yelled back. "When was the last time you brushed yours?"

During the game, we blocked out the heckling. There was a deafening din through the whole game that drowned everything out. But during the warm-ups or breaks in play, some individual voices became more audible. Which was great when they were cheering *for* us.

Most of the Rangers and Islanders alumni recognize that things that happened during the games were in the heat of the battle, and no one holds a grudge. The rivalry definitely brought out the best in all of us. The level of hockey was off the charts, and that's what made it so great. And the rivalry continues today.

CHAPTER 12

TRIO GRANDE

The original owner of the New York Islanders, Roy Boe, was neither pretentious nor snooty. He was actually affable and friendly. I liked him. He also owned the New York Nets (now the Brooklyn Nets), who were in the American Basketball Association at that time. Julius Erving, "Dr. J," was their star player.

When Roy got into the NHL, he had to pay an expansion fee to the league, and right behind it, he had to pay the Rangers an indemnification fee so that he could put his team in the New York market.

He eventually ran into money problems. I don't know the whole story, but I do remember how we found out about it. The team was checking into the Boston hotel we stayed at many times. We arrived later, after playing a game, and we were all tired as we stood in the lobby, waiting for our room keys. Al Arbour was having a discussion with the hotel manager and we couldn't help but overhear.

The team didn't send a travel coordinator in those days. That role fell to our head coach, and Al only wanted to get his players to bed so they could get a good night's sleep. But the hotel refused to provide the keys without the rooms being paid for upfront.

"The Islanders do not have credit in this hotel and we will not give out rooms without somebody paying for them in advance," the desk clerk told Al, who handed over his personal Visa card to pay for our rooms that night.

Shortly after this episode, headlines about the team's financial situation—ISLANDERS FILE FOR BANKRUPTCY—became more prominent. Then the rumours started that maybe we wouldn't get our paycheques, and thank goodness that never came to pass. I don't know how Bill Torrey did it, but somehow we always got paid.

John Pickett became the team's managing general partner and new decision maker (along with Bill Torrey) and eventually became the controlling shareholder of the Islanders. He brought stability and we seldom saw him. He never addressed the team, even at team functions, but Mr. Pickett was always very low-key, very positive, and appeared extremely confident. He and Bill were a good match, and with stability came success, at least in our case.

Clark Gillies is a couple of years older than I am, and so much bigger than me, too. Back in the days when we played junior hockey against each other, he was at least six inches taller and probably sixty pounds heavier than me. To me, he was a giant. And man, could he play hockey—score, stickhandle, and pass. And he was rugged. He was the elite power forward of his generation, before the term "power forward" was used. To me, he was the total package in that massive body. As a junior, Clark was the best left winger in the WHL.

I took a pretty good run at him in my first game and bounced off of him like a flea hitting an elephant—Clark didn't budge. But in my second year, my right winger Ian MacPhee and I sandwiched him. Ian hit like a bowling ball, and I tried to put a good sting on Clark. We all went down in a heap, and Clark was not happy about it. As I picked myself up, I wound up nose to nose with him. He dropped his chin and looked at me through his eyebrows.

"I'm going rip your fucking head off," he said.

"Gotta catch me first," I told him, and I bolted.

Clark is an athlete, a true all-around athlete. He played quarterback in high school, he's a scratch golfer, and he also was a fantastic baseball player—signed by the Houston Astros and played a few seasons in their farm system. I played baseball against him as a young teenager before I ever played him in hockey. He was playing third base for the Moose Jaw team, and I was on a six-game tryout for the Swift Current Indians. I remember looking at him and thinking, "My God, he's seventeen and he looks like a full-grown man." Clark was chiselled, well proportioned, and had uncanny reflexes. He gobbled up every ball and he had a strong arm to first base, and I was in awe of him. In one of his at-bats, he hit the ball so hard that it left the park in a split second. I think the ball is still circling the earth. When we got to the Islanders, we played a lot of charity softball games in the summer, and he was always the stud on our team.

Clark and I were both drafted by the Islanders in 1974, and he went straight to the NHL. I was excited and felt very fortunate that he was going to be my future teammate. It turned out better than I had even imagined.

By the time I got to the Islanders, he was already a leader in the locker room. He had presence.

My rookie year, we were playing an exhibition game in Buffalo, and like I said, I was bumping guys to get noticed. All of a sudden, I found myself facing the Sabres' two giant defencemen, Jim Schoenfeld and Jerry Korab. I was gliding backward, realizing that I was going to have to fight Jimmy or King Kong. *This is going to hurt, I might take a beating, but I have to stand my ground.* As a rookie, I had to show that I wasn't intimidated—even if I was. As I was backing up, I bumped into Clark. I half turned around, and my face was right at the level of the Islanders logo on his jersey.

"Everything okay?" he asked me.

I looked back towards Jimmy and Korab, and they had both veered away.

"It is now," I said.

Having Clark on my line all of those years meant I could play my game and not worry about someone taking liberties against me. In another exhibition game, we were playing the Blackhawks and Harold Phillipoff got a little too aggressive with Billy Smith. I came in to push him away and we dropped the gloves, and it wasn't much of a scrap. Clark tuned him up later in the game, I guess to send a message—"Don't touch Trottier."

I didn't want Clark to have to fight my battles, especially if I started them. But Clark was good; he knew what he was doing. He knew how to handle his role. Clark was always there for me. He was there for all of us.

God, did we have some laughs together. He had the best sense of humour and he was probably my favourite joke teller of all time. I was his best audience because I always laughed the hardest at his jokes, even if I'd heard them a hundred times. His delivery and tone tickled my funny bone every time.

He was a Westerner at heart. He grew up in the city, but he loved the cowboy way of life. Cowboy boots. John Wayne. Named his dog Hombre.

On a rare day off, we found a riding stable outside of Denver. As he mounted his horse and settled into the saddle, to me, he looked like the Marlboro Man. Ralph Stewart's horse wanted to get back to the barn and started to run away from the rest of us.

As I tried to rescue Ralph, I told Clark to take over as the trail boss. He smiled from ear to ear. The kid from the ranch passed the torch to Clark, the "perfect cowboy."

Our goalie was Bill Smith, and he became one of my very best friends on the team.

Bill could be a man of few words on game days. I knew that meant he was getting in the zone. He sat across from me in the locker room, and we had a silent language we shared. A nod, raised eyebrows, a shake of the head. I seldom got a "good morning." Just the nod.

But when the game was over and it was time to relax and unwind, he would look at me and say, "You're coming with me," and we would wind up laughing all night long at each other's stories. Smitty would not take any guff from hockey fans. He was never rude—always polite, and ever the gentleman. But don't piss him off. Don't be belligerent or a wise guy. Because that's when Smitty would decide he'd had enough. It didn't happen often, but when it did, Smitty would get in their face and smooth things over. The next thing I knew, the other guys would be apologizing, and they'd be friends by the end of the night, buying each other beers. "Silver Tongue" had smooth-talked us out of a tense situation.

Smitty's goaltending skills were underrated. In practice, he would give you three-quarters of the net to shoot at on the stick side, and then he'd stand there and deflect every shot with the paddle of his stick. He worked on everything he had to do to stop a puck. But what he really prided himself on was being a big-game player. "Put money on the line, now it's for real," he would say. When we got to the playoffs, he really ramped it up. The bigger the game, the better he played. He seemed to love the pressure, and I think he is the greatest money goalie of all time. Bill Smith might be the only guy who wanted to win more than me.

Of course, the other thing Billy was famous for was the way he always protected his crease. I watched it first-hand, but really learned what it meant in my rookie season. We were playing the Canadiens in Montreal. I was backchecking on Steve Shutt, as I'd always been taught—backchecked him right to the crease. I was tight against Steve, keeping my body between him and the puck. You couldn't put a piece of paper between us.

Steve was driving the net, and like every smart player does, he took his backchecker right to the net to cause confusion and havoc for the goaltender. I was staying as close to him as I could, trying my best to keep him to the outside. We ended up in the crease. Billy's crease. And *wham*, my ankle went numb.

I dropped to the ice, and it felt like I had been hit with a ball-peen hammer. I ended up having to ice it for the next three days.

After the whistle blew, I skated over to Smitty and said, "You know that was me you whacked on the ankle."

"If you don't like it, stay out of my crease," he said. "If they come in my crease, I'll take care of 'em."

He never apologized afterwards, not even to me, his bud.

In the '83 finals, Smitty was again protecting his crease, and he had altercations with some of Edmonton's players, including their stars. The press came running into our dressing room after the game, asking us about him. I quickly told them that story about my rookie year. "Look, guys," I said, "if even his own teammates know it's coming, the opposition is crazy to go into his crease." The reporters left shaking their heads, and I'm not sure I answered their question, but what do you say to that?

I told that same story to Mom when Billy joined us at our table at a team function. I was trying to tease Smitty a little bit. "Can you believe it, Mom?" I said. "Smitty whacked his own teammate."

Mom looked at Billy, and then she looked back at me.

"Well, you should just stay out of Billy's crease then," she said.

Even my own mom knew, so the rest of the world should have figured it out.

The first time I met Mike Bossy was at Islanders rookie camp—at Racquet and Rink in Farmingdale—in 1977. I was looking forward to watching him skate, intrigued to catch a glimpse of the scoring machine of the Quebec league. Not to be: He was injured—bleeding, alone, swollen lips, looking dejected. Mike was lying on a trainer's table in the dressing room after taking a stick in the mouth. He had taken his equipment off, and he was still sweaty. I felt sorry for him. He was thin, and had long, straggly hair, and a couple of busted teeth. I introduced myself quickly, and as I left, I thought to myself, *This is our first draft pick? This is the scoring machine from the Quebec junior league?* Poor kid.

But then I got on the ice with him in practice and was instantly amazed at Mike's talent. *This kid can fly.* He was quick, he could stickhandle and he could pass. I grew up playing with Willie Desjardins back in Saskatchewan, and I thought he had the best wrist shot I had ever seen. But Mike was in a league of his own. He had a different kind of a snap. His was quicker and heavier, and the damn puck always seemed to find a hole. He loved the one-timer—it didn't matter if he was off-balance, he'd just turn and fire. Top shelf or five-hole, his shot was very impressive. He was uncanny at shooting on the fly, too. A quick, powerful slapper. It was ridiculous how he knew what side of the net to shoot at—far post, short side, over the glove, under the blocker, wherever he wanted. I could see right away that he was a natural.

Mike looked skinny because he had no body fat. He was lean, with broad shoulders and a very muscular back. None of us realized just how naturally strong he truly was. During physical testing at training camp, we had a machine that measured grip strength. It fit in your hand and you would squeeze with all your might. Most of our team scored around forty to sixty on the strength chart. When it was Mike's turn, he grabbed the grip machine and gave it his best squeeze. The number on the scale touched ninety. And that was his left hand!

Clark Gillies and Denis Potvin, who were two of the most powerful guys in the league, couldn't believe it. "What about the other hand?" they asked. Mike torqued it with his dominant hand, his right. Ninety-eight. Clark and Denis just looked at each other. No one said a word.

I also started to get a sense of Mike's personality during his first camp. He wasn't a cocky kid—he was actually quiet—but he was confident, and quite intense.

During camp scrimmages, I didn't play with Mike at all. He played mostly with the rookies. But it was great fun squaring off against him. He was explosive. It was a challenge to keep him in check. He could deke and dive. He found ways to get lost and find open ice. I liked this guy. *Stealth,* I thought.

During that first week, I invited him to dinner and we immediately hit it off. We talked in the car all the way to my house, throughout supper, and all the way back to his hotel. I could tell he was homesick. He was a newlywed, and he'd left his wife, Lucy, back in Montreal. I said he should invite her down to Long Island, and the two of them could stay at our house. Mike and his wife wound up living with us for a month and a half.

We were building a real bond, a real friendship. I was the youngest player on the team for two seasons before Mike arrived. He's six months younger than me. We were both kids, and although I had two years of experience in the NHL, we didn't look at each other as vet and rookie. Every once in a while, I would tease him and remind him who the veteran was. I would jokingly say, "Respect your elders, young man," but really, we were equals.

Near the end of camp, Al put us together for the first time on a line with Clark. It was an exhibition game in New Haven. *Boom*. The chemistry was instant. As I remember, Mike scored three goals and Clark and I pitched in with a goal each. It was the beginning of something *grand*.

Clark and I had played most of training camp with Billy Harris, the same LILCO Line that had been together for the previous two seasons. We had some great success, the three of us. But when Al put Mike on the right side, Billy was shifted to another line. It wasn't a big deal for anyone. It happens all the time in hockey. No one complained about it, and I hoped I would still get to play with Billy here and there. But it didn't work out that way.

Instead, that was the beginning of the Trio Grande.

Mike and I were similar people, even though he grew up in the suburbs and I grew up on a ranch in Saskatchewan. We were both shy and reserved, a bit guarded. Non-drinkers, laughed at the same jokes, enjoyed the same food, movies, and TV shows. Our only differences were sleep patterns. Mike could conk out more quickly and easily than me.

We weren't roommates on the first road trip of the season, but the team put us together shortly afterwards, and we stayed together right up until Mike retired.

We both liked things simple, and were mindful of budget. After check-in, our routine became automatic. Whoever turned on the TV picked the channel and show we'd watch. Never a disagreement here. I probably frustrated Mike because I could fall asleep with the TV on, but Mike couldn't, so he'd have to get up and turn the TV off. We got to be like an old married couple. When we walked into the hotel room: your bed, my bed; my shaving kit, your shaving kit. First one up in the morning ordered coffee.

Our communication on the ice became as automatic as our roommate habits. Sometimes we didn't even need words. During a game, I'd look at Mike and he'd look at me and nod. We both knew exactly what the other guy was thinking. We'd giggle about it back on the bench, or later, back in our hotel room. That's the kind of the chemistry we had. We thought alike. We were completely in sync about how a goal scorer and playmaker should work with each other. You can call it mind reading if you want, but we understood what each of us would want and we'd adjust. We were always trying new things, to catch our opponents off guard, and not do the same thing twice.

It's exciting when someone thinks exactly like you and sees the same things that you see and you read off each other perfectly. There were a few nights when Mike would look at who we were playing and say, "It's going to be a boring shutdown game. They're a defensive team, and we'll probably play against the checking line." And then he'd score a hat trick and we'd be all excited about it, almost like little kids.

He was just the purest of goal scorers, and it was great fun to play with him, because at the same time, he was helping me. "Mike," I'd say to him, "you're making me a better goal scorer just by playing with you."

Our friendship prospered and grew throughout the years. Even when we were apart, I'd have a thought and excitedly tell Mike the next day, only to find out he was thinking something similar. Even with the success we were having, we were never satisfied.

And we didn't want the world to know what we were thinking, either. We wanted to make sure we weren't giving away any secrets. We guarded this. We would share with each other, but we wouldn't share with everybody. Clark was included, but never the media, who wanted to get into our brains. They'd ask me what made Mike a great goal scorer, and I'd say generically that he liked to shoot the puck quickly, he liked to get to the net—all of the basics, the stuff that everybody knows about great goal scorers. But the little stuff, the little intricacies, we would keep it between us.

I would constantly pick Mike's brain, asking him questions like "What do you think about when you shoot?" Nine times out of ten, Mike would say, "I don't know—I just shoot to hit the net." I thought even that was awesome, even though he might have just been trying to shut me up. But sometimes I could get him to share. I remember all of the little things that Mike would say—"If you just get it on the net, there might be a rebound." "You don't have to shoot it hard, but you've got to be accurate." "You've got to get it into a part of the net where you don't think the goalie's going to be." All of those little nuances of goal scoring. *As quick as I can, as hard as I can, as accurate as I can.* Thanks, Mike.

People would tease me about my shot—tell me I couldn't break a pane of glass with it. But for me, placement was my benchmark. I didn't shoot to score every single time. Sometimes I'd shoot to set up a little rebound for Clark to tap in. I'd shoot for the far corner, knowing that the rebound should come out to the right a little bit where Clark or Mike could get it. I knew I wasn't going to score every time, but I was going to hit the net and force the goalie to make a save.

Mike thought the same way, but he was a few levels above me as far as the ability to score went, and I used to try and steal as much from him as I possibly could. Mike was always known for his goal scoring, but his ability to make plays, his stickhandling, were things I appreciated as much as his ability to score. We'd do give-and-gos and area passes that became instinctive to us.

Clark Gillies was definitely our big brother on the ice. He was intense, hungry, and made sure that nobody broke our necks. In order for us to succeed as a line, we had to communicate with Clark as much as we communicated with each other. And Clark communicated with us, too. But those weren't just one-way conversations. In an early-season game, Mike missed the net several times in a row. He missed the far post by inches every time, and the puck went sailing around the boards. Clark and I were driving the net, and instead of getting a rebound, we found ourselves backchecking. After each shot, Mike fell and slid into the corner.

We got to the bench, and Clark said to Mike, "Hey Boss, if you miss that net one more time like that and then don't backcheck, I'm going to break my fucking stick right over your fucking head."

When Clark Gillies said something like that, it would be intimidating for anyone, let alone a teammate.

Mike looked at me and said, "Does he really mean that?"

"Oh yeah," I told him. "He means it."

"He's serious?"

"Yeah, he's serious."

Good communication.

Years later, we all talked about that game, and had a good laugh about it.

Mike and I did complement each other—on the ice and off.

We motivated each other to strive for team victories as much as individual success.

Bill Torrey and Al Arbour would use the term "prima donna" once in a while. I hate that term. "We don't want any prima donnas on the team," they said. It implied that we were entitled and that we were waiting for somebody else to do the dirty work on the ice. I couldn't understand why they said it at all. It pissed me off. Maybe that was their intent, but I didn't see any prima donnas on our team. The guys in our locker room cared about each other and everyone wanted to contribute. I thought we were the exact opposite.

Mike took pride in contributing offence to the team. So if he didn't score a goal, and didn't play up to his own standards, he wasn't happy. When he got like this, I called him "Cranky Mike."

I think in sports, there's an ugly kind of selfish—people who are all about me, me, me and don't give a shit about the team. But I think there is also a good selfish where you demand so much of yourself and you understand that the better you do, the better the team does. I liked the good selfish in Mike Bossy. We all have an ego, we all have self-esteem, they're great motivators. And it's okay to think, "I want to score to help my team win." That's how Mike was. He was a good selfish, because he wanted to score goals, and he knew that was going to help the team. And I think it's a healthy thing. A wonderful hunger.

A little bit of me rubbed off on Mike, and I think a little bit of Mike rubbed off on me. We really cared about each other, and that attitude carried over to our teammates. That's how you build a bond in the locker room and when you become a family. Everybody learns to appreciate the positives of each individual and appreciate how everyone wants to contribute to the team.

That's how I was brought up in Saskatchewan. As a neighbour, you give a shit about everybody around you. Neighbours help neighbours. Any time you have a new face breaking into the lineup, you need to welcome them and make them feel like part of the team as quickly as possible. For example, my way to make my Swedish teammates feel comfortable was to talk about how much I loved the sneaky way they played. As a Native Indian, I prided myself on being a little bit sneaky on the ice, too. Anders Kallur and Tommy Jonsson giggled with delight at my Indian humour. That was bonding, and they loved it.

In the end, I think Mike's style of play was what broke him down. He paid a heavy price to get into the danger zones to score goals. He wasn't a perimeter player. He got some greasy, grimy goals because he went to the ugly areas, too. He wanted to win. And when you get that taste of winning championships, you'll pay a price. And Mike certainly did.

In the '70s and '80s, there was a lot of mauling and grabbing. The goal scorers in that era had to be fast, they had to be quick, and they had to find a way to fight through it. Ten years of this, and Mike's back failed him. Whether it was a muscle, ligament, sciatic nerve, or disc problem, it probably frustrated Mike because it couldn't be pinpointed. The only thing the diagnosis proved was that it was the result of wear and tear, and it caused Mike terrible pain.

In Detroit, during one of his last games, and after he had scored a couple goals, Mike got rammed pretty good into the boards and went down hard, needing help to get to the bench. It was hard to get Mike back to the hotel room that night, and to get him through the flight back to Long Island. We always joked about "Cranky Mike," when he'd complain about a sore this or sore that. But when he was talking about his back this time, I knew it was different. I knew he was really hurt.

I needed Mike on the ice. I would tell him, "Once you're on the ice, you'll be limbered up." Before a game in Minnesota, he was in such pain that he couldn't bend over to put on his socks. I helped him with his socks and shoes and we walked across the parking lot to get to the Met Center through a blizzard.

"I'll never get my skates on," Mike said.

"We'll find a way," I said, and I helped him with the skates and tightened his laces. "You'll be fine after a good warm-up," I told him.

He scored a hat trick that night.

"I can't do this again," he said after the game.

Laughing, I said, "Shut up. You're going to do it again tomorrow night. We're going to get you back on the ice." I took it for granted that Mike would just keep finding a way to play because he was just a natural scoring machine. You put the puck on his stick and he would score goals.

But then . . . he couldn't do it anymore.

We were in training camp in the fall of 1987 when the news came that Mike wasn't going to be able to play that year.

I called him up and said, "Get your butt down to the rink." I was almost angry with him. Part of me still thought that once he got on the ice, he would be fine.

"I can't get to the rink," he said. "Trots—I'm really hurting."

I was devastated, of course, for Mike and his health. But I was also devastated for me, finally realizing that he wasn't coming to the rink, that one of my best friends in hockey, the guy I'd had so much success with, the guy I laughed and giggled with, was possibly done for good.

I was feeling sorry for myself, thinking about how much I was going to miss Mike. And then I thought, *Hey, wait a minute. He's got a long life to live with his family. I've got to keep reminding myself it's for the sake of his good health.*

He was still a young man. He had two little girls, Josiane and Tanya.

"Mike," I said, "take care of yourself."

When Mike moved back to Montreal, there was even more finality to it. I thought, *I've got to get over this. I've got to move on.* We did our best to stay in touch. And when we connected by phone, it was just like old times. He was still my friend. We talked about everything except hockey. I still call him Hoss, and he still calls me Trotter.

About twenty years ago, there was an alumni tournament in Tampa billed as the "Battle of the Big Lines." It had four teams, each featuring one famous NHL line. The Montreal Dynasty Line was there, with Guy Lafleur, Steve Shutt, and Peter Mahovlich; the Triple Crown Line from Los Angeles, with Dave Taylor, Charlie Simmer, and Marcel Dionne; the Buffalo Sabres' French Connection of Gilbert Perreault, Rick Martin, and René Robert; and of course, the Trio Grande line.

At that point, Mike hadn't been on skates for about three years.

Of course, he was moaning about this and that—"Cranky Mike," just like old times.

"Oh God, shut up," I said. "You don't need to backcheck. I just need you from the blue line in. And make sure you don't go offside."

He laughed. "Okay, I promise," he said

Well, we somehow ended up in the finals against the French Connection. The score ended up being 8–7 for us, and Mike scored seven of our goals, including the game winner with about twenty seconds left. It was a classic goal scorer's goal. The puck hit his stick, he turned, shot at the net, and it went through everybody's legs and was in the back of the net before the goalie even saw it. Pure Mike Bossy!

After the game, we lined up to shake hands, a great hockey tradition. As Gilbert Perreault and I clasped hands and exchanged pleasantries, he added, in his thick Quebecois accent, "Bry-un, I think that Mike Bossy come out the vagina scoring a goal."

We both laughed, and I couldn't wait to share the story with Mike.

The world will always recognize Mike Bossy as one of the greatest goal scorers ever. His goals per game average may never be surpassed. The tragedy is that, like Bobby Orr, he only got to play for ten years.

I played with a lot of great wingers before and after I played with Mike. But he was in a league of his own. *Il sera toujours ma première étoile.*

CHAPTER 13

BEST FEELING

I met my first wife, Nickie, during my rookie season. Her real name is Laura Lynn Theis. No one in her family remembers how she got her nickname. She is the youngest of five children and has a wonderful sense of family and a deep love for her mom.

We were both nineteen years old and fell in love quickly. She was attractive and outgoing and I didn't think I was either. We connected at an Islander function; we talked and laughed for a bit. Neither of us cared much for alcohol, and Nickie left early because she had to work the next morning. That was in late November of 1975. I didn't see her again until after Christmas. We crossed paths again and this time I asked for her number. She was spunky and drove a Pontiac Trans Am. She looked very cool behind the wheel of her "beast," as she called it, "a real gas guzzler."

She was a tiny gal, with an unguarded confidence I hadn't seen before. When the season ended, we were pretty much insepara-ble. Just prior to my twentieth birthday, we decided to get mar-ried. Young and enthusiastic, we bought a four-bedroom ranch house in East Northport. It was a great first home. A jet black American cocker spaniel we named John Henry was our first shared love, and he went everywhere with Nickie. We had no doubts about the future and were eager to make a home and have children, just like other young couples.

My oldest son, Bryan Jr., was born in November 1978. Nickie had a rough pregnancy. There were six months of anxiety leading up to the birth. She suffered some complications and we didn't know if the baby was going to make it, let alone be okay. But her doctor, Barry Kramer, and nurse, Terry Chapman, reassured us that everything was going to be okay. And they were right.

I had a minor shoulder injury that forced me to miss a few games. It happened to coincide with Bryan's birth. I had planned to be in the delivery room, but when there was a blip in the baby's heart monitor, I got kicked out. Sad but glad is how I describe it. To see your wife in pain is not fun. Nickie went into labour early in the afternoon and didn't deliver until around three in the morning. The expectant fathers' waiting room at Good Samaritan Hospital was pretty basic. I tried to grab a few winks curled up in a wrought-iron chair, but I was too nervous to sleep. So I just paced and talked to God. And, thankfully, He's always listening.

A nurse came out and said, "Congratulations, you have a son . . . and . . . he's perfect!"

I called everybody. Mom and Dad, Pat and Warren, all my buddies back home. Yep, woke 'em all up! "Sorry, I know it's late, but guess what? I'm a dad!!!" I was excited. An excitement I had never felt before—the excitement of being a dad. I was still talking to Mom when Dr. Kramer came out. "Your son will be out in a minute. Nickie's fine. She's resting."

When they brought him to the waiting room, he was all bundled and swaddled and my first thought was *He is perfect!* I stared at him for what seemed like hours. I counted his toes and fingers. He clasped on tight to my finger. Reflex, I was told. (The hospital put an Islanders decal on his baby onesie and a pen shaped like a hockey stick in his hand when they took his first baby photo. It was pretty cool.)

I looked at the face of my first-born child and thought, *Here I am, a dad for the first time.* It's a powerful, overwhelming moment, and the sense of responsibility that immediately comes with it felt like adrenalin on steroids. I remember Dr. Kramer asking me if I wanted to keep him. He laughed and I laughed. "I don't think I have a choice," I said, "but he's definitely a keeper."

Dr. Kramer put his arm around me, "He's gotta go back to the nursery now. So go home, get some rest, and see you tomorrow." I didn't want to leave.

I checked on Nickie, who was sound asleep. I didn't drive home that night. I went to the Amendolas'.

The next day at practice, I handed out cigars—tradition and all—and all the boys were great. Bill and Al, both dads, were so happy for me. Nickie and I asked Billy Harris and my sister Carol to be godfather and godmother, and the team priest, Father Dan, performed the christening.

I was overjoyed with the role of being a dad. But the reality of parenting kicked in pretty quickly. Feeding, burping, diaper changing, I wanted to experience it all. But when Bryan got a little colicky, we took turns rocking him. During one of these nights, I took the graveyard shift and fell asleep with him on my lap. He rolled right down my legs, and I woke up just in time to catch him at my feet.

Bryan was an early crawler and an early walker. He was very attached to his mom, but as he grew, I loved hearing his squeal when I walked in the door and he yelled, "Daddy!" He lit up. He was busy, active, and we spent a great deal of time playing. It was a new and exciting time. Me teaching him to hit a baseball, him teaching me to be a dad. We didn't bother with car seats in those days—I know it sounds crazy now—and as soon as he could stand up, he stood right beside me when I drove. He liked to see the road.

Besides having fun, I wanted my son to feel safe and secure. I just wanted to provide him with a good quality of life and an atmosphere of laughter.

Bryan excelled at just about everything he did. He was an outstanding student because he worked hard at it and was rewarded with excellent report cards. We tried to support and encourage him as much as possible, but it was his nana, my mother-in-law, Ellen, who said often that he was going to achieve great things.

Bryan is a joy to be around. He is wonderful, happy, and has a contagious laugh. He is athletic and played all sports growing up, even though he had a knee problem as a kid, Osgood-Schlatter syndrome, that caused him a lot of pain and eventually required surgery. He wore a knee brace for a few months and found a way to help his school in track and field.

Although he skated early—at age six—he didn't play hockey until he was almost ten. He started as a goalie, then moved to defence. It's fun thinking back to the time spent teaching him to hold a stick and pass the puck and how frustrated he would get because he wanted to be good right away. He became a very good skater, and his stick skills carried him all through college.

He carries my first and last name—Bryan Trottier Jr. That wasn't going to be easy in hockey, though I never thought about that until I came to Pittsburgh. I used to ask my son if he felt any pressure. "Only when they're screaming something negative," he said. I quietly hoped it wasn't going to make him stop playing. It didn't. There was some trash talking in high school. It could get very competitive. But Bryan never let it faze him. He stepped on the ice and played some great hockey. Sometimes, when I'd go to his games and the fans started getting on him, I'd tell them, "That's my son you're screaming at." That would calm them down a little bit.

Bryan was a good teammate. His teammates from high school and college are still his buddies today. Sports is wonderful at creating lifelong friendships.

Bryan went to college at Saint Mary's University in Minnesota. It was a small school with small classes, and that was important to Bryan. I was a little concerned that he might get homesick living so far from home, but he gutted it out. I thought back to when I was his age and I left home. He made an excellent choice, and I was proud of him.

Bryan graduated as a biology major, and then went on to medical school. As a resident, he put in some incredibly long shifts, which as a parent concerned me. But Bryan never complained. His hard work has paid off. Today, he's an oncologist.

To get him through medical school, Bryan and I would instruct at some hockey clinics, but he was always frugal and would spend his money wisely.

He and his wife, Joey, whom he met in college, are raising four kids—Parker, Elliott, Mattie, and Rory. Bryan divides his time between work, coaching his kids in hockey, and supporting them in any way he can. They're both wonderful parents, and I'm very proud of the great life they're building together. Every so often, he asks for his dad's advice. I like that. I've tried to not put pressure on my kids. I've always encouraged them to put in their best effort, complete what they've started, and not be afraid to try something new.

My oldest daughter, Lindsy, was born at the end of February 1982. Almost a nine-pounder. She was a bit past her due date, maybe a little overdone, maybe a little too comfy inside, but she spent some time under the bili light.

I love her name, Lindsy. Lindsy Ann Trottier. She was named after Lindsay Wagner, the actress from the hit show *The Bionic Woman*.

From the day she was born, Lindsy was nocturnal. She'd sleep all day and was up all night. I didn't mind the two o'clock feedings. I'd be home from a hockey game or a road trip—feed her, have some play time, sing to her, which she seemed to really enjoy. She was a cuddler. She didn't need an invitation to nuzzle.

Like her brother, Lindsy did everything early—walk, talk, sprint. She was almost too quick for her own good. She was a quick crawler, and loved to run once she got the hang of standing on her own two feet. There were plenty of bumps and bruises along the way because of it. When we were in public, I worried that people would think, *Child abuse?* But it was just Lindsy.

Being the father of a little girl brought out the protector in me, even more so than Bryan. Would this little girl be more delicate than my son? Maybe I thought of my son as being tougher and rougher. But to my surprise, Lindsy was not. She was a tomboy. She wanted to do everything her older brother did. Bryan Jr. sort of hated that, but he was also proud of her, because Lindsy was very, very good at sports, too. Whether it was gymnastics, track and field, or team sports, Lindsy made it fun for her family to cheer for her.

Lindsy was a terrific softball player who pushed the envelope on the bases all the time. She kept running through the coach's hold sign and would somehow slide under the tag, hop up, and be like, "What's the problem?" Anything to do with running, she was a coach's favourite. Basketball was a running game, and she could pursue and press the ball carrier like nobody else. My little sprinter was relentless running down somebody on the basketball court.

School came easy to Lindsy. In preschool, the teacher would write either "excellent" or "perfect" on every child's assignment. Lindsy was getting tired of "excellent" and "perfect." She had figured out how to read those comments herself.

One day, she came in all bummed out.

I asked, "What did you get on your paper today, Lindz?"

"Only perfect," she said, downhearted.

I said, "What do you mean only perfect? Perfect and excellent are the best you can get."

"Yeah, but I want something different," Lindsy replied.

I still love this about her today. Lindsy always looks for something new and fresh, striving for something *better*. She embraces all that life has to offer—and still wants a little more.

I call her my little dreamer. She's creative, with a great imagination and energy. She's eager to try just about everything. She learned to read and write before kindergarten. She had a great love of storybooks. As she grew, she loved hearing all my stories about growing up on the ranch, riding pigs and getting bucked off in the slop and poop. And what kid doesn't like the word *poop*?

She graduated from San Diego State University with a major in journalism and a minor in languages. Along with her love for stories, my little dreamer is also fluent in English, Spanish, French, German, and Italian. She can converse and communicate in five languages, and a prouder Papa there ain't!

Lindsy's a natural beauty—she's gorgeous. Of course, I'm her dad and I'm a bit biased. She's tall, athletic, with wavy dark brown hair. She's a loyal friend who makes a point of keeping in touch with all the kids she grew up with.

In 2001, Lindsy married Navy SEAL Zach Ruthven. I couldn't have picked a better man to be her husband. There is so much pride and love in their relationship, and they complement each other perfectly. Lindsy and Zach are raising four happy and beautiful girls—Jordan, Harper, Brynn, and Perry.

In June of 1990, my youngest daughter, Tayler, was born at the same hospital, Good Samaritan, as her two older siblings. And I finally made it to the delivery room. When the nurse wiped her off and handed her to me, I looked at this brand new baby, fresh to the world, and before I could say, "I love you," she smiled. The nurse who was standing near us said, "Babies aren't supposed to smile." But I swear she smiled at me. And she's been smiling ever since. My heart's been smiling ever since, too.

Tayler was all about being a little girl. No tomboy for her, she was into dresses and little-girl glamour—jewellery, bling, anything that had to do with fashion.

From the time she was a baby to her toddler years, her smile always got her out of trouble. No one could stay mad at her, and she loved to climb, so she seemed to get in trouble a lot! What I love about Tayler is she always made me feel like I was her Papa Bear. Tayler was a tiny little girl, and the first thing she could grab was my pinky finger, and she wouldn't let go. That was her security blanket. Tayler holding tight to my pinky finger is a favourite memory of mine.

Tayler was an agile, quick-witted, and smart little girl. Her happy demeanour would make all of us stop and drop everything we were doing every time Tayler would say, "Let's play."

Although Tayler might have been petite as a child, she grew into a courageous young woman. She graduated from New York University and thrived in the belly of the beast, New York City. Her internships were with a number of the city's major sports teams, like the Yankees and Rangers, and her networking skills landed her an exciting marketing job in Australia. And she succeeded there, too.

Tayler is a real family girl. Even when she was on the other side of the world, she had a way of keeping everybody in the family updated. She has a terrific ability to take advantage of today's technology to keep in touch with us—FaceTime, Facebook, texting. She got married in September 2019 to Brent Schaefer, who grew up in Wisconsin. They met at NYU, graduated, moved to Australia, and now live in Minnesota. Tayler's in marketing, and Brent's a financial wizard. He's a great kid, and he just adores her. I'm so proud of both my sons-in-law.

I wrote a song about Tayler's heart and I sang it at their wedding. The first line in the song is "Pretty little girl with a beautiful heart." Later, I renamed it "Daddy's Heart," because Tayler's always in her daddy's heart.

Although Nickie and I split up in the mid-'90s, we have three great kids. And now we share eight grandkids together.

When I returned home in the late spring, after my first season with the Islanders, Dad and my brothers, Rocky and Monty, were in the rhythm of the ranch, and I wasn't anymore. "You go and ride horses and have fun," they told me, "and we'll get the work done."

"You need some help?"

"No, we're good."

"Got some fencing to do?"

"No, we've got it all done."

It was my first time returning from a hockey season where Dad wasn't asking, "Where are you?" My brothers had taken more and more responsibility with the chores. It was a bit of a weird feeling. Dad now had two more ranch hands, and it was great to see that there was no longer the urgency to have me back home to help out. Monty and Rocky were growing up.

The old ranch is still there. The corrals are still standing, the barn's in need of some repair, the house stands empty, but it is still full of memories. The yard has become a campground for people who visit the national park and for those working in it. Then there's that magnificent view of Seventy Mile Butte. It's been a landmark for hundreds and hundreds of years for Native people, wagon trains, hunters. And like my parents, grandparents, and great-grandparents always said, we should never take the history or the beauty of the butte for granted. And I still don't.

My sister Kathy and her husband, Steve, live on a farm about thirty miles south of Val Marie. Their farm is over a century old. Steve is a fantastic farmer and rancher, a land and cattle man. Kathy and Steve have been married for over forty years. They have four kids and seven grandchildren, and they're still in love.

My older sister Carol and her husband, Dick, still reside in Swift Current. They're enjoying their retirement, and Carol still screams at the referees when she's at the Broncos home games.

I left home to play junior hockey when I was fifteen years old. My brother Monty was ten and Rocky was seven. I didn't get to see either of them play any bantam, midget, or junior hockey. I wish I could have seen them play more, but I'm very proud of what they accomplished. They both ended up having good professional hockey careers; Monty played six years in the American Hockey League and Rocky had a couple of years with the New Jersey Devils and in the AHL, then in Europe, before finishing up in the AHL. They both made hockey a fun part of their lives and careers and they took it to the highest level they possibly could. I hope they know that I was always pulling for them with all my might, because I know that they were always pulling for me.

Monty's always had a lot of fire in him. It was his hustle and fiery spirit that made him such a good teammate and player. In 1981, he actually attended an Islanders training camp and was the last man standing. We got to play an exhibition game together—Monty played left wing with me and Mike Bossy. He picked up a couple of assists that game, and it was so great to share the experience with him. I think he would have loved to have had the chance to play in the NHL, but we've never really talked about it that much. He was playing in Indianapolis when he met his wife, and that's where they settled. Monty started working in the insurance business after his hockey career ended. He's done very well for himself, and I'm so proud of him.

Rocky can be strong-willed and doesn't like me telling him what to do, but I support him in everything he does. He was an eighth-overall, first-round pick of New Jersey in 1982. In fact, he scored the very first penalty shot goal in Devils franchise history. After he left the NHL, he followed a different path, and played four more seasons in Europe and the AHL. I was kind of jealous of the opportunity he had to see the world while he was playing hockey.

Rocky and Monty both live in Indianapolis now, and I try to drive there to visit as much as I can. It's nice to have their families so close to me.

Whenever our family gathers, there is always music. It turns into a backyard hootenanny—everybody strumming guitars, and we all take turns singing. Like me, Monty and Rocky are both self-taught guitar players. My sister Kathy kept the family band going in Saskatchewan long after Dad passed away. Her sons, Kevin, Kelly, and Jesse, are all terrific musicians. My oldest son, Bryan, taught himself how to play guitar by watching videos online. My oldest daughter, Lindsy, can strum a guitar and my youngest daughter, Tayler, can actually read music when she plays the piano.

My grandkids like it when their grandpa gets silly and starts singing. I insert their names into songs and always find a way to get them to sing along and dance. Dad would love to know that "grasslands country" lives on.

CHAPTER 14
DREAM COME TRUE

Winning a Stanley Cup is a dream come true. But it's way better than you can imagine. Way, way better than your dream as a kid. And I became a champion for the first time in overtime! Sudden-death, just like my sock hockey days with Rowdy and my brothers. I didn't lose much in sock hockey. But it's pretty exciting to win in overtime.

Bobby Nystrom's overtime goal against the Flyers made me a champion, and people have often asked me, "Bryan, what's your greatest moment, your biggest thrill in hockey?" and my answer is always the same: becoming a champion for the first time. The mayhem and atmosphere at Nassau Coliseum will be forever etched in my mind. That Saturday afternoon hit every nerve in my body.

We earned that 1980 Cup. It wasn't handed to us—we went through the toughest teams in the NHL that year. Every team we faced in the playoffs was a contender—tough, solid, and skilled. In the first round we played the Los Angeles Kings and faced the Triple Crown Line of Marcel Dionne, Charlie Simmer, and Dave Taylor. This was also the first time the two teams involved in one of the most impactful trades in NHL history faced off against each other. Butch Goring became an Islander at the trade deadline that year, and our former teammates Billy Harris and Dave Lewis were now LA Kings. It was the preliminary round, a best-of-five, and our team found its groove early—especially our special teams. I had a hat trick the first game. In pivotal Game Three, Alex McKendry scored the overtime winner, which shifted the momentum of the whole series. We closed it out in Game Four, winning the series, 3–1.

In the second round, we found ourselves facing Boston, a team with a blend of talent and intimidation. Although it was the '80s, the reputation of the Big, Bad Bruins of the '70s was still intact. Gerry Cheevers was still solid in net. There were some incredible battles between Clark and Terry O'Reilly, and between Garry Howatt and Wayne Cashman, including a bench-clearing brawl in Game Two. That series was an incredible display of team unity, strength, grit, and combativeness, led by Gillies, Nystrom, Lane, Bourne, Howatt, Sutter, and Smith. That series against the Bruins was a battle in the best sense of the word and was a watershed moment for us. We stood our ground, we initiated, we didn't retaliate, we stayed aggressive on the forecheck and on the body, and we stayed disciplined. We won the series, 4–2, both teams played great, and it felt like an all-out war.

In the semifinals, we were up against the heavily favoured Buffalo Sabres, with the legendary French Connection line of Gilbert Perreault, Richard Martin, and René Robert leading the offensive attack. Danny Gare was a scrappy fifty-goal scorer, and they had a big, strong defence with Jim Schoenfeld, Jerry Korab, Bill Hajt, and Larry Playfair. The goaltending tandem of Don Edwards and Bob Sauvé had a Vezina Trophy–winning season. They were a strong, stingy, and explosive team.

That series really highlighted the importance of special teams. Our penalty kill was a little bit better than their power play, and our power play found a way to penetrate their great defence. With every win, we gained more confidence. We ended up defeating the Sabres, 4–2, which propelled us to our first Stanley Cup final, against the Philadelphia Flyers.

Throughout the playoff run, our young team was building character. We realized that to win the Cup, you had to keep reaching a higher level of play from the previous series. Now we were facing the Flyers, who had been the best team in the league during the regular season. They went thirty-five consecutive games without a loss that year, a record that still stands today.

The Flyers still had the Broad Street Bullies reputation. Bobby Clarke, Bill Barber, Paul Holmgren, Ken Linseman, Bob Dailey, André "Moose" Dupont, Behn Wilson, and Jimmy Watson could mix it up with the best of them. Rick MacLeish, Reggie Leach, and Brian Propp could put the puck in the net.

We found out that the Stanley Cup finals are a different beast than any other playoff round. The Flyers came into the series determined to win, playing at the top of their game, and so did we. We were going to have to match them or be better. Through six games, I heard Dad's voice in my head, saying, "Rest fast, rest fast." I had no chance to be tired. I had to be ready at a moment's notice.

That series against the Flyers was the greatest test of our fortitude in Islanders history. We had to fight through every check and bear down on every shot, and it was the truest test of our special teams. Our power play was firing on all cylinders, and our penalty-killing unit was the stingiest it had been in the entire playoffs.

It was a war of attrition. The corners and the front of the nets were battle zones. Nobody was backing down. I went nose to nose with Clarke and Linseman that entire series, both of them tough as nails. We also found ways to contain their scorers. And the physical war also became a mental war. Al Arbour's mantra—"Initiate, don't retaliate"—paid off.

We had learned from the past. Every win and every loss over the previous seasons provided lessons for us. This final series gave us a sense of mastery—we had finally learned how to win. We'd put together everything we'd learned over the previous years and were finally champions.

They could have picked anyone on the team as playoff MVP and it would have been a good choice. But *somehow* I was chosen. I was ecstatic to be chosen, but I was also humbled by the honour. Like all hockey players, we know how an award like that reflects on all teammates. I'd set a new playoff point record that year and had a solid final series, but we wouldn't have won the Cup without an MVP effort from everyone on the team. I could have gone down the roster and any of the guys would have been a worthy recipient.

As I was handed the Conn Smythe Trophy, I saw Jean Béliveau's name—he was the first recipient of the trophy. I immediately flashed back to the time when I was eight years old, watching the Canadiens win the ultimate prize on that old black-and-white TV back home, and Béliveau skating around with the Cup. I wondered if I was having the same feelings that he'd had then. Jubilation. Satisfaction. I couldn't stop thanking my teammates as each one came up to congratulate me.

The 1980 playoffs taught me something that I'll always carry with me about hype and expectations. When we lost to Toronto in the '78 quarter-finals, we weren't ready to win. We were distracted. With each disappointing loss, we learned how to win. I learned to differentiate between media and fan expectations and my own expectations and reality. It was important to keep the media and fans in check. You had to set your own realistic expectations. I had to bring my best game; no shortcuts; everything detailed, to be ultra-dependable in every situation—every face-off, every shot—with no distractions. As I said earlier, those lessons we learned in '78 and '79 were valuable. They made us appreciate the success more. We avoided being distracted by the hype, but kept our focus and our discipline. We controlled what we could control.

We had a few days to celebrate prior to the Stanley Cup parade. One of the celebrations was at the Beaver Dam Country Club. The party was winding down, so I asked Bill Torrey where the Cup was going to be that night. He said he was taking it home.

"Can I have it?" I asked him. "I want to wake up in the morning and open my eyes and the first thing I see will be Lord's Stanley Cup."

"Absolutely," he said. And then Bill smiled and chuckled. "Just remember to bring it to the parade tomorrow."

Today, when a team wins the Stanley Cup, each player gets to take it home and have a day with it. But it wasn't like that then. I didn't know what the protocol was; I didn't know if I'd have any time with it. All I knew was that I wanted to have my time with Stanley. I wanted to be discreet and I didn't want to make a big fuss. So I quietly snuck the Stanley Cup to my car and gently laid it out on the back seat. The keeper of the Cup asked what I was doing, and I said, "I'll be right back." It was a lie.

When I got home, I put the Cup at the foot of the bed and opened the bedroom curtains, knowing that when I woke up, the morning sun would be shining right through the east-facing window. I couldn't have written a better script. When I woke up, the Cup was glowing like you couldn't imagine. It was magnificently perfect.

It is not easy to repeat as champions. Injuries, referee calls, bad bounces can all go against you. You can run into a hot goaltender or a team that suddenly has a red-hot power play. Sometimes, an opponent you'd least suspect developed hot hands. Anything can happen that works against you, it's no one's fault. The important thing to remember is that you can't let it bother you.

I heard an interview with Scotty Bowman once, and he listed five things you need to repeat as champions: you need goaltending; your top players have to perform in a big way; your foot soldiers need to be huge contributors; your special teams have to be better than the opposition's; and you have to stay healthy and disciplined. Years later, when I wound up being coached by Scotty in Pittsburgh, he repeated those exact words to us in a team meeting during the season.

We've all heard about the Stanley Cup hangover—a team that parties too much during the summer. Stanley Cup fat cats. I wasn't going to be satisfied with just one Stanley Cup. I wanted more. Al prepped us well, too, stating that "complacency would be a challenge. Don't let it become a problem. When you're on the top of the mountain, you've got to be ready, because every team is looking to knock you off. Every team wants to beat the best team. There's going to be no nights off for the Stanley Cup champs."

Me, I just wanted to win, and I didn't want to lose that feeling of being a champion. It goes all the way back to my youngest days, when I won my first race at a school field day. When they pinned that ribbon on me, it lit a fire in me. Competition! It was a good feeling to compete and win. I wanted to find a way to win at everything. So as I got ready for the 1980–81 season, I knew that if I won the last game of the year, I'd be a champion again.

This sense of never being satisfied and always wanting more made me reflect on something that happened when I was younger. I was about nine years old. Dad and I were checking cows on horseback. Dad was a horseman and a good cowboy—he looked good in the saddle and in a cowboy hat. I emulated him as much as I could, doing everything he did. I was behind him, as usual, my horse following his, as if in tow.

Like all kids, I was probably daydreaming about wanting stuff I didn't have. A new this or a new that—or even a used one that was in good shape. And out of nowhere, I blurted out, "Hey Dad, how come I always want something?"

Dad turned quickly in his saddle, looked back at me, paused, and in the most matter-of-fact tone, he growled, "Because when you stop wanting, you die."

Then he spun back around and kept riding. It shut me right up. And did it hit home! I never forgot it. What he said, and the way he said it, left an everlasting impression on me.

It was one of those moments. *Holy shit,* I thought to myself. *I'd better want to keep wanting . . . or I'll die.* Dad's message was pretty clear to me: wanting is a good thing; pursue what you want and don't have.

Mike got off to a hell of a start at the beginning of the 1980–81 season, and with it came his run at scoring fifty goals in fifty games. At that point, only one player in NHL history had ever done it: Maurice "Rocket" Richard, in 1944–45. Mike was a scoring machine and we all wanted to be able to help him accomplish something that hadn't been done for such a long time.

Mike stayed hot, and he kept getting closer and closer to tying the record. The media circus surrounding the chase for fifty in fifty didn't faze him in the least. Mike was in the zone. One night, we were in Pittsburgh, and when we walked into the arena, there was security everywhere. Mike had received a death threat. I guess somebody didn't want him to match that record. And NHL security was not taking the threat lightly. Understandably, he was a little rattled by it, and for a while we were all a bit unnerved. But of course, we were also a bunch of ding-dong hockey players. So during the warm-up, we tried to lighten the atmosphere. Why? I don't know, but we made it a point to keep our distance from Mike, to see if he would notice. As he skated around, we all stayed fifteen to twenty feet away. No one made eye contact with him. We split in half at centre ice to take our warm-up shots at the goalies. Every time Mike would skate to one side of the ice, the rest of us would move over to the other side, leaving him all alone. "You bastards!" Mike said, shaking his head.

As Mike closed in on fifty goals, teams started really clamping down on him. No team wanted to be the opponent of record if and when Mike accomplished his feat. If Mike was feeling any pressure, he didn't show it. We were roommates and I loved pumping his tires, keeping his confidence up before each game. "We're going to do this, Hoss," I kept telling him. We both liked it because he said the same thing to me when I was going for the scoring championship in '79.

Our fiftieth game of the season was against the Quebec Nordiques at the Nassau Coliseum. He had scored forty-eight goals in forty-nine games. The stage was set, and our whole team was wired on adrenalin. He scored his forty-ninth with a backhand shot on a broken play. Later in the game, a strong forecheck by John Tonelli resulted in an errant pass finding its way to me. I sent a horrible pass Mike's way. He was about twenty feet away from me. It was the ugliest pass imaginable. But Boss stopped the puck just briefly, spun and half-slapped it. It was a typical Bossy snapper, and it found its way through Ron Grahame. Five-hole. Record tied. The fans in the Coliseum went insane. Mike and I celebrated some goals over the years, but that embrace was special. Probably one of my all-time favourites.

Mike had a chance to break the record shortly after scoring his fiftieth. I slid the puck over to him for a one-timer. Under triple coverage, he calmly slid the puck back to me and I had an open net. *Should I give it back to him? No, I've got a tap-in,* I thought quickly.

Afterwards, I said to him, "Mike, that was unselfish."

"It was the right play," he said. That tells you what a pure hockey player Mike was.

We all knew when Bill Torrey was mad. Most of the time, he was jovial and upbeat. He'd greet you with a "Hiya, kiddo." Both he and Al were always very positive. But when they got mad? Oh, you knew it.

Al would ask Bill to come in and lower the boom once in a while, especially if he felt we needed a reminder about who was calling the shots, a little dose of reality. Al controlled our ice time, but Bill had the big hammer—he could trade you! "If you don't want to play here, just come see me and I'll make sure it happens." That was one of Bill's best lines. We didn't hear it often, maybe once a year, but it never lost its impact on me.

There was a pillar in the middle of the dressing room, and there was a shelf that surrounded it. It was the perfect place for stick boys to place the sliced oranges, gum, skate laces, and the Gatorade kegs and cups. Everything was organized and in its place. Picture-perfect.

During one team tête-à-tête, Bill paced the room a while, saying nothing. Silence can be a powerful moment. Then *wham*, he slammed his fist on the shelf and everything on it went flying. Shit went everywhere. What an effect. *Uh-oh, he's really pissed*, I'd be thinking.

It was never good to see Al or Bill angry, and I really didn't like it. It made my stomach clench, and I hated for the whole team to catch shit if it was me they were mad at.

Trades aren't fun. I hated to see guys leave. Trades are one of the ugly aspects of the business. They weighed on me because I felt a bit responsible—as if, for some reason, I didn't do enough to help them. It wasn't just a teammate leaving, it was a friend. As tough as it was to see an old friend leave, I had to quickly pivot to welcome the new player coming in to help him fit in.

Playing against a former teammate was equally as hard. But as professionals, come game time, there were no friends on the other team, so I dealt with it.

Near the end of the 1980–81 season, we traded goalie Glenn "Chico" Resch to the Colorado Rockies for Jari Kaarela and Mike McEwen. McEwen wound up making some big plays and scoring some big goals for us. But Chico was one of us and was part of the climb to that first championship. He was as popular and friendly with the fans as he was in the locker room.

That trade really stung me.

In the '81 playoffs, we drew the Toronto Maple Leafs in the first round. The hype in the press was that we owed these guys for beating us in the '78 quarter-finals. We were a different team by now, and there were only a few players left on the Toronto roster from that earlier series. Our Islanders team was on a mission to repeat as champions, and we were on fire in that series. We won the first game, 9–2, then finished off the best-of-five with a 5–1 victory at home and a 6–1 win in Maple Leaf Gardens.

Next up were the Edmonton Oilers, who had upset the Montreal Canadiens in the first round. They were a bold young group. They seemed to be having fun, singing and smiling on the bench at times. It pissed some of our guys off, but I kind of liked it because they were having a blast. This Oilers team played fast-paced hockey. Their approach to a game seemed to be: if you get fifty shots, we'll get seventy. If you get seventy, we'll get ninety. We'll outshoot you, outskate you, and outscore you. Oh, and our goalie will get some sleep, too.

They kind of reminded me of our team a few years earlier. They had a young nucleus. They were destined to be a force to be reckoned with. They had some phenomenal players at every position. It wasn't just Wayne Gretzky. They had Mark Messier, Jari Kurri, Glenn Anderson, Paul Coffey, Kevin Lowe. All future Hall of Famers.

Al warned us not to get caught up playing fire-wagon hockey against them, but somehow we did. And we didn't mind it. The Oilers pushed us hard, and they were the only team to win a playoff game in our rink that spring. We beat them in six games, and I enjoyed the series immensely.

We got the Rangers in the conference finals, our crosstown rivals. The hype around the rivalry was magnified this year because the Rangers had knocked us out in the '79 semifinals. Again, there was a whole new crew. We were a different team in '81 than we were in '79. We beat them in four straight games, maybe because we didn't want to give them any hope of winning one game and building their confidence.

Waiting for us in the Stanley Cup finals were the red-hot Minnesota North Stars. The Stars had a lot of great young talent, including Dino Ciccarelli, Bobby Smith, and Neal Broten. Steve Payne and Al MacAdam were racking up a ton of points, too.

Don Beaupre was their goalie. He had the hot hand, and Mike was getting a big kick out of scoring goals against him.

After winning the first three games, we lost Game Four in Minnesota.

I dislocated my shoulder late in the third period of that game. I tried to hold up Bobby Smith, and I felt a ripping pop. I tried one more shift, then Al shut me down. I iced my shoulder the whole plane ride back to Long Island.

That next morning at home, I couldn't reach the milk to pour on my son's cereal. I had to eat and brush my teeth and wipe my butt left-handed. Every motion hurt. I thought my right arm would put me out of commission. But our trainer, Ron Waske, turned into a miracle worker. He kept my range of motion and flexibility. I found that if I held my elbow in tight to my body, it stabilized my right shoulder and the pain was significantly lessened. So Waske strapped my shoulder tight to my body, which kept my forearm free to move up and down and sideways. I was excited and grabbed my stick, and was relieved that it felt okay. Even more so when I got on the ice and found out that I could stickhandle and shoot.

The harness that Waske made for me that night worked perfectly. So I got to play in Game Five. We got out to an early lead and Al didn't use me a lot, but I had a consecutive playoff point-scoring streak going, and it stayed alive when I assisted on a Mike McEwen goal. We won the game, 5–1. Back-to-back champions —my shoulder didn't hurt anymore.

It was extremely rewarding—not so much because we beat the North Stars, even though they played extremely well to get to the finals—but because we had been determined to repeat as champions and we were going to find a way to beat anybody, and we did. Mission accomplished.

It's funny when I think back to the celebration on the ice. I wanted to be involved so much. I wanted to pump the Stanley Cup over my head the way I had the year before, but my arm was strapped to the side of my body. Mike and Denis flanked me because I could only get it so high. It kind of pissed me off, but I also appreciated the gesture.

There was also a bit of a dark cloud over the celebration that year. Mike's father passed away a couple of days after we won. Going to the funeral, we all tried to put on a good face, but it's tough when your buddy loses his dad.

CHAPTER 15

AGAIN AND AGAIN

Heading into the 1981 Canada Cup, I was a two-time Stanley Cup champion. Our Islanders team was not a cocky crew. We aspired to be like the Canadiens dynasty of the '70s and conduct ourselves like champions. Integrity seemed to ooze from those Montreal teams.

Walking into the Team Canada dressing room, we had a tempered confidence and reserve. Myself, Mike Bossy, Clark Gillies, Denis Potvin, and Billy Smith had all been invited to attend the camp. Smitty, unfortunately, broke a finger on his catching hand during a practice and didn't get to compete in any games. Denis played great and our Trio Grande line did very well. Mike led all goal scorers, and he and I finished right behind Wayne Gretzky in points. But that is no consolation when you don't win.

Scotty Bowman was our coach, assisted by Red Berenson and Al MacNeil. Scotty was almost intimidating—not because he barked or yelled at us, but because of his demeanour. Scotty always seemed deep in thought. He was definitely the man in charge and had a strong presence and confidence. I liked him immediately and really liked how he spoke to me in private conversations.

Scotty's meetings were quite similar to Al Arbour's. Maybe he had influenced Al back when he coached him in St. Louis? The meetings were short and concise. Like Al, Scotty left room for offensive creativity but made it a point to focus on our team's strengths. I was most impressed with Scotty's bench management.

Mike and I enjoyed Berenson and McNeil, too. Both had highly respected coaching careers, and to a man, they made us all feel valued. Red and Al seemed to take a shine to Mike and me, which made the training camp much more enjoyable and a very rewarding experience. In the back of my mind, I wondered if Al Arbour had called his friend Berenson and said, "Keep an eye on these two idiots. They might be silly and full of laughs during practice, but they'll be all business come game time."

Training camp was full of superstars. There was a young, dynamic Wayne Gretzky, and Guy Lafleur was still at the top of his game. But to me, the best player in camp was Gilbert Perreault. His speed, puck control, and confidence were something else—wow! And that trio played on a line together—*holy cow!*

The Canada Cup was an opportunity to improve the NHL pension plan. And as a group of elite athletes, we also wanted to compete against the best in the world. That summer and early fall, we had the opportunity to do so. The Soviet Union, Czechoslovakia, USA, Canada, Sweden, and Finland: the top six hockey powers in the world were all part of the tournament.

When you are playing for your country, it's a different experience. I thought back to the time I represented Canada in the World Junior Championship years earlier. And now, I was wearing the maple leaf proudly on my jersey again. The hockey fans in Canada are as passionate as the players about the game, and we understood that. It gave us incredible motivation.

The Soviet Union had defeated our group of NHL All-Stars during the 1979 Challenge Cup in New York, so here we were, two years later, looking for redemption.

Team Canada had a terrific tournament. We went undefeated in the round robin, four wins and one tie. What was great was the fact that we got to play in different cities across Canada, and to be cheered on by hockey fans from coast to coast.

In the finals, we faced off against the Soviet Union in a best-of-three series. We won the first game, 4–2, and lost the second, 5–4. But what most people remember is the third and deciding game.

My memory of that final game was very different than what was reflected in the final score. We had a lot of chances early and had the Soviets on their heels. But they were a great team with great players, and that makes for great completion. Sometimes it can come down to one big play or one lucky goal that influences the outcome of the game. It's why we play the games. As we got into the second and third periods, it became clear it wasn't going to be our night. It happens. We ended up losing, 8–1. The final score might have looked like a rout, but hey, we had our chances. They just scored on theirs.

As disappointing as that Canada Cup loss was, we couldn't dwell on it. We had to pull ourselves together and get ready for the upcoming season.

Like the previous seasons, defending Stanley Cup champions don't get any nights off. Al reminded us that the regular season is a marathon, not a sprint, and although we would have to pace ourselves in order to have enough gas in the tank for the playoffs, we also had to stay disciplined, keep our good habits, and execute with pride. The 1981–82 season turned out to be very productive for me and the team. The Islanders finished with the best record in the league, and I scored fifty goals.

Our team was all about maintenance and injury prevention. Stretching, off-ice conditioning, proper rest, and ice-time management were just as important as on-ice strategy. Again, credit goes to our trainer, Ron Waske, who created our team and individual workouts. Mike set a regular-season record for right wingers with an incredible sixty-four goals and 147 points. We were as fine-tuned as a championship team could be, going into the playoffs. Everybody on the team knew their role and we were firing on all cylinders.

In the opening round, we played the Pittsburgh Penguins. In the first two games, we put the pedal to the metal and filled the net, but then the momentum shifted. The Penguins got some life by winning Game Three—in *overtime*. In Game Four, they beat us, fair and square, 5–2.

Everything came down to Game Five. We were actually trailing, 3–1, in the third period and it was looking as though our championship reign might be over. Here was a pesky, determined group of Pittsburgh players with nothing to lose, while we had everything to lose. We were throwing everything at them, trying to change the tide. On a power play in the middle of the third, Mike McEwen brought us within one. But what I remember most about that goal was what happened before it. Al made the brilliant tactical move of changing goalies, which meant a three- or four-minute warm-up that gave our power-play unit a breather. And it worked.

We knew we had to build on the sudden momentum. Lose and there was no tomorrow, so we kept up the pressure. Good fortune struck when John Tonelli tied the game with less than three minutes left. He jumped on a dump-in shot that hit the boards and jumped over Randy Carlyle's stick. He then snapped a far-side zinger, sending the game into overtime.

At the six-minute mark of OT, John, a tireless worker, struck again, winning the game for us. The entire team breathed a huge sigh of relief, and it was a reminder to all of us to take nothing for granted.

In the next round—the Battle of New York—we found ourselves against our greatest rivals, the Rangers. If anyone wanted to knock us off, we knew it was going to be them. The near-loss to the Penguins had sharpened our mental focus, and we didn't want to find ourselves in that position again.

The Rangers pushed and pushed and wouldn't give up. They beat us in the Coliseum, 5–4, in the first game. It was a tight one. We came back to beat them convincingly in Game Two, 7–2. Game Three was another tight game, and we won it in overtime. Guess who scored? It was initially meant as a pass to Bob Bourne, but my backhand just caught the far corner past a surprised Eddie Mio. The victory shifted momentum back our way. We beat them in the Garden, 4–2, and had the Rangers on the ropes. But they wouldn't give up and came back to beat us, 4–2, on our ice. We closed out the series back in New York with a pretty solid 5–3 win. Smitty was brilliant early.

In the semifinals, we faced a very talented and scrappy Quebec Nordiques team. They had a terrific lineup that included the Šťastný brothers (Peter, Marian, and Anton), Michel Goulet, pesky Mark Hunter, and goaltender Dan Bouchard. We were firing on all cylinders by this point. We found ways to keep their scorers off the score sheet, and it seemed everyone on our team was contributing offensively. Wayne Merrick scored a huge overtime goal in Game Three that put us up 3–0 in the series, leaving the Nordiques with a steep hill to climb. Thoughts of the opening series against Pittsburgh stayed with us, and we didn't want to give them any opportunity to come back. We swept the series with a 4–2 victory, and we were off to our third consecutive Stanley Cup final.

Our opponents in the finals: my good friend Tiger Williams and the Vancouver Canucks. The team had had an amazing run that spring. They were a feisty bunch. Along with Tiger and another junior teammate, Ron Delorme, they had Harold Snepsts, Stan Smyl, and Curt Fraser. Goaltender Richard Brodeur, also known as King Richard, was at the top of his game. The Canucks knocked off Calgary in the opening round, then eliminated a Los Angeles Kings team that had shocked the hockey world by dispatching the heavily favoured Edmonton Oilers in the opening round.

Tiger was the spark plug of that team. They had skill, but it was Tiger's grit, determination, and passion that inspired his teammates. It was a salty series. The Canucks wanted to stir the pot and get us in the penalty box. Al was all over us to turn the other cheek. "Initiate, don't retaliate," he kept telling us on the bench.

The Canucks played us tight in Game One. They were a four-line team, which meant we paid a price with every shift. And Brodeur stayed absolutely brilliant in net. The first game went to overtime, and as the seconds ticked away in that first extra period, the greatest goal scorer ever, Mike Bossy, gobbled up an errant clearing pass from Harold Snepsts and ripped the puck past King Richard. It was one of the hardest, most accurate shots I've ever seen.

The rest of that series was incredibly combative. They took more penalties than they should have, while we stayed disciplined, avoiding scrums and retaliation. This final was Mike Bossy's time to shine. On his way to being named playoff MVP that year, he scored seven goals in the final, some of which left me and the hockey world shaking our heads. *Amazing* isn't a good enough word to describe it. No matter what the Canucks did to Mike—clutching, grabbing, slashing—he rose above it and proved how great a player he was.

We swept the Canucks in four games and won Stanley Cup number three. It ended up being the only championship that we won on the road. I felt badly for Tiger, because I love him. But I loved my Islanders teammates, too. It sure felt good to head home to Long Island as a champion. The feeling of being a champion—man, it never gets old.

CHAPTER 16

DYNASTY

Between the regular season, playoffs, and international tournaments, I ended up playing a lot of hockey over the years. I don't think that any group of guys in the history of hockey played more games as me and my Islanders teammates over this four-year period.

The 1982–83 season offered a new challenge: wear and tear. Besides that, injuries are also part of the game, and they kept a bunch of our team out of the lineup for extended periods, including Ken Morrow, Dave Langevin, and Denis Potvin who were rehabbing knee problems. Others nursed groin pulls or minor shoulder aches. It seemed like everyone was a bit worn, and it took a toll on the team.

The regular season was a grind, but nobody was complaining. "Tape and aspirin to it" and "brace up" became common sayings prior to games. We all continued to ready ourselves, and we were willing to give our best on the ice. We did, however, get off to a hell of a start, with eleven wins in the first thirteen games. But the season is long, and there were some dips along the way.

By early March, we found our groove again. As battle-worn as we had become, we still finished second in the Patrick Division and sixth overall in the league standings. We knew we had to find another gear come playoff time. This would be the third time we defended our reign. Experience prepared us for the obvious. Once again, every team was looking to knock us off.

The opening series was against the Washington Capitals, and it featured two pairs of back-to-back games, four games in five nights. Another challenge for the battle-worn Isles. The thing that comes to mind is how we were always finding ways to win hockey games. We became very good at capitalizing on all of the chances that were presented to us. Opportunistic, some might call it. We took care of Washington, 3–1, and for the third year in a row, moved on to face the Rangers.

There's nothing like an Islanders–Rangers playoff series to get the juices flowing. The intensity is so high, it's hard to measure. We knew them well, and they knew us well, and neither team was going to go down lightly. Under Herb Brooks, the Rangers were playing freewheeling hockey and skating like they had never skated before. Mark Pavelich and Rob McClanahan were scooters from Herb's Miracle on Ice team that won the 1980 gold medal. Ron Duguay was equally as quick, and he and the Maloney brothers were now veteran leaders. There were plenty of goals scored in the series, but we outscored them on our way to winning the series, 4–2.

Our opponents in the conference final were the Boston Bruins. They were loaded with stalwart veterans that year, like Peter McNab, Rick Middleton, and Brad Park. Young guns Raymond Bourque, Mike Krushelnyski, Barry Pederson, and Tom Fergus brought youthful energy, along with rugged Gordie Kluzak, who grew up in Mom's hometown. They marched through a very solid season and came into the playoffs as a force to be reckoned with.

The Bruins were determined to shut Mike down during the season and had assigned a kid named Luc Dufour to cover him. They were both French Canadian, and they went back and forth with their *français* jawing. I always wondered what the hell they were saying to each other. In spite of having a Bruins blanket on him throughout the series, Mike still ended up with nine goals, including four in Game Six.

The series was a typical Islanders–Bruins clash. Every puck battle was won with grit and determination. We eliminated Boston in six games, which sent us to the Stanley Cup finals against the powerful offence of the Edmonton Oilers.

I had my own nickname for Edmonton. I called them "the creepy Oilers," for good reason—no offence or malice meant. It was because they wanted to take away something we had, namely the Stanley Cup. It was just my way of motivating myself and getting ramped up.

The Oilers studied us the way we had studied the late-1970s Montreal Canadiens. They watched our practices, just as we'd watched Montreal's. We felt them studying us, breathing down our neck. They had built a core of young, skilled players through the draft, much like the Islanders did. They were younger than us by five or six years. But we didn't feel like old-timers. We were only twenty-seven to thirty years of age, but the media made us out to be old, long in the tooth, worn out. We had played a lot of hockey, but adrenalin and pride wouldn't let us feel tired.

The series started in Edmonton, and they came out flying. They looked fresh-faced and eager. We'd had a tough regular season and been through some battles against the Rangers and the Bruins to get to the finals. Not that they had a cakewalk. They had earned the right to represent the West in the finals. They were dominant during the earlier rounds of the playoffs.

Boss was sick for Game One. In fact, they put us in separate hotel rooms. Without our sniper, we had to be that much better defensively. Al was all about discipline, and reminded us to rely on the system, apply pressure in a smart way, maintain body position, and protect the good ice. We weren't to take any stupid penalties, and we needed to be mindful of when Coffey was on the ice. And to our good fortune, we had "Mr. Cool, Calm, and Collected": Billy Smith.

We wanted to get the lead against the Oilers. We didn't want to play catch-up hockey against them. We needed to force their offence to take more chances, which would open up opportunities for us to counter with our attack.

Mike was back for Game Two, and he scored a huge goal. It was great to have our best offensive weapon back in the lineup. We stayed with our strategy of jamming up the middle and keeping them to the outside. Everyone stayed dependable defensively, limiting quality chances and rebounds. Denis was a tank, and he, Butch Goring, and I were tasked with every defensive-zone faceoff during those first two games.

Although we won the first two games in Edmonton, 2–0 and 6–3, it felt like we were sitting on a keg of dynamite. The Oilers were so explosive, and we knew they could blow things wide open at any moment. We couldn't let their offence get going. Don't let that lid get off the barrel.

I can't say enough about Billy Smith and the way he played in that series. He gave up little to nothing, and to me, he never played better. Smitty didn't talk about his game all that much. I came to know that he was going to make every save he should, and some that he shouldn't—the spectacular ones, the game savers that would leave us all shaking our heads. If they were going to score a goal, it wasn't going to be a shitty goal, a back-breaker. The puck would have to find a perfect spot to get into the net.

Going back to Long Island with a two-game lead, we hadn't dominated the Oilers. We had played some good defensive hockey. And we had Smitty. At this point, I think Smitty got in their heads a bit. He was coming up big and the Oilers were having trouble getting anything past him.

When Kenny Morrow nailed the empty-net goal in Game Four, we completed a sweep of the Oilers with a 4–2 win. That fourth Stanley Cup was extra special. We developed a reputation for finding ways to win, no matter who we were playing against, whichever way our opponents wanted to play. Washington and the Rangers came at us with speed, the Bruins were all about grit, and the Oilers had a powerhouse offence. And we found a way to win. If you are going to wear the moniker of being a dynasty, you have to earn it. And I think we did with that championship. It felt a bit uncomfortable, but it was also empowering. We didn't call ourselves a dynasty, we *felt* like a dynasty.

CHAPTER 17

THE DRIVE FOR FIVE

There was plenty of attention on the Islanders as we started the 1983–84 season. The Montreal Canadiens had won five Stanley Cups in a row, from 1956 to 1960, and we were on the doorstep, trying to match this incredible accomplishment. Our group was totally invested in it, and it ended up being our toughest challenge yet.

A couple of highly touted draft picks arrived that year. Pat LaFontaine and Pat Flatley joined the team right after the 1984 Winter Olympics. They were young, they were excited to be in the NHL, and they were obviously really talented. Lafontaine was a dynamic player, with skill and speed. He was eager to learn and a wonderful student. Flats was a strong physical player with a ton of competitiveness. Both wanted to contribute, had a strong work ethic, and were natural leaders. Their hunger and youthful enthusiasm were welcome in our dressing room. We embraced them.

Both were like young puppies. LaFontaine followed me around everywhere. He was full of questions. Flats was the same, and almost over-apologetic, saying he was sorry for not making a pass or going to the right place. I would tell him, "Stop fucking saying you're sorry and bear the fuck down." It's fine to keep saying you're sorry for the first week or two, but after that, you're a professional now and it's time to up your ante, kiddo. It was fun watching those kids mature and become part of the team.

A day off here and there was always appreciated. Al Arbour and our trainer, Ron Waske, kept a pretty good eye on things and knew when it was important to rest guys. When you factor in the grind of travel, the demands of the schedule where you may play three games in four nights or back-to-back games, the season can really take its toll. On the road to a fifth Stanley Cup, Al, the coaching and training staff, and all of us knew we had to keep sharp and stay healthy.

Looking back, I realize that there will never be another run like the one we had in the 1980s. It was a unique time in hockey because of the Canada Cups in the fall. Nobody is ever going to play that many games in a four- or five-year span again.

The 1983–84 season was a strong one for the Islanders. We won the Patrick Division and finished second to Edmonton in the overall standings. Mike had another solid fifty-goal season, and I led the team in assists, and we both notched over 100 points. Al was experimenting with line combinations throughout the regular season, and all of us were working hard to maintain our mojo for a run at a fifth Cup.

Al did a very good job of making sure we didn't burn ourselves out during the season—especially me, for some reason. "Do you remember how hard I played you when you won the scoring championship in '79?" Al asked me once.

"Yeah, thanks for that," I said. "You double-shifted me quite a bit the last month of the season."

"And I burnt you out, Trots," Al replied. "That was my fault, not yours. We both learned from it, right?"

Did I want a scoring championship or a chance to have enough gas in the tank to compete for Lord Stanley's cup? Enough said!

I denied it at first, of course—my pride wouldn't let me admit it—but Al was probably right. Thinking back to the 1978–79 season, he was playing me thirty to thirty-five minutes a game down the stretch. He, as much as my teammates, helped me win the Art Ross Trophy that year. In the regular seasons that followed, my playing time was reduced to twenty minutes, max. Our team had good depth and it became all about quality ice time rather than a quantity of ice time.

This was our fourth defence of the Stanley Cup. We were going to rest ourselves and conserve energy for the playoffs. As we finished off the regular season and prepared for the playoffs, it was "business as usual." A laser focus, along with individual workouts, rest, and diet, were paramount for what lay ahead.

Getting out of our division wasn't going to be a cakewalk. But we didn't assume anything. We drew the Rangers in the first round, and once again the rivalry produced high-calibre hockey. The momentum of the five-game series ebbed and flowed, with the final game ending in overtime—classic! Kenny Morrow scored the winner for us. It was one of those shots where Kenny got all of it. I've always thought he was underrated offensively. His reputation as a stay-at-home defenceman hid his puck skills. He's a strong man, and a smart hockey player. He wasn't a bruiser, but he was incredibly effective. I called him the "Long Arm of the Law" with his six-foot reach and poke-checking ability. When you practised against players like Kenny and the rest of our defence—Stefan Persson, Gord Lane, Dave Langevin—every day, you just became a better hockey player. Headlines were few for them, and they never complained. But we all came to appreciate their immense talent and abilities. In my mind, we would never have won four Cups without this defensive corps, and wouldn't have been in a position to push for a fifth.

Next up, the Washington Capitals. Here we were, facing them again, like a perennial weed that kept showing up every year.

They won the first game in the second round series, and they took us to overtime in the second game. The Capitals had three solid lines that year, featuring Mike Gartner, Bobby Carpenter, and Bengt-Åke Gustafsson. And their defence included future Hall of Famers Rod Langway, Scott Stevens, and Larry Murphy (my future teammate in Pittsburgh). I felt that the difference in the series to me was going to come down to goaltending, and in my mind, we had the best goalie. The best money goalie in NHL history, Billy Smith. We ended up winning the series in five games.

As fate would have it, we found ourselves in a best-of-seven conference final against the Montreal Canadiens. They seemed determined to block our attempt to equal their franchise's historical record of five consecutive Cups. Even though we had won fifteen more games than the Canadiens during the regular season that year, we had to go on the road and play the first two games in the Forum—a crazy change in the NHL playoff format that season that I can't fully explain, but it somehow gave them the home-ice advantage for the series.

The Habs of the late 1950s were the only team in history to win five Stanley Cups in a row, and now the modern-day Canadiens had a chance to prevent us from matching that record. Obviously, that storyline was top of mind among the Montreal fans and media. They were all rooting against us, and that's understandable. It's human nature. Somehow, we wound up being the bad guys in this series for pretty much anyone who wasn't an Islanders fan, and for the most part, I understood and accepted it.

There was also a core of veterans on that Montreal team who had been part of the Canadiens' 1970s dynasty—Bob Gainey, Larry Robinson, Guy Lafleur, Steve Shutt. They are a proud group, each one a true Hall of Famer, and I'm sure they wanted to show their younger teammates how to battle. How to play with the pride of *les Habitants*.

Quite a few things were written by some great hockey writers, comparing the *bleu, blanc, et rouge* teams of the '50s to our Long Island blue and orange team. They played a seventy-game schedule back then, and there were only two rounds of playoffs. If we beat Montreal, it would be our nineteenth consecutive playoff series win. Montreal had only needed to win ten series, total, to win those five Cups back in the '50s. There were no Challenge Cups or Canada Cups in the midst of their journey to add to the wear and tear on their top players. And those were the days when a team stayed short-handed no matter how many times you scored on them during a power play. Those great Montreal teams probably had a lot to do with the rule change. Now, when a team scores on a power play, the other team goes back to full strength.

The contrasts and comparisons didn't matter to us, to either of the current teams. We had so much respect for history and for what those Montreal Canadiens teams had accomplished. If we tried to make any sort of point about the differences, it would sound like we were diminishing their accomplishments. We could have talked about how they were different eras, how we didn't play in that era, how there were always going to be comparisons, whether they were right or wrong. Hockey players aren't like that. At the end of the day, you still have to score more goals than the other team, regardless of headlines or media narratives.

We lost the first two games to the Canadiens, and you can imagine the reaction in the Montreal media. There were not a lot of positive things being said about us. We didn't enjoy it, but after four Stanley Cups, we were used to it. We'd developed a thick skin. I was looking forward to going back to Long Island for the next two games, knowing that we had to take advantage of our home ice the same way the Canadiens took advantage of theirs.

We had the experience and the confidence of a team that usually found ways to win. Our Islanders identity was going to be a factor: dig deep, boys.

And we did. We won the next two games.

Montreal, too, could play any kind of game. Their identity has always been "The Flying Frenchmen," and this team was quick and fast-paced, but no one talked about how good they were defensively. Playing from behind against them would not be fun. If we didn't grab a lead in the series, they might smother us.

In Game Three, we got out to a blazing start, scoring five straight goals to win the game, 5–2. Then we won Game Four, 3–1. Mike put us ahead in the second period before Gord Dineen put the game away in the third. In both these games, Smitty made the difference for us, as he had so many times before.

That set up a big Game Five back in Montreal, and pretty much everyone figured the outcome could tip the series one way or the other. I got the first goal on a power play early in the first period, and then Brent Sutter scored a shorthanded goal—up 2–0, so far, mission accomplished. They got one back in the third period on the power play before Pat Flatley put the game away with an insurance goal. I praised him afterwards, "Way to bear down, Flats."

He smiled. "I listened to you, Trots." No apology needed.

I have one awful memory from that night: I took one of the worst hits of my career. Three Canadians turnbuckled me, and I can feel it like it was yesterday. How I didn't break my neck or dislocate every frickin' joint in my body, I don't know. It was like getting hit from three different directions by three different trucks all at once. The benches in the old Forum were unique because they had these tiny little doors, and there was always a logjam of guys getting on and off the ice. I actually can't remember if I was going on or going off the ice, but I got waylaid right by that door.

Hits like that stick with you.

The crowd went crazy. I thought to myself, *I can't let anyone know I'm hurt. I gotta survive this somehow.* I took some deep breaths, and Al gave me a little bit of extra bench time to help me shake it off.

By winning Game Five, we put the Canadiens one game away from elimination. We were determined to take as much momentum as possible into Game Six at the Coliseum. Mike's two goals, a commanding performance by Denis and another solid effort from Billy Smith sent us to the Stanley Cup finals. Who else but the Edmonton Oilers were waiting for us.

When we played the Canadiens, the headlines were all about winning five Cups in a row. When we walked into Edmonton, it was all about how beautifully the Oilers played and how ugly the Islanders' style was. We had great respect for the Oilers and loved how they played. They did have a grace about the way they played hockey, and they were spectacular. But after winning four Cups and nineteen straight playoff series, maybe we weren't as "ugly" as everyone thought. I think the media gets tired of seeing the same team win. It happened to the Montreal Canadiens in the seventies. They were a great team, and people just got mad at them. Sports pundits and the hockey world wanted a new champion. It's true in all sports. It's the reason people started hating Tom Brady. It wasn't his fault that he kept winning. For any professional athlete, achieving and maintaining the feeling of being a champion is what we crave.

In this era, for two teams to meet in the finals in back-to-back seasons was incredible. One of the things we focused on was to not beat ourselves. I believed that if we brought our best game and they brought their best game, we'd let the chips fall where they may. Just good, honest hockey.

Like no other series before, the format for the Stanley Cup final was 2-3-2, instead of the usual 2-2-1-1-1. The series opened in

Uniondale, then shifted to Edmonton for Games Three, Four, and Five. Odd? Sure. But it didn't matter. Both teams were going to have to deal with it, whether the outcome was good, bad, or indifferent. It's hard to say whether the result would be any different if the 2-2-1-1-1 format had been kept.

In the first game, I felt we had our chances, but Grant Fuhr played remarkably. We outshot them, 38–34, but they beat us, 1–0. Neither of the team's big guns scored a goal that night. Kevin McClelland, with eight goals all season, was the only one who scored. We came back in Game Two and beat them convincingly, 6–1, but everything went our way that night.

It stung to lose Game One, because we lost the psychological edge that home-ice advantage gave. We dug in and won Game Two, and now it was our turn to win one of the next three games in Edmonton. We had to turn the tide, regain home-ice advantage, and return to Long Island. I didn't want them closing out the series at home. My mentality was rooted in determination as much as desperation.

To their credit, the Oilers won the next three games. We gave it a valiant effort, but it wasn't meant to be. Although much has been said about the Oilers changing their style to play us in the finals that year, we didn't notice it a heck of a lot. They won the Stanley Cup, fair and square. If you are going to lose to somebody, lose to good champions, and they were a great team.

Personally, it was devastating. It was painful to go all the way to the finals and lose. There are no words to express how it feels to look a teammate in the face after that. It's an apology with no words. You feel like you've let each other down. There is no celebration when you come in second. It doesn't take the pain away when Al and Bill are thanking you for a great year and you haven't won.

I felt a heavy responsibility for the loss, and it took a while to shake that awful feeling. I didn't feel I played my best in the finals. I worked hard, I had my chances, and created some chances, but I needed to do more offensively. I also didn't do anything game-changing when it was needed.

You've got to give the Oilers credit. They went back to the drawing board after losing to us in 1983, they showed up in the finals again, and to their credit, they beat us. We lost to a great team, great players, and as I found out later as I got to know them over the years, great people. I have great respect for that Oiler team.

The summer after we lost to the Oilers in the final, there was another Canada Cup, which meant another short summer after a long playoff run. My mind wasn't on the tournament; I was thinking about getting the Stanley Cup back.

But I was looking for a little change. Because of my birthright and Indigenous heritage, I thought now might be a good time to go through the process of playing for the United States. Because I was married to an American girl, because all my kids were born in the USA, and because I was a North American Indian, it felt like a good time to give back to a country that had been so good to me for the last ten years of my life. My application for United States citizenship was already in progress, so I asked if I could play for Team USA in the Canada Cup. The reaction was mixed. The general manager of Team USA, Lou Nanne, was pretty excited, but there was some disappointment from Team Canada.

The decision raised eyebrows and made media headlines, which was not my intention. Holy cow! It hurts when someone calls you a traitor. Crap like that was written in the papers. But other Canadians had done it before—goaltenders Tony Esposito in the 1981 Canada Cup, and Chico Resch in the 1982 World Championship. Lou Nanne was born in Canada but was general manager for Team USA. My decision was hard for the media and some hockey fans to grasp, and it became exhausting to continue to explain myself.

Al Arbour and Bill Torrey were supportive, and many of my friends on both sides of the border wished me well, but it was extra difficult to explain to Mike, because it meant we would be split up for the tournament. I didn't give him enough consideration when it came to our friendship. After the tournament, we discussed it and I apologized to Mike.

I never said anything bad about Canada. I wasn't playing *against* Canada; I was playing *for* the USA. And when we played a game against Canada, I wasn't playing against the country—I was playing against those players. At least that's how it felt for me. The Canada Cup was a series of exhibition games that improved the pension plan for the players.

I do admit that I didn't think about the patriotic part of my decision, given the importance of hockey in Canada. Was it the right thing to do? It was at that moment in my life. If I had to do it over again, I'd think it over a little longer and get more input from friends and family. Maybe I'd do it differently. Probably; maybe not. But my nature is not to dwell on stuff. So I kept moving forward.

It was very strange to play against Mike in the tournament, which was another thing I hadn't considered. In one game, he had possession of the puck along the boards, and I found myself hesitating to take the body. So I let up and attempted a stick check instead. He snuck around me, dammit!

"Mike, I could have lit you up there," I teased him afterwards.

"No way," he said. "I saw you. I left you there holding your jockstrap."

"That was a pretty good move," I chuckled, "but if it was anyone else, I would've put them in the third row."

"Yeah right, you wish."

That was us teasing each other.

Our USA team included Neal Broten, Joe Mullen, Chris Chelios, Pat LaFontaine, Bobby Carpenter, Rod Langway—a highly skilled and competitive group. There was also a young Chris Nilan in the lineup, who I got to know as a teammate. He prided himself on execution. He impressed all of us with his heart and hustle.

Team USA had a good tournament. I played on a line with Joe Mullen and Mark Johnson and was one of the leading scorers for Team USA. We tied Canada, 4–4, finished second to the Soviet Union in the round-robin, and made the semifinals, where we lost to Sweden. Sweden then lost to Canada in the finals. I was proud of my Team USA teammates, and very happy for Mike and Canada.

It was the last time I played international hockey.

CHAPTER 18

IT HAD TO HAPPEN

I returned to the Islanders' 1984 training camp with what I thought was a nagging groin injury. It wasn't improving with therapy, and then I was diagnosed with a deep stomach muscle tear. I played through the pain for the first thirty games of the '84–85 season, while strengthening the injured area at the same time. The injury was right beside the hip flexor and it impacted my skating. I could cross over to my right no problem, but the injury didn't allow me to cross over to the left. It turned out to be the most challenging injury I've ever had, mostly because it took so long to heal. In hindsight, maybe I should have just rested and rehabbed.

While I dealt with the impact of years of wear and tear on my body and worked to maintain my ability to stay in the lineup, changes were going on with the team over the seasons that followed the end of our Stanley Cup run. When that happens, the chemistry of a team starts to shift and players begin to assume different roles. The mojo of our Stanley Cup roster was gone, and we were building a new identity with the kids coming in. We still competed, we were still there, but it was different.

We didn't know it at the time, but Al Arbour was struggling with some issues that were affecting his health. In the 1986–87 season, he stepped away from the bench, and I felt like I had lost my commander.

We all realized how many hours he had put into preparing the team. It's different than being a player. As a player, you show up for practice, you go home, you show up for the game and you go home. The coach puts in hours and hours of work during a day, reviewing game film, power-play and penalty-killing breakdowns, getting the team ready to compete every night. The demands are incredible. Al was highly respected, and his presence was going to be missed.

I didn't know what to expect. Al was the only coach I'd ever played for through an NHL season.

Brian Kilrea had been our assistant coach the previous two seasons, and I assumed he would slide into the head coaching role. To me, it would be a natural transition. It didn't turn out that way. Brian went back to Ottawa to the junior 67's. So, who was going to be Al's successor?

Bill hired Terry Simpson.

Terry was intense and came with a solid résumé. His Western Canadian work ethic was evident, and it pushed us to compete hard every night. Me? I really didn't care who they hired as Al's replacement; I was going to give him respect and continue to play my heart out.

In the end, it didn't work out with Terry. They fired him during the '88–89 season. I felt badly for Terry, that somehow I had let him down and didn't play well enough for him. And who would've thought that the guy they brought in to replace Terry would be my old commander, Al Arbour?

Al was a different coach the second time around. I can't quite put my finger on it, but he wasn't the same Al from our Stanley Cup years.

Before long, there weren't many of us left from the Cup teams besides me and Ken Morrow. Bill was extremely active with trades and roster changes. We were officially rebuilding, and the team was feeling growing pains all over again. Gone were Wayne Merrick, Gordie Lane, Dave Langevin, Duane Sutter, Bob Bourne,

John Tonelli, and eventually Butch Goring and Clark Gillies. The guts of our Stanley Cup teams were either picked up on waivers or traded.

Throughout this time, I found myself surrounded by an array of young talent. Mikko Mäkelä and I had a few good years together. LaFontaine and Flatley started to assume a greater leadership role, and I found myself as the veteran welcoming in this wave of new young talent.

I was still trusting Al when it came to my ice time. "I know what you can do out there," he'd tell me, "but I've got to try some things out there with these kids." We were winning some games and losing a lot of them. My ice time started diminishing, even though I was playing hard. It was tough to get much going with five to six minutes a game, and I was getting a little frustrated.

You can say it sounds like sour grapes, but when you're not playing much and you're not winning, you start to question things. I didn't want to question management, I just wanted to understand where I fit in with the team. When you're not playing, the whole world reads into it. When your stats start to go down, people start to wonder whether your skills are fading. This situation is hard for any player to understand.

Towards the end of the 1989–90 season, we had a home game against Pittsburgh. Again, I didn't get much playing time. So, after the game, I rode the bike and did my strength training to maintain my cardio and stay ready. While leaving the arena, I ran into Mario Lemieux and Danny Quinn, who were waiting for a cab. Knowing what taxis were like on Long Island, I knew they might be waiting awhile, so I offered them a ride back to their hotel.

Mario, who was twenty-four at the time, thanked me for the lift. Then, out of the blue, he asked me, "Do you think you'll get traded?"

It was the first time in my life anyone had ever asked me that!

I told him I had a couple of years left on my contract and I planned on honouring them. But as I drove home that night, I kept thinking about it. Why had Mario asked me that? I parked it in the back of my mind.

Talk about a premonition.

When the season ended, Bill called me in for a quick meeting. It was June 22, two days after my daughter Tayler was born. We had a typical quick conversation. He asked me how the baby was, how the family was, and how I was feeling. I was feeling better—I'd rested for a few weeks and the old injuries had pretty much healed. I had a new baby in the house, so things were good.

What happened next, I didn't see coming at all. I was notified that the final two years of my contract were being bought out.

Bill tried to explain the rationale, but none of it made sense.

I asked him, "Can we look for a trade? I'll call a few teams to see if there is any interest. At least this way, you'll get something in return." Buying out my contract would leave them with nothing. I was owed $1.9 million for the final two years of the deal. The NHL's collective bargaining agreement stipulated that two-thirds of the remaining salary would be paid over twice the number of years remaining. For me, that meant $1.25 million, paid over the next four years.

But that wasn't what Bill explained that day. The Islanders interpreted the CBA as meaning they would owe me $50,000 a year for the next twenty-five years, or the present-day value of that amount, which turned out to be just under $500,000.

What I understood, and what the team understood, were two different things. I thought to myself, *This isn't Bill's idea. This is somebody else's idea, telling him to do this, and Bill is being the stand-up guy who has to deliver the awful news.*

In my mind, what the team was proposing completely violated the spirit of my contract and the CBA. I was rattled, and it hurt. The blood, sweat, and loyalty I'd given the Islanders were being discounted. It was like they were saying, "We appreciate everything you've done for us . . . here's your parachute. It's not a golden parachute, it's got a lot of holes in it, so good luck on the landing."

I drove home from that meeting knowing that I had to move on. For the next few days, everything that was written in the press was basically saying that I was finished and that my career was over. That was a crock of shit.

My business advisors had no plan in place for this type of buyout. They listed some of the challenges that I was facing, but offered no advice or solutions on how to deal with it.

I was determined to move forward and trust my instincts. There were going to be lots of changes and some unknown challenges, but one thing I knew was that I needed a new advisory team. I believed there was more hockey in me, and somewhere in my gut, I felt there was a team that wanted whatever I had left to give.

CHAPTER 19

A NEW IDENTITY

On July 1, 1990, for the first time in my life, I became a free agent. Putting my emotions aside, I pushed forward, and realized there were more players like me who were on the market. *Get comfortable with it*, I told myself. I wasn't sure how to navigate these uncharted waters, so I started by identifying teams I thought might like some help.

Detroit had a young Steve Yzerman. Wayne Gretzky was in LA. And there was Mario in Pittsburgh. I'd always wanted to be a Maple Leaf, and I admired how a young Wendel Clark played, so I put Toronto on the list. Neil Smith, an old friend from the Islanders, was now general manager of the Rangers. These were going to be exciting calls to make.

It was great to talk to some of the people, like owner Bruce McNall in LA; Jimmy Devellano in Detroit, whom I won some Cups with when he scouted for the Isles; and Craig Patrick in Pittsburgh, who was methodical and thoughtful. It was a bit of a whirlwind, but each conversation was genuine and friendly. I wasn't trying to rush anybody, but I told everyone I was ready to sign with the first team that sent an acceptable contract.

There were a lot of financial consequences as a result of the buyout, and I was able to find new representatives to help me navigate my way through it. Ken Horowitz and Barry Klarberg, my attorney and tax consultant, were absolutely terrific. They were cool and calm, and hell-bent on getting everything in order. I'm forever grateful to them.

I was enjoying the time I was taking to reflect on what I could offer a potential team and the kind of game I was capable of playing at thirty-four years of age. It was motivating to identify and talk to potential teams, and energizing to have that feeling of desire and belief that I still had some good hockey left in me. I figured I might not be part of a team's first wave of attack, but I felt I could be part of the second or third wave, while still being dependable with my defensive skills and providing some leadership in the locker room.

Of all the people I talked to, Craig Patrick seemed most interested.

In one of our discussions, he asked me. "Why do you want to play in Pittsburgh?"

My answer was simple: "I want to win a Stanley Cup with Mario."

"I'll have a contract for you within the hour," Craig said.

Craig might remember it a bit differently, but that is my memory of it all. We also talked about Bob Johnson, who was going to be coaching the Penguins. Of course, I had played for Bob at the Canada Cup in 1984, and I liked him a lot. We talked about Joe Mullen and Paul Coffey. Craig had mentioned that he wanted to add a little more Stanley Cup–winning experience in the dressing room. I was really looking forward to playing with them.

The contract that Craig sent needed very little tweaking, so negotiations were minimal. When the subject of bonuses came up, I told him I was happy with everything he was offering, but would like to bump up the bonus for the big one—the Stanley

Cup. When Craig agreed to that, I signed the contract and faxed it back to him.

Within the hour, Bob Johnson called me right after I signed the contract. His voice was filled with excitement. "Hi Bryan, Badger Bob here." We were on the phone for an hour, and I think I talked for three minutes of it. He told me who I was going to play with, and how the team was going to be put together. "You're going to feel like an eighteen-year-old again," he told me. I got off the call and thought, *Bob is the best.*

After I finished speaking to Bob, the proper thing to do was to contact the other teams and let them know I'd made my decision. Everybody was understanding, and they all wished me luck. I was now a Pittsburgh Penguin. It felt great to have this new identity.

With a one year contract, the decision was made to keep the kids at home, at the same school—to give them a sense of "normalcy"—so my family stayed on Long Island.

I didn't know how hard it was going to be to leave my kids. *Wow.* Packing up and getting ready to go to Pittsburgh, I felt just like I did when I left Val Marie to go and play junior hockey: homesick. I got on the road and I cried for the first hour of the drive. I pulled into a rest stop on the Pennsylvania Turnpike and called the kids, who had just finished school. "Hi Dad!" Their voices cheered me up.

After fifteen NHL seasons, my only knowledge of the mighty Steel City was the airport, the Civic Arena, the Marriott hotel, and the restaurant known as The Common Plea. After three and a half hours of driving on the Pennsylvania Turnpike, I turned west onto 376, which took me through the Squirrel Hill Tunnel. It's the first time I had seen the city coming from this direction. *Wow,* I thought to myself. *What an impressive skyline.* It's gorgeous. I spent the next hour driving around, familiarizing myself with all the downtown streets and bridges.

Next I called the Penguins' PR director, Cindy Himes, just to let her know I had arrived. I was telling her about the drive, the tunnel, and the view, and she stopped me dead.

"Did you hear about Mario?" she asked me.

"No. What?"

"Mario just had back surgery."

I didn't even make it to the hotel. I asked Cindy which hospital Mario was in. She gave me directions and I drove right there.

When I got to the hospital, I asked the woman at the reception desk which room Mario was in. "We have no Mario Lemieux," she replied frankly. Bewildered, I called Cindy back. "Ask for Ron Jones," she laughed. I went back to the same nurse and asked, confidently, "Ron Jones, please."

Suspiciously, she asked, "How do you know Ron Jones?"

"He's my teammate."

Entering the room, I introduced myself to Mario's wife, Nathalie. They were both gracious and appreciated that I had stopped by. I just wanted him to know that I cared.

"You've got to get yourself better," I told him. "I've only got a one-year deal. We've got to win a Cup together."

I didn't really know Mario that well. I had only met him a couple of times and knew he was a first-class kid. We never went head to head much on the ice. But now we were teammates.

Steve Latin, the Penguins' equipment trainer, had been around the league for quite a while. We knew each other, and he was the first guy I met when I walked in the locker room. He was the perfect ambassador. He had Penguins blood in his veins, and he was as excited as I was that I was now a Penguin.

Training camp orientation opened with Craig Patrick addressing the team. Then he did something I thought was brilliant. He asked everyone to introduce themselves and state where they were from. A lot can be learned from a simple self-introduction. It really helped us to get to know each other. Bob Johnson started, followed by the coaching staff, the training staff, and each individual player. When it was my turn, I said, loud and proud, "Bryan Trottier, New York, hometown Val Marie, Saskatchewan."

My first roommate as a Penguin was an eighteen-year-old Jaromír Jágr. He was tall and lean and had the perfect '90s mullet. He was a shy kid with a big smile. He was trying to learn English quickly, and he learned by watching MTV and stealing lines from common songs. I checked into the hotel a few days early, and when he arrived, he only had a couple of duffle bags.

"Hello, Mr. Trottier," he said.

"Call me, Bryan," I responded.

"Okay, Big Bryan," Jaromir said. And the name stuck. He still calls me "Big Bryan," and for some reason, I like it. We remained roommates until Craig traded for Jiři Hrdina, a Czech native who could help him with his English and his adaptation to American customs and the culture. It was a brilliant move by Craig.

I was eager to see if the training camp in Pittsburgh would be any different than the ones I had attended in New York for fifteen years. It turns out that the locker room and training camp atmospheres are constant, no matter what city you're in, which made me happy. My stall was between two goaltenders, Tom Barrasso and Frank Pietrangelo. Rob Brown sat directly across from me, and man, could this kid talk. I liked him immediately. It was a typical locker room with all the jabber and teasing. *Normal*, I thought. I loved getting to know all of the young players, like Kevin Stevens, Mark Recchi, and John Cullen. It was also great getting to know the players who had been there for a while, like

Jimmy Johnson, Troy Loney, Phil Bourque, and Bob Errey. They made me feel accepted and comfortable.

And then there was Bob Johnson, who made every day a great day for hockey. "We're a great team now, but we're going to be a better team in October," he'd say. "Then we're going to be an even better team in November. And December's going to be our best month, because, come January, nobody's going to skate with us. Then in February and March, we will really be hitting our stride." The team meetings we had every day with Bob were spectacular. We would all be sitting around like little kids, listening to him.

Bob's practices were not only upbeat, but also entertaining at times, especially when Bob would narrate. Bob would say things like, "Here comes Phil Bourque . . . look at the hop in his skates, kid loves playing the game of hockey. Joey Mullen . . . look at that stickhandling. Watch that sneaky little New York shot he's got. He loves to score goals." He always had something to say about everybody.

The whole world knows how positive Bob Johnson was in life and hockey. And somehow, no matter how bad we played, he always found something positive about our game. We lost a game at home once, 8–1, a horrible loss, and we thought we were going to get our asses handed to us afterwards. We sat quietly at our stalls as Bob walked from one end of the room to the other, hands on his chin, pensive, probably trying to find the right words. "Nine goals scored tonight. Nine goals!" Then he paused. More walking. "Nine goals. And we scored the prettiest one. See you on the ice tomorrow morning. Ten-thirty. Get some oatmeal, walk the dog."

One game, we left Frank Pietrangelo out to dry, and he get shelled with more than fifty shots. After the loss, Bob's whole speech to the team was about how well Frankie had played and not how poorly we'd played in front of him. "Frankie, I just loved all of those big saves you made tonight. You made some glove saves that no one's going to make again for decades. What a game."

As Bob left the room, Frankie leaned in to me and whispered, "Holy Christ, Trots, we just got thumped out there. Does Bob know we lost the game?"

Obviously, we started the season without Mario, who was recovering from his back surgery. The young trio of Cullen, Stevens, and Recchi stepped up and provided our offensive punch. I found myself playing with Jágr quite a bit. Our left side was split between Phil Bourque, Troy Loney, or Bob Errey.

For me, it seemed like every little thing I did was appreciated. Bob, the fans, and my teammates were constantly complimenting me. At thirty-four, I found myself with renewed enthusiasm and felt rejuvenated. Any little contribution, offensively or defensively, was ridiculously magnified, but it sure added to my desire to be part of this group.

This might surprise you, but I only have a vague memory of the first time I played against my old Islander team at Nassau Coliseum. I really wasn't looking forward to it, and there wasn't a lot of attention on it until game time. When I arrived at the ol' barn, it felt weird. I had never taken the ramp into the building to play a game, and I had never dressed in the visitors' locker room. The familiar faces of the ushers and security guards were full of good wishes and smiles. They didn't treat me like an Islander; they didn't treat me like a Penguin; they treated me like Bryan.

I don't remember the warm-up; I don't remember my first shift. But I remember that the fans gave me a salute, a standing ovation. Somehow, I ended up picking up an assist early in the game. I don't even remember the play. Go figure. I didn't even finish the game, either. I blocked a shot and had to go get my foot X-rayed at the hospital. It was sore and I wanted to finish the game, but our trainer, Skip Thayer, said he needed to make sure there was no break. It was protocol. I grabbed my hockey bag, clothes, and a waiting cab and went to Winthrop Hospital in Mineola. The X-ray proved negative, so I put my clean clothes on and met the team at the airport. I knew my kids were at the game, and I didn't have a chance to see them and get some kiddy hugs. That damn homesick feeling hit me again.

Moving through this season with the Penguins, my self-esteem was higher than it had been for a while. I felt valued and my teammates were now my friends. Bob's daily dose of positivity, I'm sure, was working on everybody.

But there were still some challenging moments for our team. Injuries and a few too many losses called for roster and lineup changes. There were also some important trades. Besides Hrdina from Calgary, there was Larry Murphy, a skilled and clever defenceman, and Pete Taglianetti, a complete competitor on the ice, came in from Minnesota. I liked Pete's attitude. Then there was the blockbuster trade with Hartford that sent John Cullen, who was having a fantastic offensive season, skilled defenceman Zarley Zalapski, and Jeff Parker to the Whalers in exchange for future Hall of Famer Ron Francis, Ulf Samuelson, and Grant Jennings. It can't be easy being a general manager and trading popular teammates and fan favourites, but these trades proved to be some of Craig's finest moves ever.

In late January, more than halfway into the season, we still didn't know Mario's status until one day we received the exciting news, a mini-miracle, that he would be returning to the lineup. Down the stretch, five teams battled for four playoff spots, but over the last ten games of the season, our team hit its stride, finishing first in our division, and we were able to ride that wave of success right into the playoffs.

Leading up to the 1991 playoffs, my cranky back was acting up, so Bob was using me conservatively. He would continuously remind me, "The playoffs are coming, get ready." My thirty-four-year-old back was diagnosed with stenosis and osteoarthritis in several discs. The stenosis I'd had from birth, while the osteoarthritis was the result of the wear and tear of everyday life—oh yeah, and sixteen years of professional hockey.

Then came the playoffs, and when Bob asked me, "How are you feeling?" I told him I'd never felt stronger or better. I wasn't lying. I don't know if it was the limited ice time during the season, or the playoff adrenalin, but the more I played, the better I felt. It seemed like Bob was putting me on the ice for more defensive-zone faceoffs and last-minute situations. Ronnie Francis was one of the best faceoff guys around, so, much like my previous connection with Butch Goring on the Islanders, Ronnie and I would tag-team and divide up the draws. "I got 'em . . . you got 'em." Different team, same dynamic.

The first playoff round against New Jersey was a tough seven-game series. General manager Lou Lamoriello had assembled a strong team that included Peter Šťastný, Kirk Muller, Brendan Shanahan, and Ken Daneyko.

We split the opening two games in Pittsburgh, and did the same with Games Three and Four in Jersey. It was a seesaw battle through the first six games. Frank Pietrangelo saved it for us in Game Seven with an amazing stop on Šťastný, propelling us to a 4–0 victory to close out the series.

The Washington Capitals were a team built on speed and grit. Every game in the second round was close. We lost the first game, 4–2, and knew that we had to win Game Two or risk going into Washington in a hole it would be hard to dig out of. One of the unsung heroes on the team, Randy Gilhen, scored a huge tying goal to make the score 6–6 with about four and a half minutes left. He hopped over the boards for an extra attacker when Barrasso sprinted to the bench on a delayed penalty. When he scored that goal, his face lit up with the biggest smile. It lifted our entire team, and then Kevin Stevens scored the winner in overtime. We won the next three games to advance to the conference final against Boston.

The Bruins had a fantastic team that year, led by Ray Bourque and Cam Neely. We lost the first two games at Boston Garden, then stormed back to win the next four in a row. After the first two games, Kevin Stevens boldly predicted that we would come back and win, and he became a force they couldn't stop. Mario Lemieux scored a goal with Bourque on his back, and Tom Barrasso was stellar in net. After a seven-year absence, I found myself back in the Stanley Cup finals.

We were facing off against the Minnesota North Stars for the Stanley Cup, a team that had a really nice blend of youth, experience, and toughness: Mike Modano, Dave Gagner, Brian Bellows, Neal Broten, Mark Tinordi, and Bobby Smith were all solid. Both teams had earned their way to the finals. We anticipated their best game every game, and Bob ramped us up to bring out ours.

A standout moment in this series was Mario's signature goal. It came in Game Two, when he danced through two defencemen and went forehand, backhand, empty net for the tap-in. It was one of the most remarkable goals I'd ever witnessed. We split the first two games in Pittsburgh, and then the next two in Minnesota. Mario missed Game Three due to a flare-up to his back. It's never great news when your captain goes down, and our guys really wanted to win for him, but we came up short that game, losing, 3–1. Incredibly, Mario was back in the lineup for Game Four. Our captain inspired the team again by scoring a big goal for us in that game. Ronnie Francis, the "ol' two-niner" Phil Bourque, and I chipped in as well to win, 5–3, and send the series back to Pittsburgh all tied up at two games each.

Things went our way in Game Five. The power play—Mario, Kevin Stevens, Mark Recchi, Larry Murphy, and Paul Coffey—was red-hot that night, and we jumped to an early lead. But Minnesota wouldn't roll over. They battled back to tie the game at four, but late goals by Ronnie and Troy Loney sealed the deal and sent us back to Minnesota for Game Six with a 3–2 lead.

We were one win away from a championship, and we didn't want to give the North Stars an opportunity to gain any momentum. Just prior to puck drop, coach Bob Johnson's message to us was simple: "Win today and walk together for the rest of your life."

We took the wind out of their sails early in the first period. I won a faceoff and got the puck cleanly back to Pete Taglianetti. Tags put a perfect pass across to Ulf Samuelson, who had the room to wind up and step into a slapper that slipped by a partially screened Jon Casey.

We were up 3–0 by the end of the first period. We stayed calm during the intermission, mindful to stay disciplined and focused and stay together. We didn't want to give the North Stars any life. The message was: keep their chances minimal and take advantage of ours. By the end of the second, we had added three more goals to our lead—and we were just as calm during that intermission. Keeping our emotions in check and not getting ahead of ourselves. Giving them nothing.

In the third period, we stood our ground. Jim Paek scored early in the third and Larry Murphy scored a power-play goal late in the game to make it 8–0. Still, the clock just wasn't moving fast enough. When the final buzzer went, all mayhem broke loose.

Mario picked me up and lifted me high in the air like a five-year-old. His smile was incredible, and mine was probably just as big. That moment brought back thoughts of that phone call with Craig Patrick months earlier, when I had said, "I want to win a Stanley Cup with Mario."

There was an eight-year gap between the last Cup with the Islanders and this first one with the Penguins. And *oh*, how I wanted to experience the feeling of being a champion again. I was older, so the sense of accomplishment was more appreciated. I was ready to celebrate with my new teammates and a new city. I was going to enjoy this Cup with the Penguins. When we got back to Pittsburgh, forty thousand people met us at the airport, and I found out why they called it "the City of Champions." The fans know how to celebrate a championship!

Bill Torrey called me right after the game to congratulate me. "I couldn't be happier for you, kiddo," he said. It was great to hear from him. There was some vindication, but it was good to know that my old GM was still Bill Torrey, my friend.

I had done what I had set out to do. I believed that I could do it. I gave it my all, my best effort, just like my dad taught me all those years back. Holding the Cup and pumping it up over my head again—pure glee. I'm eight years old again. Mario is my Jean Béliveau—and there's this incredible resemblance between *"Le Gros Bill"* and *"Le Magnifique."* When my turn came to hoist the Cup, I sprinted out of the pack alone, savouring my moment. Just like Clark Gillies did in 1980. The other guys on the team looked at me and said, "Wow, you're thirty-four years old, you've won four Cups and you're acting like it's your first."

I said to them, "Yup! And ain't it awesome?"

The celebrations continued on the plane ride back. During the chaos, Craig plopped down next to me and asked, "Hey, do you want to do this again?"

"Hell yeah!" I said. "Same contract?"

We agreed to another one-year deal.

CHAPTER 20

FINDING A WAY

Upon reflection, maybe our second Stanley Cup in Pittsburgh should never have happened. You don't lose your coach the way we lost Bob Johnson and then win a championship.

In training camp before the 1991–92 season, the sledgehammer came down. *Boom.* It was horrible. One day, Bob was healthy; the next, he was in a hospital with brain cancer.

I went to Mercy Hospital to visit him. He was the same old Bob, happy and upbeat, but he was having trouble talking. The prognosis was terrible—it was terminal. There was no fix. We were going to lose the Badger, and in my mind, it wasn't fair.

Bob's condition really weighed on my mind. My thoughts were with his family, but the selfish part of me wanted my coach back. The rink became my haven where I didn't have to think about anything negative. The joy of playing hockey took me to a place where the outside world was blocked out, but only for a while. Because the dreaded day came anyway. We buried Bob.

At the funeral, I held Bob's wife Martha's hand and passed her a silver whistle. I shook hands with his sons, Mark and Peter, and offered my condolences to the rest of the family. The Johnson family is very strong and they'll be special people in my life forever.

Off the ice, the ache of losing a fallen commander kept returning. Bob's presence was enormous, and now so was the void. Even when he came to Colorado in a wheelchair and watched us play an exhibition game, I couldn't make myself say goodbye to Bob. It was too hard and too final. But I should have. And I should have thanked him for everything that he ever did for me.

Craig Patrick, always calm and always direct, gave us the news that Scotty Bowman would take the helm as head coach. Scotty had been working in player personnel for the Penguins. To me, it seemed like a pretty smart move for a whole bunch of reasons. He had an incredible coaching résumé, great experience, and was respected around the league. I had some experience with Scotty at All-Star Games and international tournaments.

Under difficult circumstances, I thought Scotty did a masterful job. In his brilliant style, he opened up by saying, "Let's do this: let's dedicate the season to Bob. Let's keep his memory strong and try to keep Bob's energy flowing." And that set the tone for the season. Scotty ended up being a pillar for us.

I can't say we played Stanley Cup–calibre hockey in the 1991–92 season, because of the distraction of losing Bob. Yet players were still doing some amazing things on the ice. Mario played only sixty-four games and still notched an incredible 131 points. Kevin Stevens had fifty-four goals that year; Joe Mullen had a forty-goal season; Paul Coffey and Larry Murphy were solid on defence, and young Jaromír Jágr was coming into his own.

The team chemistry changed when Mark Recchi and Paul Coffey, two popular Penguins, were traded. Kjell Samuelsson, Rick Tocchet, and Ken Wregget joined us in this exchange. Losing two friends was tough, but Tocchet proved his grit and hunger. Kjell, with his long reach and dependability, offered more strength on the blue line, and Kenny offered solid support behind Tom Barrasso.

Just after the trade, I asked Scotty if I could have a meeting. He said, "Absolutely." I stopped by his office and our exchange turned out to be my favourite meeting ever with a coach. I was having an okay season, but I wanted to tell him that I could do more.

"Bryan, I know what you can do. I'm going to play your legs off in the playoffs."

Scotty in private is very different from Scotty in public. Behind the bench, he's a man of few words, always deep in thought, analyzing the game. In a one-on-one situation, however, Scotty's warm and unguarded, and he smiles a lot. During our meeting, his confidence was evident. We finished the season strong and went into the playoffs on a high. The special teams were rocking. When Mario did come back, his back was so stiff and sore that he sometimes had to get his skates tied by "Seve"—Steve Latin, our equipment manager. Seve had the Civic Arena carpenters build a box for Mario to rest his skates on while Seve tied them. Mario would tell him he needed them a little looser, a little tighter. He couldn't tie them himself. And then he'd go out and score a couple of goals and ring up five points. Even with all of this, Mario was still the best player on the ice.

Mario's reserved and poised, not a rah-rah kind of guy. He inspires by his action. When he does say something, it's impactful, thoughtful. And everyone pays attention. To me, Mario is a natural-born leader. Ron Francis, our assistant captain, has similar leadership instincts. Any time Mario or Ronnie would run an idea by me, my response was always the same: "I love it!"

During the first round of the '92 playoffs, we found ourselves down three games to one against Washington. The Capitals had finished the season with eleven more points than us and were a good team that year. Mike Ridley, Dino Ciccarelli, Dale Hunter, Dave Christian, Sylvain Côté, Kevin Hatcher—solid lineup.

Ronnie and Mario approached me before our morning skate ahead of Game Five in Washington. "We've got an idea."

"Whatcha got?"

Mario said, "We should do a 1-4 on the forecheck. Sending two guys in isn't working." He was right. We were sending two guys in and getting caught—the Caps were beating us on the transition.

"Let's do it," I told them.

In the pre-game meeting, Mario was great. In his matter-of-fact style, he said to Scotty, "Maybe we should send in one fore-checker and do a 1-4."

Ronnie jumped in and explained the reasoning. And without hesitation, Scotty turned to Rick Kehoe, one of our assistant coaches. "Chico, show the boys the 1-4."

Here was one of the greatest players in the world and one of the greatest coaches in the world having an instantaneous exchange. This adjustment turned the tide for the series, and we stormed back to win in seven games.

Tom Barrasso proved to be an important part of the 1-4 system, too. We stacked the blue line and forced the other team to dump it in as much as possible. Tommy had terrific puck handling and shooting skills for a goaltender. Every time the Capitals dumped the puck in, he'd corral it and dump it right back out of the zone while their forwards were trying to forecheck. We were now catching *them* in transition. His performance was great the year before, but this playoff run, he went to another level. I always loved his demeanour and the way he prepared for a game. He was all about focus. In '91–92, Tom was a piece of plywood—it was tough to get anything past him.

I will always remember this season. There were big trades, there were all kinds of different challenges and dynamics. We didn't win the President's Trophy—we were third in our division—we had to come back from being down 3–1 to Washington, and we had a tough series against the Rangers in the division final. Our opponents in the Stanley Cup finals, the Chicago Blackhawks, came into the series red-hot, riding an eight-game playoff winning streak with Denis Savard, Bryan Marchment, Ed Belfour, Chris Chelios, Jeremy Roenick, Steve Larmer, and Michel Goulet leading the way. But we got on a roll at the right time and beat them in four straight.

We had tremendous skill and depth. We had leadership. Scotty and Craig manoeuvred us through a difficult, tough season in which we faced a whole bunch of incredible, unique challenges. And we did it. I had a sixth Stanley Cup, and I got to party again with the city of Pittsburgh.

Back-to-back championships, both won on the road. It didn't matter. Pittsburgh went crazy. There was a light rain during our celebration at Three Rivers Stadium, which postponed the festivities. Craig asked me to grab a few of the guys and run around the field with the Stanley Cup to break the lull. I enthusiastically agreed. Phil Bourque, Troy Loney, Bob Errey, and Rick Tocchet agreed to join me. I grabbed the Cup and charged down the stairs to the open infield. With the Cup high over my head, pumping it up and down like a crazy man, I looked back. Where were my buddies?

They hadn't moved a muscle. All four were standing, waving at me. "You're on your own, Trots!" they seemed to be saying. Bastards! They left me out to dry, but I didn't care. I noticed that the tarp had been laid out to cover the baseball infield, and it had a nice layer of water on it from the morning drizzle. I thought back to rain delays I'd seen when watching ball games on TV. I remembered seeing players from both teams running, sliding, on the basepaths. Fifteen, twenty-foot slides, slopping around playfully while killing time. But they weren't carrying around a forty-pound Stanley Cup.

I wondered how far I could slide on a wet tarp. I hugged the Cup tightly and dropped into a feet-first slide on my back. Shit, I went only about three feet. I got back up, thinking I could do better. *I need more speed*, I thought, and did it again. This time, I went about ten feet. The place went crazy. My Stanley Cup slide has become part of the team's lore, and is a wonderful connection that I'll always have with the City of Champions and the old Three Rivers Stadium.

When I went home for the summer, Steve Walsh, Bob Rosenthal, and Ralph Palleschi, the Islanders' new ownership group, offered me a front-office job, learning the sales and marketing aspect of the hockey business. When Craig Patrick and I discussed the possibility of taking a third run at a championship, I let him know about the offer I had in New York. I was missing my kids, who were still there, and my thirty-six-year-old body was saying, "Maybe now is the time." But in my heart, I would have liked to take a third run at that Cup.

There was a part of me that didn't want to let go. Pittsburgh wasn't saying no, but my instincts were saying my future was back on Long Island. I was going home to my family; I was going home a champion.

As painful as it had been to leave Long Island a few years earlier, I was now excited to be back. Islander fans welcomed me home as I jumped into the role of vice-president, sales and marketing. Jerry Grossman was named president of the new ownership group. He became my daily mentor, and we were instant friends.

During the 1992–93 season, I got an education on the business of hockey—advertising, sponsorship, ticket sales, suites, and game operations. I was in on every meeting, and I loved it. It was stimulating and fresh. The ownership group were successful businessmen. Along with guidance, they gave me responsibility. I got to see, participate in, and understand everything and anything that had to do with the revenue and expenses of the hockey team. Some days were overwhelming, but like I said, every day was stimulating. I never knew what was in store for me from day to day, but it was always a welcome surprise.

I was also working with two good friends, Jim Johnson and Ralph Sellitti, who were in charge of ticket sales. We were softball buddies, and friends for many years. Ticket sales were a major source of revenue for the team, so we spent a ton of time together. Jimmy and Ralph had incredible energy, and their experience was extremely valuable. It was great to work with them on a daily basis. It was fun being back with friends. Good friends and loyal employees.

The hockey team was rolling along under Al Arbour's leadership and Don Maloney's guidance as GM. But there was a part of me that hoped to be involved in the hockey side of the business. In the 1993 playoffs, my Islanders eliminated my Penguins in a seven-game series. Allegiances don't leave quickly, and I found myself cheering for both teams. When the series was over, I was happy for my Islanders, but I felt horrible for my Penguins.

As the summer approached, I got a most interesting call from Craig Patrick.

"How'd you make out this year?" he asked me. "Did you miss it?"

"Miss it? Only every day," I said. "I'm feeling really good. I've got no aches and pains. I'd really like to take another shot at playing."

We had a great chat. We talked about family, my current role with the Islanders, the Penguins' season. Then he asked me:

"Have you ever thought about coaching?"

"Not really," I told him.

"I've got an idea," Craig continued. "I'll call you back."

The phone call got my adrenalin pumping. *Holy cow! I might get back into hockey!* I might not be playing, but I'd be back in the game.

When he called back, Craig asked, "So, what do you think of, like, a player-coach? Think about it, and let's talk in a day or two."

I wasn't sure what I thought about it. I talked to my family, Mom and Dad and my kids. And then I called Bobby Clarke, who had been a player-coach in Philadelphia his final couple years, to ask him about this kind of transition. Bobby's a meat-and-potatoes guy. He's honest and he's frank. It's not that Bobby and I were best friends, but every time we talked, I knew I was going to get a straight answer, like it or not.

"Bryan, I think you're going to love it," Bobby said. "You'll play, and all of us want to play until our legs fall off. Coaching is the closest thing to playing. You'll be part of the team. You'll be in the action. Bryan, it's tough to let go as a player, but I bet you make the transition faster than you think."

I took everything he said to heart.

The next step was sitting down with the Islanders' ownership. When I explained the opportunity the Penguins were offering me, they couldn't have been more supportive. They recognized my desire to get back into the game. When Craig finally called me back, I eagerly accepted the player-coach role. Craig and I worked out the details and I signed a five-year contract.

No sooner had I signed the deal than Eddie Johnston phoned. He had replaced Scotty Bowman as the Penguins' head coach. His first words to me were "Trots, you're going to be terrific." Eddie couldn't have chosen better words to greet me.

Then he explained to me that I was going to be playing full time, so I should come to training camp in shape. "We want you working that locker room. The guys will be excited to have you back. You're the lucky charm. We won two championships with you."

From that phone call to this day, E.J. became one of my favourite people in or out of the game of hockey. He's an amazing person.

I was getting more and more excited about the season. I told the kids we'd be moving to Pittsburgh—I wasn't going to leave them behind again. Pittsburgh was to be our new home—a new address, new adventures.

Walking back into the locker room was even better than I could have imagined. Even though the players knew I had a player-coach contract, I wanted all of them to know I understood that the locker room was a sanctuary.

As the season progressed, I found myself fighting the urge to be in the coaches' room more and more. I didn't want to walk out of the locker room, go into the coaches' room, then come back to the locker room, because it felt like I was neither a coach or a player.

I played 40 games that season. What the experience taught me was that I could still play, but I couldn't stay healthy. The guys on the team were great to me. They were encouraging. "Oh, good game, Trots," they'd say even though I didn't quite feel it yet and my timing wasn't there. I kept figuring I'd get it back, but I never quite did.

I worked hard, and put in a lot of time on the ice—and a *lot* of extra time off the ice. Then I tweaked my knee, and it didn't recover all that quickly. That was a little frustrating. But it gave me time to work on some coaching stuff, like watching video with Rick Kehoe. It was a good learning experience. I learned a lot that year just being around Eddie and Rick, and it was a lot of fun.

But it got to be more fun at the end of that year. I hadn't played in a good month, and we met Washington in the playoffs again.

"You're going in the lineup tonight," Eddie told me.

I was shocked. "E.J., I haven't played for a while. But I'll give you all I got."

"You're going in, and you'll play great," he said, encouragingly.

I was excited, but I hadn't been in the room for a long time. I had to give myself a second to pump myself up. This was playoff hockey. But the guys were all pumped up about having me around.

It turned out to be an uneventful game for me. It was frustrating. I wanted to do more, but I didn't. We lost—the game and the series. It was my last NHL game ever. There was no joy in that locker room.

The next fall, there was a lockout looming, with the real possibility that, whenever we came back, it would be for a shortened season.

I skated through August of 1994 with the guys. They were always looking for extra skaters to get in shape. Somewhere in my heart, but not my brain, I realized I didn't have a step, and I didn't like it. I was having fun, I was working out, staying in shape, but in the scrimmages, I realized that nobody was hitting me—and I found myself thinking that was okay. I remember wondering what was wrong with me—I used to love the banging. Now, I wasn't first into the corners and I wasn't looking to absorb any physical punishment anymore. When you lose that reckless, fearless feeling, and you're not engaging in battle, the realization slowly sets in: *I can't make my body do this anymore.*

I kept myself busy during the eventual lockout. I went to Portland, Maine, and watched our farm team play three or four games. I could feel myself letting go of the game, letting go of the locker room.

Getting the summertime chores done at the ranch.

Mom, Dad, Monty, and Rocky skating with me for the first time in New York.

Performing at Lonestar, New York City.

The Trio Grande.

No better feeling in the world.

© B Bennett/Getty Images

Lindsy in the Cup!

Sixty-minute battle against Messier and the Oilers.

Me and *Le Gros Bill*.

Sharing another happiest moment with the city of Pittsburgh.

Me and Stanley visiting Danny Gaudet and the community of Deline, Northwest Territories, celebrating hockey's birthplace.

My brother Monty and I taking Bryan and Lindsy horseback riding.

Lindsy's always waitin' for Dad to get home.

Laughter and smiles galore when family unites.

The whole family at Brent and Tayler's wedding.

Grandpa with his California beauties.

A great honour.

I wanted to be more involved in coaching. I wanted to learn more about it. E.J. and Rick were great, and I learned a lot by watching. But I wanted to be more hands-on. There was really no transition plan—for player to end, and the coach to start, at least full-time. E.J. and I never discussed it, but with the shortened season, something inside me made me stop by Craig's office one morning.

"Craig . . . I'm not sure, but I'm pretty sure. I think I want to coach this season, and not play."

"I knew you'd be saying that," Craig said. "Let's talk with E.J. when he gets here."

Craig's a wise old owl. When E.J. arrived, we gathered, and they made my final decision very smooth. E.J. has a knack for making everything easy, no complications. He's a terrific resource, he shares everything, and he's as honest as the day is long. His hockey knowledge is vast; his knowledge in life is vaster. And he talks so fast, you're forced to listen closely.

Rick was fantastic, too. I had won two Stanley Cups with him while he was an assistant coach with the Penguins, so we shared that bond. And having played against him for ten years, I knew his intensity and now valued his expertise, too. To work with Rick on a daily basis and get to know him as a coach and a friend was a real pleasure.

When the four of us huddled—me, E.J., Rick, and Craig—there was an energy. An enjoyable energy. Craig's not the biggest talker, but he provokes good questions. I had three of the best people in hockey to talk to, listen to, and learn from.

The fire within me returned as I accepted this new role. Everyone I spoke to about this new challenge was right. I adapted to it much faster than I thought. Whether it was pre-game or post-game think tanks, my coaching education was one I couldn't have paid for.

Whether it was a Mario idea or a Ronnie Francis suggestion, nine times out of ten when I took it back to E.J., he was receptive, and usually, it worked. I was very respectful of guys like Kevin Stevens, Rick Tocchet, and all of the young leaders who were coming up through the ranks on the team. I had a reputation for being an honest and straightforward player, and I think that carried over to my new role behind the bench. I felt like I was a trusted conduit to get the right information from the players to the coaching staff. For example, Mario would give me a nod on the bench, and in a whisper, say, "Hey, I'm going to post up. I'll tip the puck left or right. We might beat the trap. Tell the wingers, tell the defence." That kind of insight from elite players is so helpful. E.J. liked it, Rick liked it, and I think it helped us adjust on the fly sometimes, to shape and reshape our game plan.

Players talk to each other on the bench all the time, stuff like "Hey, I'm open here" or "Give a shout if you're open—I didn't see you."

There's some comedy that happens on the bench at times. The forwards would get a little frustrated, and come back and yell, "Trots! Tell those fucking defencemen to wake the fuck up!" Three shifts later, the defence would come back, screaming down at me, "Trots! Tell the fucking forwards to wake the fuck up!"

"You heard 'em, boys! Wake the fuck up!" It felt like I was part of the fun action once again. The guys were looking to me to deliver the message.

The internal conflict between my heart and brain was disappearing. I was letting go.

CHAPTER 21
ALONE

Grasslands National Park is a pristine area of Saskatchewan where much of the wildlife that is endemic to the area has been restored. In the late 1970s and early 1980s, Parks Canada purchased large blocks of land from ranchers and farmers around Val Marie. Our family ranch was one of the last to go. Dad wasn't getting any younger, and his boys had all moved away. Mom was working full time at the bank in Val Marie. Change is a part of life. Running a small ranch without the lease land wasn't really feasible, so I understood Dad's decision to let it go. He sold the ranch to Parks Canada.

Mom had moved to town, and Dad was making music albums and performing. He wanted Mom to be with him while he toured, but it just wasn't realistic since she was working full time. They just sort of drifted apart. Their breakup was a little awkward for me, maybe for all of us kids. But in the end, I just wanted my parents to be happy.

Dad was off on the road, playing and singing, and neither one of them had to worry about the ranch. I figured they were settling into the next stage of their lives. Dad had made some terrific cassettes and CDs, and he truly enjoyed performing. On the road, he got to see so much of the prairie countryside that he loved so much. Dad travelled all over the western provinces, into Alberta and eventually British Columbia. He even thought he might settle in BC because the landscape was so spectacular and he had some friends who had retired out there.

During one of our phone conversations, he was explaining his future plans to me. I said, "Dad, BC's a long way from Saskatchewan and your grandkids. And think of the hills. When I get into British Columbia and deep into the mountains, I get a little claustrophobic." I thought Dad might get homesick for the open spaces of the prairies and his family.

He had toured BC and done well with his music. The weather was a whole lot warmer in Kelowna and the southern part of the province during the winter months, unlike Saskatchewan. Dad had very good instincts, and I always tried to end our conversations on a positive note. But Dad was determined and I didn't try hard to convince him otherwise.

Dad called me back in February. "The plains of Saskatchewan are calling me home." I didn't say a word.

And suddenly, in March of '95, Dad passed away. He was sixty-three. Heart failure. *Goddammit!* I was angry at God. He took my dad. *Why?*

I remember the last time we spoke, and his last words to me. It was on his birthday, February 16. We were laughing and he was happy. It was a wonderful conversation.

"Are you coming home this summer?" he asked me.

"Yeah, I'll be home."

"Well, don't take too long," he said.

It still pisses me off to think about our last conversation. It seemed a strange thing for Dad to say, but it turned out to be prophetic. Son of a bitch. He was only sixty-three. I stayed angry for a long time.

Nobody had any idea that Dad had heart problems. A few of his sisters and his younger brother had pacemakers, but there were never any signs or symptoms that he was having problems.

He drove himself to the hospital one day after lunch. "I don't feel right" is all he said to the nurse. Then . . . gone. It was so fast and sudden, it didn't seem real.

I was in Montreal with the Penguins when my sister Carol called me.

"Dad's gone," she said. "It was his heart. He had a heart attack. He's gone." She was crying.

Tears poured out of my eyes like never before. "Was he in pain?" I heard myself asking Carol. "Do you know if he had any pain?"

"No" was all she could muster.

I asked Carol for the phone number for the hospital. I called, and they told me Dad had passed out, they had resuscitated him and started talking to him, and then he passed out again. They tried everything but couldn't bring him back.

After I got the call from Carol, I phoned E.J. and told him the news. He immediately came to my hotel room. "Take all the time you need, Bryan. Rick and I will take care of the team until you get back." He sat with me for what seemed like forever, making sure I wasn't alone. E.J. just knew what I needed at that time—a friend.

My oldest daughter, Lindsy, took time from school to come home with me. I filled her full of Grandpa stories on the plane and in the car. We laughed and cried together. She didn't interrupt me once.

Dad's funeral was indeed a celebration of life. His friends and fellow musicians he had performed with through the years came to share their memories. And yes, there was music. So much music. Dad's sisters sang; his nieces and nephews sang; and, yes, even his own kids sang at their father's funeral. Our little Val Marie church was packed with people who had been touched by Dad through the years. People came to pay their respects and show their appreciation. Whenever music was needed—rodeos, weddings, holidays, any celebration—Dad was there to provide it. Music would be Dad's legacy.

He was cremated, and we spread his ashes at the ranch.

After the service, family started to leave, and Lindsy and I spent a few more days with Mom. Something inside me said, *I've got to get back to work. Lindsy's got to get back to school.* Mom understood. I told her I would be back in the summer. Hockey once again became my safe zone and would be a sanctuary away from the grief.

I went back home again in July that year, and stayed for almost a month and a half with my sister Kathy and her husband, Steve, on their farm. I took the time I needed to heal. It was great to be in Val Marie and to have friends of ours share their stories of Dad. It was cathartic.

Fatherhood has been the best thing in my life. Winning the Stanley Cup was awesome, but being a dad is way above that. There's no better reward—none. My kids are the first thing I think of when I wake up in the morning, and I look forward to being a Dad every day. There are no days off, there are no sick days. There's no financial payoff—the payment is a smile or a hug. Watching them excel in their lives, their health, their welfare. All of these things I wanted, but most of all, I wanted them to feel safe and loved.

As my first marriage ended, my children became my main focus. I needed 100 per cent access to my kids. If they called or needed help, I wanted to be right there. So I was, every day. When I took off for jobs in Portland and then Colorado, I still made it a point to stay connected.

In the spring of 1996, the Penguins were in Boston for a game near the end of the season. That's when I met Jennifer Mekovsky. She had finished up her master's degree in global communications at Emerson College and we got married in 1999, when I was coaching in Colorado. She was pregnant through our Avalanche Stanley Cup run in the spring of '01. We affectionately called it our "good luck pregnancy."

We had our son Christian in November of 2001.

The ultrasound revealed we were having a son, and I fell in love immediately. I found myself talking to him even when his mom was sleeping. I'd be talking to her belly, telling him about all the fun we'd have. I told him we'd get a boat and an RV and we'd go fishing and camping all over the country. And as promised, we did it all.

I was again in the delivery room for Christian's birth. He fit in both my hands. He opened his eyes early—slits at first, then gradually wider and wider. He was eager, taking the world in, anxious. He didn't want to miss a thing.

As he grew, Christian wanted to do everything much sooner than usual, whether it was slapping pucks before he learned how to walk or whacking a ball with a plastic baseball bat. He is a handsome boy, a quick learner, and a natural athlete. Christian was definitely the apple of his mom's eye. And for me, he was an incredible gift. I was once again the teacher, and he was my perfect little student.

There's a big age gap between Christian and his brother and sisters. He's eleven years younger than Tayler, my youngest daughter; he's nineteen years younger than my oldest daughter, Lindsy; and he's twenty-three years younger than his brother, Bryan Jr. They all love and care about each other, but I especially enjoy how protective and concerned the older kids were when Christian was young and growing up.

Because of the age gap, Christian became an uncle when he was five years old. Bryan and his wife, Joey, had their oldest child—my first grandchild—Parker. He's really grown up with his nieces and nephews, and they look up to him as much as he cares and loves them.

Of all my kids, Christian has spent the most time in Val Marie because I was able to get back home more often when he was younger.

Dad passed away in 1995, so he never got the chance to meet Christian. I know in my heart that Christian would have loved the cowboy in Dad, and Dad would have taken to Christian's great athletic ability.

Christian spent a lot of time with Mom—Grandma Mary. During our summer visits, Mom loved to spoil Christian, and he loved when she did.

Christian became a staple in my little town. Everyone knew him as Mary's grandson. He joined Grandma on her coffee visits with friends around town, enjoying treats as he listened to their stories. One year, on Canada Day, we bought him a quad so he could decorate it and ride in the parade. He ripped a donut on Main Street. He was four!

Christian walked around Val Marie as though he owned it. Mom bought him an old bike with a banana seat and he'd head down to the store, pick up a bag of groceries, and tell them to put it on his grandma's bill. Mom gave him carte blanche to buy anything he wanted. Christian would come back with the strangest combination of foods you'd ever seen—a bag of potato chips, a pint of milk, an orange, and jujubes. Grandma Mary happily paid the bill.

We'd spend a week at my sister's farm every summer, and he'd get to ride on the tractor, the combine, and his cousin Stephanie's horse, Wildflower, a beautiful sorrel mare. He loved Uncle Steve's farm and getting to spend time with his cousins.

We would also go up to Swift Current to visit my sister Carol and her family, and spend some time with Tiger if he was around.

Tiger fell in love with Christian and vice versa. Tiger's grandson Ethan is the exact same age as Christian, so we all went fishing once, up north in the Lac la Ronge area at my cousin's fishing camp. We had a blast. To this day, Christian still talks about that fishing trip. The highlight was when Tiger stripped down naked and jumped into forty-eight-degree water to push the pontoon boat off the sandbar. Christian, who was eleven at the time, turned to Ethan and said, "Your grandpa's crazy."

"I know," said Ethan.

All of my kids have embraced our family heritage. They're proud of their First Nations, Irish, and French bloodlines. They're especially aware of their First Nations roots and their natural love of sports and nature. On my visits to First Nations communities, I'm often presented with handmade rugs, jackets, and fur-lined beaded mitts. These gifts are as gorgeous as they are warm, and my kids revere them.

Growing up in Val Marie, I've shared many entertaining stories with my kids. Now, my grandchildren laugh as hard as my children did when I tell them about Grampa's childhood and all of the floating animals in Gramma's bouillon, the potatoes at every Irish meal. They also enjoy the hunting, rodeo, and ranching stories. Music continues to play a part in our lives. It's a constant and continues to get passed down to the next generation. Tayler plays piano and Bryan Jr. and Lindsy play guitar. Christian played the saxophone in his middle school band, and I know at some point he will also pick up an instrument. It's in our blood.

—

When Mom passed away in January 2011, I felt like everything crumbled beneath me. With Mom, I felt I had my one person I could always count on, come hell or high water. Now she was gone. I was alone. *How will I stand?* I lost the floor to my world.

She beat pneumonia the previous December, but I could hear in her voice how exhausted she was during that battle. I said to her, "Mom, I need you, I need you in my life," urging and encouraging her.

"How much longer do you need me in your life?" she said, weakly.

"I need twenty more years."

"Twenty more years? That's a long time. I'm tired," she whispered.

"Mom, I think you turned a corner," I said to her.

She was getting stronger, but her voice remained weak. The night before she passed, we had what turned out to be our last conversation. She was happy. She was laughing. She had been watching comedy on TV. It was so good to hear her laugh.

The next day, she was gone.

It was devastating.

Saying goodbye to Dad was tough, and I still miss him every day, but losing Mom is an ache that won't heal. And yes, we sang at Mom's funeral, too.

Winning a championship is a wonderful accomplishment. But that doesn't protect a person from something unexpected, let alone something unrecognizable. Mental health issues are a different challenge, and they can sneak up and bite us. It bit me, and I didn't even know what it was.

In training camp in September 1994, I thought I had a bad flu. I wasn't sleeping, I wasn't eating, everything tasted terrible. It was lingering, and I wasn't getting better. I went into the trainer's room, saying, "I can't shake this." And he asked what my symptoms were. I told him how I was feeling

"Take the day off and go see the doc," he said.

I called Dr. Philbin, our team internist, and gave him my symptoms, and he gave me a phone number. "Go see this guy," he said.

I went to see the specialist. He took all of my vitals and basically gave me a quick physical. Afterwards, we sat in his office. "Bryan, I think you're depressed."

Depressed? Me? Why? I have nothing to be depressed about.

"Seriously?" I said to him. "Get the hell out of here. Can I just get a shot of B_{12} or something?"

He kind of chuckled at me. "You can fight it for as long as you want, or you can find help. My suggestion is that you find help, and find help now. There are tools to help you recognize it and help you through it."

Go figure. I felt sort of stupid. Asking for help seemed silly. I felt weak and embarrassed about asking for help. Then came the lockout season, so there was no hockey being played. I met with Craig and E.J. and told them, "I've been diagnosed with clinical depression. I'm going to get some help. I might need some time—a week or two, I'm not sure." Their reaction was reassuring, and almost unexpected.

"Go. We'll see you when you get back."

I entered a facility in Upper St. Clair, Pennsylvania, called Lakewood Farms. I signed myself in and stayed ten days. The staff there helped me recognize some issues that were undermining my self-esteem. There were some really dynamic group therapy sessions where we'd share our stories and gain valuable insights. We would focus on how folks perceived us and how we saw ourselves—self-analysis; introspection. I realized my self-esteem needed a boost, and I needed to focus on taking care of myself so that I could take care of those I loved. It all made sense.

Asking for help is a strength, not a weakness. When friends, family, or neighbours asked for help, I jumped in with both feet. The staff of professionals helped me recognize my issues.

I was in transition, I guess. I had been a highly competitive professional athlete thriving on adrenalin for most of my adult life, and that period was now coming to an end. On top of that, I was trying to get on top of some business pressures that continued to weigh on my mind. Then, out of the blue, Tiger called. Then Mike and Clarkie. They all said that getting help was the wisest and most important thing I could do for myself. Even my oldest children said, "Dad, we're fine. Take care of you."

The stigma of depression is ugly. Nowadays, there is growing awareness about mental health. In sports, and society in general, there are more people sharing their stories and inspiring others to get the help that they need. My self-awareness and my journey through that dark period of my life showed me how far we've all come.

CHAPTER 22

COACHIN' 'N' LEARNIN'

Eddie Johnston was relieved of his coaching duties after the Penguins went through a bad stretch of games in March 1997. He came in early to tell Rick and me. "They're making a change. I'm not going to be coaching anymore."

As Eddie cleaned out his desk, we talked. "It's part of the game," he said. "It's nothing personal. I'm going to still stay on with the organization."

I felt horrible, and partially responsible. Why was Eddie the only one fired? Why didn't they let the rest of us go, too? I told E.J., "It reflects on all of us." I also said that if he went, then I quit.

"Oh no, don't do that," Eddie was quick to respond. "Craig's going to finish up the year. You'll enjoy working with him. You guys keep going. Hang in there. I appreciate your loyalty. Support Craig the same."

Craig Patrick went behind the bench for the rest of the season, and he was good to work with. We lost to Philadelphia in the first round of the playoffs, and as always, to exit quickly is a painful pill to swallow, whether playing or coaching. That said, hockey teaches us not to dwell on losses or disappointments, but rather, to look forward quickly.

I left for Val Marie shortly after our team wrap-up.

That summer, I was inducted into the Saskatchewan Sports Hall of Fame. It was a great celebration for our family. Mom was proud. She was asked to find artifacts from my playing career to donate to the Hall of Fame. "More people will get to enjoy it now," she said. In a way, she was creating her own son's shrine.

Before I left for the induction ceremony, I had a short meeting with Craig, asking if I could interview for the head coaching job. Even if he didn't choose me, I wanted the experience of going through a job interview. I was wrapping my head around that hope, and I made quite a few notes in preparation. Maybe I was ready for this, maybe I wasn't. Rick had more coaching experience, and I would have enjoyed being his assistant. He's a friend, he has tremendous hockey knowledge, and we had three solid years together.

During my trip to Saskatchewan, the Penguins made the announcement that they were hiring Kevin Constantine, who had been the coach of the San Jose Sharks. I knew very little about Kevin, but I knew he had a solid coaching record.

I was a little disappointed about not getting a chance to interview, but I had a great chat with Craig when I got home. "I don't need to interview you, Trots," he said, "I know your history as player and these last few years as an assistant. You're close. You'll get your shot at head coaching one day." Craig had always been a straight shooter with me, so I trusted his judgement and guidance.

My meeting with Kevin was cordial and quick. I met Craig right afterward and he asked, "How did it go with Kevin?"

"I'm not sure if it'll work. I think I'd rather go get some head coaching experience," I said. "Would it be all right if I looked around?"

"I think that's a great idea," Craig said.

I started to make a few phone calls. I was enjoying the direct contact with teams and having the sense of being responsible for my own career path. The Chesapeake Bay Icebreakers of the East Coast Hockey League gave me my first interview. The ownership flew me down, and to my surprise, they said they would present me with a contract the next day.

On the flight home, my mind raced with erratic thoughts about letting Craig and the kids know. When I landed in Pittsburgh that night, I bumped into NHL referee Paul Devorski.

"Hi, Devo," I said. "What brings you to Pittsburgh?"

He told me he had just been at an NHL event and was heading home. He asked where I was coming from. I said I was getting back from Chesapeake Bay after an interview for a head coaching position.

"I think George McPhee is looking for a coach up in Portland," Devo said. "Here's his number. Why don't you give him a call."

George had just taken over as the general manager of the Washington Capitals. Their AHL farm team were the Pirates in Portland, Maine, and the Pirates' head coach, Barry Trotz, had just been hired by the Nashville Predators.

Thanking Devo, I immediately walked to a pay phone and called George.

"This is the call I have been waiting for," George said. "Meet me in Portland tomorrow."

I flew into Portland, and George met me at the airport. We spent the day together. "I think you'll be the perfect fit," he said. He offered me the job and a two-year contract.

It's exciting to be wanted. I liked George immediately. I knew him as a player—he was tough, intense, and fearless. Upon meeting him, I found him to be pensive, poised, calm, and sincere.

I told Craig I was going to accept the Portland job, and that I hoped he understood.

He wished me luck and added, "This will be a great experience for you, and I know you'll do great." Eddie Johnston stopped by the house to wish me well. I explained to him that the role of head coach and director of operations meant I was in charge of all hockey decisions. He said, "This is exactly the kind of job you need." E.J.'s words always seemed to be exactly what I needed to hear, and at the right time.

I took off for Portland in early September 1997. I hired Jay Wells as my assistant. Jay was a great hire. He basically ran the defence. He's a tireless worker and a proud family man, and we remain friends to this day.

It felt good to have this responsibility, and I was determined not to let George down. I didn't quite have carte blanche, because we had a limited budget. Jay and I had to be very cognizant of finances, and we were. The first couple of times I wanted to make a player move, I called George to run it by him. Eventually, he said to me, "Will you stop calling me? Just get it done." I loved his trust.

I inherited a terrific mix of veterans and young players on the team. I think we made the most transactions in the history of the American Hockey League that season. George was calling our players up to the Capitals left, right, and centre, which is good, but it left us short-handed. So, in turn, we were constantly calling Hampton Roads, our ECHL affiliate, to plug the holes. John Brophy and general manager Al MacIsaac were terrific. They never let me down, supplying me with scoring or muscle. When the Capitals called up our top scorer, Andrew Brunette, I called Broph and asked if I could borrow his leading scorer, Victor Gervais. He was so good, I didn't want to send him back, but he was on a full-time ECHL contract. They sent him up for a week, and I kept him for a month. They called me every day, reminding me that he was going to have to go down eventually.

We got off to a rocky start. The ongoing call-ups and some injuries meant that we were always juggling the lineup. Coaching in the AHL was much different than the NHL. I was now developing players so that they could get to the next level. I was enjoying the opportunity to teach, push, and encourage these players, and the reward for me was to see guys like Andrew Brunette, Stew Malgunas, Steve Poapst, and Nolan Baumgartner get their chance in the big leagues.

We finished the regular season strong and won our first round in the playoffs. J.S. Giguère and the Saint John Flames finished our year off. Jay and I felt confident about the impact we had on our young players. They played their hearts out. And the city of Portland really supported us. We had great fans, and it was a wonderful place to live. I'll treasure that year always.

I still had a year left in my contract, but respectfully, I called George and asked him if it would be all right if I interviewed for NHL jobs.

"Absolutely," he said. George was supportive, but he reminded me, "I like what you're doing. I really don't want to lose you."

You can dream about playing in the NHL, scoring a goal, and winning a Stanley Cup—but you don't dare dream of making the Hall of Fame.

At Capitals training camp that fall, George McPhee, grinning from ear to ear, said, "Bryan, there's a phone call for you."

We walked into George's office and all of the hockey staff were sitting around the conference table. George asked, "Do you mind if I put this on speakerphone?"

"No," I said, still not quite sure what was going on. Everyone in the room was in on the secret, so they were smiling, too.

Then a voice came through the speaker. "Bryan, it's Scotty Morrison. You've just been unanimously selected to be inducted into the Hockey Hall of Fame." The room exploded into applause. Handshakes, congratulations, and fifteen minutes later, we're back to work evaluating players, business as usual. That's life in pro hockey. Calling home to tell Mom would have to wait.

I don't mean to backtrack, but there's a lot of excitement surrounding the Hall of Fame. Incredibly, I was being inducted with one of hockey's greatest players—my teammate from Pittsburgh, whom I won two Stanley Cups with: Mario Lemieux. The ceremony happened in November. It was two days of mayhem. Media tours, autographs, friends and family coming in from all over the place. On the morning after the event, I was having breakfast with my family, and Gordie Howe came and sat next to us, chatting away with my mom. *Who wrote this script?* I get inducted into the Hall of Fame *and* the next morning, Gordie Howe joins us for breakfast? After this mind-blowing experience, we said goodbye to Toronto and it was back to Portland, back to reality.

As my first season in Portland ended, so too did Marc Crawford's coaching tenure in Colorado. I called Pierre Lacroix, the Avalanche's general manager, who had been Mike Bossy's agent back in the good old days, and I left a message with his secretary, Charlotte Graham. I had actually met Charlotte the year before—our sons played hockey together out in Albuquerque, New Mexico, of all places, and ended up being roommates. I didn't know Charlotte was Pierre's secretary at the time, but it was interesting how that all came to be.

Pierre called me back right away. "Be on a plane tomorrow," he said with his wonderful French accent. "I have an idea." I thought, *Oh my God, this is exciting. I'm getting an opportunity to interview for a head coaching job in the NHL.*

I prepped during the entire flight to Denver, writing down thoughts and reviewing all of my notes. When I got off the plane, I walked into the men's room and got myself all dolled up in a suit and tie. With my presentation in hand, I felt ready.

I was ready for the conversation with Pierre and was feeling pretty confident.

I got deflated pretty quickly.

"You're not going to be my head coach," Pierre said. "I'm hiring Bob Hartley, but I want you to come in as assistant coach here. We're going to win the Stanley Cup."

I felt my heart sink a little bit. Pierre hit me with a hammer, and then, right behind it, he put a bunch of balloons on my butt and lifted me right back up in the air with the part about winning a Stanley Cup. Now I was intrigued.

"Meet Bob. Meet François Giguère [the Avs' assistant general manager], and Jacko [goaltending coach Jacques Cloutier]," Pierre said to me. "You already know Michel [director of player personnel Michel Goulet]. This will be a great group."

And it was. Bob was fantastic. He was engaging. We had coached against each other in the American Hockey League the previous year—he was in Hershey and I was in Portland.

Jacko's love of the game is infectious. I liked him instantly. His insights and the joy he got from coaching were evident. François was younger, yet he oozed hockey intelligence.

So there was a whole bunch of fun stuff to talk about. But I still wasn't fully sold on the idea of going back and being an assistant. I had loved being a head coach up in Portland. I loved being able to hold the reins and make all of the decisions. It was one of the most fun jobs I'd ever had.

"Sleep on it, and let me know in the morning," Pierre said to me. "I know I can convince you." I stayed at his house that night, and Pierre wouldn't let up. He was tireless and ever-positive. "Call your kids. They'll love to visit you in Denver."

I called Mike Bossy that night to get his thoughts, and he had only nice things to say about Pierre and his wife, Coco. I phoned the kids and, as usual, they were in Dad's corner.

Denver and I had history. It was the city where Dad bought me my first baseball glove when I was a small boy. I went to school in Fort Collins, and lived in Strasburg for a while when Dad was doing road construction. It felt like I was revisiting old memories, and I had a comfortable feeling there.

I woke up pretty early the next morning and went for a walk. It was a crisp, clear morning. When I got back to the house, Pierre was standing there. Before he said anything, I told him, "I'm in."

Calling George McPhee to let him know about my decision wasn't easy. As usual, George was great. He gave me his blessing and wished me luck.

Bob is very intense. He's vocal, has plenty of energy, and is demonstrative (the opposite of me). He's also honest and direct, traits that I admire about him. And French swear words have a different energy. When Bob said "*tabernac!*" on the bench, Ville Nieminen turned to me once and asked, "Trots, what does '*pappernac*' mean?"

"Nothing good, Ville," I said. "Just know Bob ain't happy right now."

I went to Colorado and settled in. We had a great group of players in Colorado: Joe Sakic, Peter Forsberg, Ray Bourque, Robbie Blake, Adam Foote, Patrick Roy. And behind them the young kids like Chris Drury, Alex Tanguay, Milan Hejduk, Martin Škoula, Steven Reinprecht, and Danny Hinote. The young guys are all big ears and big eyes, trying to absorb everything. Coaching magnifies your appreciation of players like Stéphane Yelle, Shjon Podein, and other unsung heroes.

Our first year, we picked up Theo Fleury at the trade deadline. He was a great addition to an awesome lineup. Unfortunately, we lost to the Dallas Stars in the 1999 Western Conference finals.

We came out for the 1999–2000 season ready to make our run for the championship. We moved into a beautiful new arena, the Pepsi Center, and had a great regular season, but we were again eliminated in the conference finals by Dallas—Mike Modano, Ed Belfour, Derian Hatcher, and crew.

I really enjoyed the different approaches and philosophies that Bob and Jacko and I sometimes had. We had some really good disagreements and a lot of good debates. Nobody was angry, but everybody would hold their positions really well. But we always came out of there united—we had to. Just like every dressing room, different personalities and different opinions add to the overall preparation and insight.

A coach's day can be long. We'd get to the rink at 7 a.m. and, on a game day, we'd get home at midnight—long after that if it was a road game. Somehow, we'd all be excited to get back to the rink the next day. Sleep was optional. But it helped to work with a group like this.

We were able to rise to the summit with that group of players because they were so special.

Adam Foote was a solid defensive-minded defenceman, but we wanted to try him on the power play. "I've never played on the power play," Adam said to me. "Well, you are now. We want to utilize that half-slapper of yours on the point." He was grinning from ear to ear. And Adam embraced that new role so successfully.

Getting to know the players on a personal level is a side benefit for me. Yes, Patrick Roy is a dynamic personality. He has fire, he's competitive, and has an incredible desire to win. He's also a loving father, a devoted family man, and has great respect for his teammates. He wears his heart on his sleeve, and I love him as an athlete and a person. Oh, and he's a damn good goalie, too.

I affectionally refer to Joe Sakic as "Miracle Joe." He would amaze us with low-percentage plays and create magical scoring chances. Like Bobby Orr and Mario, he could make these plays work more than anyone else. He's a very confident, disciplined man who carries himself off the ice the exact same way. He's also quick to laugh and has a great sense of humour.

Peter Forsberg never saw himself as a goal-scoring superstar, but he was as tricky as anyone I've ever seen play the game. I nicknamed him "Sneaky Pete." He laughed every time I called him that. "You've got a little Indian blood in you," I'd tease him. He played on full instinct and had a special sense about the game.

As a coach, you get to know these players as people. I've got stories about every one of them, and I've got a wonderful personal history with all of them. We shared a few defeats, but we also shared some great celebrations; including one glorious celebration in 2001.

It's also easy to find humour and joy every day. It's not just the *Xs* and *Os*, screaming and yelling. There's a lot of fun during the day, teasing and razzing with the guys, back and forth.

In 2001, we beat the defending champion New Jersey Devils in a classic seven-game final. That team had Scott Niedermayer, Scott Stevens, Martin Brodeur, Alexander Mogilny, Patrik Eliáš, Scott Gomez—*holy cow*, what a team! They had such a good mix of grit and skill.

It was great to watch Joe grab the Cup as captain and lift it over his head, and then hand it to Ray Bourque, who was winning his first Cup after twenty-two years in the league. Ray had tears streaming down his eyes. It was as emotional for me to witness as it was for everyone in hockey. I knew exactly what Ray was feeling. The long wait for Ray was over, and now we were all connected, having survived the ultimate war of attrition.

They're all warriors, to a man. I was excited for Rob Blake, winning his first Stanley Cup; for Adam Foote, winning his second; and for Patrick Roy—his third, along with his second Conn Smythe Trophy as playoff MVP. As I hugged every player, the Cup was getting passed back and forth. And then it was my turn. My first time wearing a suit and tie. I found my family in the stands in the Pepsi Center and felt my eyes tearing up. Special moments are treasured moments. As I pumped Lord Stanley as high as I could, I was hoping Mom was watching on TV.

I didn't score any goals, didn't make any passes, didn't make any big hits or block any shots. I didn't sweat and I didn't bleed. But I appreciated this Cup as much as any I had won as a player.

We spent the summer celebrating with the city of Denver. I wanted to defend and repeat with this special group, realizing that head coaching could wait.

On October 20, 2001, as the Avalanche and I started the season as defending Stanley Cup champions, I had the great honour of having my number retired by the New York Islanders. It took a few years because the team had gone through a number of ownership changes and schedules never seemed to align.

There had been some speculation in the press that I was being difficult about the effort to make this happen, but nothing could have been farther from the truth. And that must have been confusing for the fans.

It was Charles Wang, the team's current owner, and I who made it happen. He invited me to come to Long Island so that we could pick a date. We had breakfast, and his sincerity and trust were immediately evident. We became instant friends. We chose an afternoon game against the San Jose Sharks. The atmosphere was electric, and I was both humbled and stoked. My three oldest children were there to share the moment, and I had Pat and Warren Amendola, my Long Island "family," raise the banner to the rafters of the Nassau Coliseum.

It was all so perfect! My banner slid right between those belonging to Clark Gillies and Mike Bossy. The Trio Grande was reunited. I joined money goalie Billy Smith, captain Denis Potvin, and Mr. Islander, Bobby Nystrom, whose numbers were already up there. The honour that we all share, with our numbers side by side, is a tribute to our history together, our connection with the fans, and the wonderful enjoyment we all got from bringing those championships to Long Island.

Near the end of the 2001–02 season, a head coaching job opened up with the New York Rangers. I went to Pierre and told him about the opportunity, and he nudged me to put my hat in the ring. Glen Sather, the Rangers' GM, sent every candidate a questionnaire. Through the playoffs, I slaved over the questions one by one and treated each one like I was writing my thesis. Fifty-seven answers later, in written essay form, Glen called and told me he was impressed with my answers and diligence. We spoke several times by phone. When the playoffs ended for the Avalanche—a seven-game loss to Detroit in the Western Conference finals—I flew to New York to meet Glen face to face.

We talked hockey philosophies and concepts, and about our Islanders–Oilers history. I thought this would be the first of several conversations, but Glen surprised me with the nuts and bolts of a contract that was too good to refuse.

"We'll have a veteran team," Glen said. "Do you think you can handle it?"

I told him, "Give me twenty Idi Amins and a couple Al Capones and I'd find a way to win." We agreed to the terms that day.

I was excited to learn of the final lineup and free agents he had signed. We already had Ranger veterans Brian Leetch, Mike Richter, Eric Lindros, Mark Messier, and a nineteen-year-old goalie, Danny Blackburn.

I hired Terry O'Reilly and Jim Schoenfeld as my assistant coaches. And Ted Green remained from the previous year. All of my assistants had great résumés as players and were experienced coaches.

The first time we played the Islanders, the media had some fun with it, and I understood it all. I had applied for Islanders coaching jobs in the past and nothing had really materialized. For hockey fans, especially Islanders fans, the job opportunity that opened up just across the river was with one of the team's greatest rivals. Naturally, some—especially in the media—were going to look at the situation and try to stir up some controversy and headlines. As far as I was concerned, I was going where the job was.

There were players who moved between the Rangers and Islanders organizations before. I wasn't the first, and I'm certainly not going to be the last. That's just hockey—no big deal. But we won the game.

The whole experience with the Rangers was first class, even though it only lasted fifty-four games. The best memory I have of being the coach of the New York Rangers was the effort the players gave. I couldn't have asked for anything more. Owner Jim Dolan and GM Glen Sather gave me all the tools to succeed. And the fans of New York City are second to none. I got a full dose of "Blueshirt loyalty."

Everybody wants to win, and nobody wanted to win more than me. It's a little bit tough being the guy that's got to face the media after a loss and bring a good message, a positive message. But that comes with the territory.

We were seven games under .500 and a few points out of a playoff spot. I wish I had a little more time. Some of our players were out for the year, while others were coming back from injuries.

No one likes to get fired. Even the word has some sting to it. When Glen made his final decision, I felt disappointment—like I had let the players and Glen down. Maybe it's my pride, but I wanted to do something more to help. I wanted the team to succeed.

But life keeps moving, and it will move even without me. So I decided to keep moving forward, like I've always done. I've stayed hungry and I've stayed tuned in.

When I bump into the Big E today, he still calls me "Coach," and I love it. He's a first-class kid with a giant's heart. He'll always be recognized as a dominant player, and I was as proud as anyone when he was inducted to the Hall of Fame.

I moved my family back to Pittsburgh, ready and eager and hopeful about getting another crack at coaching.

Pittsburgh was an easy choice. I had a wonderful history there, it was familiar, and it had become a great place to raise my family. I stayed in touch with the league and the players, watching games; it kept my juices flowing. But my youngest, Christian, now two, was occupying the bulk of my time and my heart. I was a dad 24/7. I fell in love with that role—maybe a little too much. Then Tiger called.

CHAPTER 23

ALWAYS KEEP MOVING FORWARD

I still wanted to stay active in the game, so I threw my name out there a few times for a coaching position, but when things didn't happen right away, I didn't push too hard. I was enjoying life with Christian and sneaking in a lot of visits with my older children.

In the fall of 2003, Tiger called me.

"Are you done moping, yet?" he asked, referring to my Ranger job. "Get on a plane and meet me in Prince George." He didn't say hello, didn't ask me how I was. He just bossed me around like he always did. Here was my old buddy Tiger, dragging me into this wonderful world of the NHL Alumni.

I tried to ask him some questions about the competitive level of these old-timers' games. I told him I didn't even know if I could play and keep up.

He said, "Shut up, you're coming. Mark Napier will be calling and will give you the whole agenda. See you in Prince George."

It was like I was sixteen years old again, when Tiger drove out to the ranch through a snowstorm and hauled me back to Swift Current. This time, I was on a plane, thinking, *Dammit, Tiger, you're doing it to me again!*

On the plane ride, I was having second thoughts. I wasn't sure I'd be accepted by the guys. Who else would I know other than Tiger? I've never been so wrong in my life. Hockey players are all pretty much the same, cut from the same cloth. We all played the game. It didn't matter if you were a fourth-liner, an All-Star, or a Hall of Famer. I was part of the brotherhood that had played in the NHL.

Tiger had been involved in these games for a few years, and again, I followed him like a puppy. He got my ass going again. It revitalized me, and I believe it reminded folks that I was still alive and kicking. Before and after games, we signed autographs and mingled with the fans. They thanked us for helping raise money and how willing we were to support charity fundraisers.

And then the phone started ringing. Not for coaching jobs, but for community events, speaking engagements, and celebrity golf tournaments. The Stanley Cup of Golf and the Baycrest Hospital Hockey Tournament events were great fun for me. We raised millions of dollars, and I got to spend time with legends like Gordie Howe, Red Kelly, and Yvan Cournoyer.

Between 2003 and 2014, Tiger and I played forty to sixty games a year, travelling all across Canada, coast to coast to coast, and touching hockey fans in remote communities in the northern provinces. Michael Burgess, one of Canada's most gifted singers, who had wowed audiences in productions of *The Phantom of the Opera* and *Les Misérables*, skated with us sometimes and would perform between periods. I always went out to listen to his golden voice.

When the NHL Old-Timers were playing an exhibition game in Victoria, we had a hootenanny one night and a local band was playing country music. Tiger and Steve Shutt talked them into letting me play and sing a few Merle Haggard standards—"Mama Tried" and "Working Man Blues." I'm just an okay singer, and I'd taught myself chords on the guitar from my bass-playing days. My family band history was coming to the fore. After my renditions of those classic songs, Shutt convinced me I should do a song on the ice. Cathy Sproule, who was our event coordinator for the Old-Timers, did a terrific job of setting up the sound check in each arena. And somehow it all worked: me, a guitar, and a microphone, at centre ice, rocking Johnny Cash's "Folsom Prison Blues." The Rexall Centre, the Air Canada Centre, the Saddledome, and small venues across Canada would get the crowds clapping their hands and stomping their feet. In Verdun, Quebec, I sang a Willie Nelson classic, "On the Road Again," in French, and the place went absolutely crazy.

I was able to perform with Burgess during our alumni tours for several years, again at centre ice. He'd sing one verse of "You Are My Sunshine," with me on guitar. Then, on the next verse and chorus, I would join him with the harmony. Mom heard us in Saskatoon, and my sister said she cried. I asked Mom afterward, "How was it?"

"It was beautiful," she replied. "And Michael's a pretty good singer, too." You've gotta love your mom!

I'm very proud of my hockey family and how we represent ourselves as ambassadors of this great game. Tiger was a leader, a respected voice. The way he conducted himself was how I conducted myself—proudly.

He made playing again remarkably fun. We either played on a line together or we were defence partners. The calibre of hockey of the teams we played against was top-notch. Local police, RCMP, emergency service workers, and firemen usually made up our competition. All had played some junior hockey or at a semi-pro level. The revenues generated usually went to a national charity, such as the United Way, but it was ultra-rewarding when the money stayed in the community to benefit local arenas or minor hockey organizations.

I was forty-seven years old and my juices were flowing like a teenager. We played twelve games in twelve different cities in fourteen nights. We bused, we flew, and, amazingly, went 12–0. Our NHLers just knew how to move the ol' biscuit around.

And then the First Nations called. Throughout my career, I had always made myself available to speak to Native students, whether it was at inner-city schools or communities near NHL cities. Now I was going to the western Arctic, visiting communities in the Mackenzie Delta, and along the Beaufort Sea. We would get to do some amazing things with our hosts, like tracking a herd of dall sheep in a helicopter or participating in a traditional muskox hunt, which was one of my most precious memories. Our guide skinned and quartered the carcass in fifteen minutes in minus-forty-degree weather—no gloves, just the heat of the animal keeping his hands warm. The meat was prepared for a community feast that evening in Paulatuk. The muskox stew was delicious and fed over six hundred people. Our guide was presented with the muskox hide in a powerful ceremony. A spiritual appreciation of nature, animal, and community.

Storytelling is very natural in First Nations culture, and I love stories. I try to be a good storyteller. I share my story: my life path, my decisions (some good, some not so good), my rewards and achievements, and, most importantly, my dream: my dream of playing hockey at the highest level in the world, the NHL, playing against the very best of the best, and achieving my dream of winning a Stanley Cup.

So I went on the road, and every community I visited was more welcoming than the last. The hospitality was genuine and the humour and laughter were ever-present. The phone kept ringing and I kept visiting. It was rewarding, enriching, and exhausting work. I was reconnecting with my First Nations people, my heritage.

During one of the feasts in the great white north, a local sat down next to me to share his love of hockey. During the discussion, he proudly stated, "Do you realize you are the most decorated Indigenous athlete in the world?" He listed all of my awards, achievements, championships, and halls of fame. Hockey players tend to be a little humble, so I graciously said, "Thanks, but can I steal this line?"

We're one nation/one blood, and First Nations are such an important part of everything that is going on in Canadian life today. When I'm in the North, the Native communities want me to experience their local culture and customs. It's mind-blowing.

In Inuvik, I visited a student centre, and it was mayhem. There were kids everywhere, but the centre was really short on supplies. There was a pool table with no cues, a Ping-Pong table with no ball and a couple of broken computers. There were also a few musical instruments. So I grabbed a guitar and started to tune it. The kids gathered and asked me to sing them a song. I could tell they were shy—they wouldn't make eye contact. I looked at everyone and asked, "Do you know 'Country Roads'?" Slowly, one by one, they joined me. They all started singing, smiles everywhere. Mine was the biggest. One little boy, maybe six, walked up and sat next to me. He pressed the side of his face and ear against the guitar while I was playing. An older girl, probably his sister, came up and pulled him back and sat him on the floor with everyone else.

I asked her, "Does he always do that?"

"He's deaf," she explained. "He just likes to feel the music." Hockey is for everyone. So too is music.

Invitations to First Nations communities have increased over the last decade. As the number of Indigenous players in the NHL has increased, it has also meant that there are also more who are former players, too. Pioneers Fred Sasakamoose and Jim Neilson, who aren't with us anymore, were groundbreakers, and we've honoured their memory by forming an Indigenous alumni hockey team. John Chabot is our coordinator, and our team includes fan favourites Gino Odjick, Arron Asham, and the "Riverton Rifle," Reggie Leach. Our Indigenous team also invites a *mooneeow*, Cree for "white man," to join us. Former players who have joined us have included Ric Nattress, Chris Nilan, and the late Bob Probert. Our message to the children is always the same: be proud of your blood, embrace your talents, continue your education, and make choices that are going to help you to achieve your dream. We all have a dream.

The Indigenous alumni team has been together for a decade. We've been through Yellowknife and communities of the Great Bear Lake, as far north as Old Crow, and as far east as Labrador and the Maritimes.

Life isn't always fair, and it is never anyone's fault. It's just life. My second marriage ended in 2018, and I found myself at home with a seventeen-year-old twelfth-grader and a ding-dong dog named Rowdy. "The Three Musketeers" pushed forward. Christian graduated with honours and chose West Virginia University as his college. He's a solid student and athlete, just like his brother and sisters, and will do fine in any profession he chooses. Christian has his eye on Air Force ROTC, when things open up after COVID. His generation is resilient. Christian started college during this "dampanic" and is in Morgantown, West Virginia, which is forty miles from home.

I'm living in Pittsburgh. Christian being close is good for me . . . and maybe a little bad for him, because he's going to be opening his college apartment door and saying, "Jesus Christ, Dad, *you* again?"

Our kids watch us as parents. I can't thank my parents enough for being such terrific role models. I might not have listened to everything they said, but I watched and learned from them. Their examples of hard work and dedication—from sun-up to sunset—without a doubt, reflects on my career as a hard-working and dedicated athlete. But it also goes deeper—to my grandparents, my aunts, my uncles, my cousins, my teammates. These are the people who helped me to achieve the kind of success I had in the NHL. Eighteen years as a player, another ten as a coach. And only seven Stanley Cups—twenty-one losing seasons. Still, it's one hell of a ratio.

I'm very proud of my accomplishments as a hockey player. But I'm equally proud of my heritage, my children, and where I come from. I'm proudly Canadian and truly North American.

I'm sixty-six years old now. Two of my children are now parents, and they're terrific parents. Bryan Jr. and his wife, Joey, have four children; my daughter Lindsy and her husband, Zack, have four beautiful daughters. And Tayler and her husband, Brent, were newlyweds in 2019. No pressure, but I bet they'll be starting a family soon.

Christian will be graduating college in a couple years. Then he'll be starting his life. I'm pretty sure there are more grandchildren coming. I giggled when Bryan Jr. was going to become a dad. "This is going to be interesting," I thought to myself. *Bang.* He's terrific. I still remember when my son, the oncologist, paid me the highest compliment as he said, "I want to be a dad just like you." *Gulp*. And when Lindsy became a mother, she added that she'd learned how to be a parent just by watching me.

I think we all want our children to be healthy, happy, and educated. I see mine as wise, confident, and ambitious. A prouder father there could never be.

As proud as I am, it is difficult. I want all of my kids to be closer to me. But they're thriving and building their own lives. My home is quiet now with Christian away at school. Rowdy sleeps most of the day. He's eleven . . . that's seventy-seven in dog years!

I'm not as homesick these days, but I do miss Mom and Dad. I honour them by living life to the fullest every day. I have their memories, my Val Marie Canadian roots, and the importance of hard work, strength, and family. I also have their lessons. Mom's "treat people the way you want to be treated" and "you can only make a first impression once." Dad's "firm handshake and look them in the eye" and "*A* for effort is the most important grade on your report card." "Don't do it to get it done, do it to get it done right." I'm mindful, and I love to share these words of wisdom.

Home is in your heart. I hope my children feel the same as I do, and that they carry me in their hearts. They can always look to me as a foundation. Home was where I always felt safe, secure, and loved. And like those all-important words my parents said to me, "You can always come home."

DAVE "TIGER" WILLIAMS

Blood brothers. That's what Bryan Trottier and I are. I am most fortunate and blessed to have been able to call him my friend for fifty years, and I thank him for that.

Everyone knows Bryan Trottier is one of the greatest hockey players who ever played. In my estimation, Bryan is the best hockey player to hail from Saskatchewan. Nobody can take anything away from Gordie Howe, but Bryan Trottier has seven Stanley Cups.

It is one thing to be a tremendous hockey player, but that is just the tip of the iceberg when describing Bryan. He's even a better person than he is a hockey player. The great influence he had on me, and I believe on everyone else around him, is incalculable.

As a sixteen-year-old, he was always smiling, he was always happy. Everything was just a bowl of laughs to him—till the game started, and then that little grin went away and it was all about winning.

And so tough. Not the "drag 'em down and beat 'em up" tough, but guys could hit him, run him down, and like a genie in a bottle, he was so quick to get back up and skating, you didn't realize he'd been down. And then he just kept on going. He was very sturdy on his feet; his balance was incredible. When he hit you, it hurt because of his low centre of gravity and his great skating ability. He was like a modern-day fast tank.

As a young player, he got sick of the rough-and-tumble and being a marked man. He quit and went home at one point. When he left, I was horrified. It would have been such a waste. I went to his home at the ranch and brought him back. I told him not to worry about those guys coming at him; I would take care of him and he could play the game.

I would never have made it to the NHL without him. He's just that good. He was so good at the game that he made you look better, and play better, too. He took a lot of players with him on the way to the big league. He dragged us lesser beings along behind him. Without Bryan, I would not have been drafted. I would not have had the career I had, or the life I have now.

Bryan is always kind, and always treats everyone with respect. I mean everyone. When he talks to you, you feel like you are the only person who matters in that moment. Young or old, weak or strong, plain or beautiful; you all get nothing but respect and kindness from Bryan.

He was so very shy as a sixteen-year-old. This is one thing that changed in him as the years went on; the shyness went away and his kindness, respect, and genuine interest and concern for people could shine through more brightly.

Many former players travel to the big communities for various appearances. Bryan does, too, but has spent more time travelling to—I swear—every northern community up to the Arctic Circle and back to help people in those communities. The time and effort to do this is hard to imagine, but I know he loves every minute of it. He has been, and continues to be, a great ambassador for the NHL, and for all players, and does so with integrity and class.

Back in my days in the NHL, the other team was your enemy and the opposing players were, too. You didn't hang out with them before or after the game, but I broke that rule with Bryan. I would sneak out after a game and meet him and catch up a bit. That was Bryan's and my little secret for the next twenty-five years.

I wish we lived closer to each other. I wish we could see each other more often than we do. When we do get together, it is always fun. Bryan is a very accomplished guitar player and has a wonderful singing voice. His guitar is as fine-tuned as his hockey skills and the way he conducts himself in every aspect of his life. I have spent many happy hours listening to him sing and play, and it was so special to hear him play and sing with his brothers, sisters, and dad.

Bryan once said to me that every time he is going through a low in his life, I seem to call. I feel that with him, too. In his own quiet way, Brian has always been there for me. So carry on, Bryan, my blood brother, my friend. The best may be yet to come!

Tiger Williams

LINDSY CHARLIE RUTHVEN

Everyone grows up thinking their father is a superhero, right? He's a pillar of strength, security, and happiness. In the case of me and my siblings, it's actually true. Our dad was a titan on the ice. His career is laden with individual achievements and incredible victories. Now imagine witnessing many of those events firsthand as a curly headed kid. Queen's hit song "We Are the Champions" floods the chilly arena but you can barely hear it over the thousands of fans celebrating. They are screaming your father's name and banging the glass while he raises the prized Stanley Cup over his head and skates full speed around the rink, hair blowing in the wind, megawatt smile blazing. He thanks the city for the opportunity to play for them, for believing in him, for making him a champion.

People often ask me what it's like to grow up with a famous athlete as a father. It's all I've ever known so I can't offer any comparison. But I'll give it a go here and tell you a bit more about my father, Bryan Trottier, as a dad.

Simply put, he's the best. He's playful, smart, encouraging, hilarious, humble, strong, and always available to help solve a problem. He makes it so easy to be proud of him because of the way he handles himself and the way he treats others. Currently, one of Dad's former teammates is struggling with his health. Dad is lending his strength to the family, spending hours on the phone, telling funny old hockey stories to brighten their days. He's so good.

I have three siblings: Bryan, Tayler, and Christian. Our dad loves us. He tells us. He shows us. We know it in our bones. As kids, we'd find Dad in the kitchen cooking our breakfasts, at our events cheering the loudest, or in the laundry room folding our clothes. Many nights, I'd seek him out to give him a goodnight hug or invite him to play a few games of cribbage. He'd always drop whatever he was doing to hear anything on my mind while we played a few hands. He cheered the good stuff and offered solutions for the bad. He always assured me, "We'll figure it out," and most of the time we did. It's funny how your parents' words come out of your mouth when speaking to your own children. Recently, my daughter swore up and down that her orchestra piece was impossible to learn. "We'll figure it out," I promised her, and when the time came, she performed it perfectly. I wanted to help ease her tension and show her I was in her corner like Dad did countless times for us.

Sometimes, road trips meant missed birthday parties, or playoff games conflicted with school performances. Sometimes Dad's career forced him to relocate and live separately from us for multiple months on end. But he still showed up for us when we needed him. One of Christian's favorite "Dad stories" is how Dad taught himself calculus while coaching the Sabres in Buffalo. Christian was struggling with his math assignments back home in Pittsburgh, and he called Dad, frustrated, worried he might fail. Dad left school in tenth grade to play pro hockey, but that didn't stop him from grabbing a textbook and calling Christian every night to help work out equations. He even roped in his Russian goaltending coach, Artūrs Irbe, to help tutor them. Most times, Christian came up with the answer on his own. But it helped to have Dad on the phone talking to him, encouraging him, offering suggestions and when the report card came, "they" earned an *A*.

Dad has infinite patience for us, even during our teenage years. One time, my brother yelled that he had a million things to do and no time to get it all done. Dad calmly replied that he should just do one thing so he'd only have 999,999 things left. It didn't go over well at the time, but it's true. I believe all of us remember that lesson, and smile when we start to feel overwhelmed.

Despite the tough-guy-hockey-persona, our dad is an attentive nurturer dedicated to putting his kids first. He fixes projects in our homes, changes our babies' diapers, constructs gingerbread houses, gives piggyback rides, and nurses our wounds. When my older brother Bryan had knee surgery as a kid, Dad carried him around the house for months. He'd plop him on the couch in front of his favorite TV show, bring him to the kitchen table for his favorite meals then carry him upstairs to play Nintendo. He even toted him back and forth to the bathroom, making colorful jokes both ways. When my younger brother Christian suffered a bad concussion, Dad lowered all the lights in our house so they didn't hurt Christian's eyes. Dad placed cool washcloths on his head and requested extensions on Christian's school assignments so he could rest. When a dog bit my cheek an hour away from home, Dad heard my cries for him in the background of the call. Less than 30 minutes later, he scooped me up in his strong embrace and I knew I'd be okay. The doctors weren't able to put me under for fear I'd move during the operating procedure, so Dad held my hand for every stitch and distracted me from the moving needles with his funniest material. "Look at me," he'd say. "Did I ever tell you about the time on the ranch . . ."

Our welfare always beat out Dad's concern for local speed limits. One time, when my sister was about two, we were all playing in the basement when she took a header onto the concrete floor. The *thunk* was mighty loud. Dad immediately grabbed the keys to his sports car and drove like a demon to the emergency room. As Dad lifted Tayler out of the back seat and gently tucked her blanket around her, murmuring comforting words, a hospital employee jogged up. He told Dad he couldn't park there. Without hesitation, Dad tossed the random stranger his keys and told him to move it or keep it but his little girl needed a doctor right away. Tayler was perfectly fine, thank goodness, and the car stayed right where he left it. Still, Dad was a hero in my eyes that day, proving nothing was more important than his kids.

He's been heroic many days, in many ways. In 2016, I flew with my two young daughters to chilly Toronto to celebrate Dad's induction to the Canadian Athletes Hall of Fame. I planned to grab a cab at the airport and meet my family at the hotel. Well, guess who was waiting for us at baggage claim with open arms and a warm pickup truck? That's right—the man of the hour. Dad flung our bags over his shoulder and tickled my kids, kissing their ears, making them squeal with delight. I asked him if there was somewhere he needed to be the day before his big event. He replied, "Yes. Right here with my girls."

Dad always makes everything more fun. Whether it's playing card games like Old Maid, or making us kids chase him around in a game of tag, or playing ball in the backyard, he always makes sure we have a good time. Dad is a good-natured tease with a great sense of humor. When he brought us kids in the players' locker room, he'd suggest we tie Pat Lafontaine's skates together or help hide Paul Coffey's glove. The small nuisance for a teammate got big laughs from us. Now, it's the grandkids that get the benefits—no one makes the grandkids laugh like Grandpa.

—

In a way, hockey is the family business. Both of my uncles played in the NHL. Both of my brothers played collegiate. My nephews are lighting up youth hockey in Minnesota, destined for greatness. Dad has taught thousands of hockey camps across North America, usually with a son, nephew, or brother in tow. For many summers, Dad ran a hockey camp in Lake Tahoe, which is absolutely gorgeous. The guys did all the hockey-related things, while Tayler and I mostly tagged along just for the fun. One of my best memories involves an invite by a Squaw Valley employee to climb on the roof of the gondola at night to admire the view. Dad firmly declined. He doesn't like heights. But I scampered up the ladder and out the hatch so fast all Dad could do was hold on to my pant leg to make sure I didn't fall. It was incredible! It's also indicative of Dad as a parent. Despite his discomfort, he didn't hold me back, but he also didn't let go of my ankle.

If hockey is our family's business, then music is its heartbeat. As anyone who's attended *Hockey Night in Canada* will tell you, Dad is a terrific musician. He inherited his talents from his dad, my grandpa, Buzz Trottier. Buzz had a song he performed with each of his five kids. It was their special duet. He cut a record of "Rose Colored Glasses" with my Aunt Kathy who performs with her own family band today. We have extremely talented cousins in Canada, Nashville, and Indianapolis. My cousin Jordy's band, The Midwest Originals, is nothing short of fantastic. At any family get together, you can expect to find the whole Trottier Tribe strumming an instrument, singing their hearts out, or just clapping along. My kids love singing, "You are my Sunshine" with Grandpa every time he visits.

Dad brought his guitar to my wedding rehearsal dinner in Florida. After delighting the room with a few of his best numbers, he convinced me to come up and sing our favorite duet

"Little Girl Awaiting" for the 70+ guests. I was dying but as soon as he started strumming, it was just the two of us singing and I was six years old again. Everyone loved it and guests still bring it up today. It's arguably one of my favorite memories. But it pales in comparison to what Dad had in store for my sister's wedding reception.

Tayler knew he had a surprise, which if you know my dad, could be anything. As he walked up on stage and began his introduction, my gorgeous bride-of-a-sister sat up a little straighter, bracing herself. Dad has been singing nonsensical numbers all our lives. But that evening, he unveiled a brand new original song called, "Save a Little Room in Your Daddy's Heart." He spent months writing it, tweaking it, making it just perfect. It's a brilliant tribute from an adoring father to his grown-up little girl. Almost everyone in the room was crying, including the groom.

Dad is a poet. He pours his heart into every birthday card or Christmas letter. He even wrote the sweetest, sometimes silliest, messages on my brown paper lunch bags when he was home to pack them. One day, I was especially tickled by his note so I tore it off and kept it. I did that the next day and the next. Then I started gluing them to empty pages in a notebook so they wouldn't get lost. By my senior year, the notebook was full and I can now flip through a whole collection of handwritten love messages from my dad.

Our dad taught us all to love hard, enjoy life, pursue our passions, and give our best in all situations. It's not about the grade or the score, but knowing that we put forth our best effort. That's all he asks.

I enjoyed the rare privilege of sitting in the Stanley Cup as a baby, posing awkwardly next to it as an adolescent, and later holding it high as an adult. It's a testament to my dad's talents and long success in the game. He was an amazing hockey player, but truly an even better father. I am so incredibly honoured to have the chance here to share a bit of our dad with the world. I couldn't be prouder of the man my father is nor could I love him more.

Lindsy Charlie Ruthven

ACKNOWLEDGEMENTS

My family has always been my foundation. Everything starts with Mom and Dad. They instilled in me a work ethic, family values, and the importance of living each day to the fullest. Rest high!

My kids, Bryan Jr., Lindsy, Tayler, and Christian, continue to motivate me and instill a pride that every father should feel. Your spouses—Joey, Zack, and Brent, and my grandchildren—Parker, Elliott, Mattie, Rory, Jordan, Harper, Brynn, and Perry—have all added a unique richness that magnifies the love we all share.

My brothers and sisters, who know all the good and the bad and love me anyway. Thank you, Carol, Kathy, Monty, and Rocky. You guys were all horrible goalies, but terrific allies and we continue to rally and stand strong together. I love and thank your families, Dick, Jonathan, Chelsey, Steve, Kevin, Maureen, Sam, Sophie, Kelly, Richa, and Aria. Jesse, Sam, Max, Stephanie, Aaron, Matt, Mia, Terry, Ryley, Jordy, Adrienne, and Dallas.

Thanks to all the Trottier, Gardner, de Montigny, Wirtzberger, Grunderud, Bellefeuille, Ecklund, Curley, and Kuntz families, and all of the aunts, uncles, and cousins that I'm proud to call family. We can be a bunch of renegades at times, but I wouldn't trade a one of ya!

My hometown of Val Marie will always have a special place in my heart because the people there are my roots, my beginnings, and my longest friendships. Mom's hometown of Climax shares this space, too. I was lucky to feel at home in both places.

Thanks to my earliest minor hockey teammates and my best friends—Bernie Syrenne, Claude Jeanson, Will Desjardins, Mike Kirk, Leslie Mything, Grant Goodall, and Kim Laidlaw. You guys laid the groundwork.

Thank you to Swift Current for providing a huge stepping-stone through my Legionnaires and Broncos days.

I am grateful to everything that Earl Ingarfield and Gary Kirk did for me, and to the incredible fans in Lethbridge who cheered me on, despite me making a bunch of mistakes.

I want to thank the NHL, especially the New York Islanders, the Pittsburgh Penguins, the Colorado Avalanche, and the New York Rangers, for allowing me to chase my dreams and provide a magnificent life for my family by playing and coaching the game I love. Thanks to all of my teammates and to the fans of Long Island, Pittsburgh, Denver, and Manhattan. We had some fun, didn't we?

Thank you to Bill Torrey, Al Arbour, Ed Westfall, Mario Lemieux, Craig Patrick, Bob Johnson, Scotty Bowman, Eddie Johnston, Rick Kehoe, Pierre Lacroix and his wife, Coco, Charlotte Graham, Bob Hartley, Jacques Cloutier, Paul Fixter, George McPhee, Dave Fisher, Glen Sather, Chuck Dolan, Ted Nolan, and Artūrs Irbe.

To my Aboriginal Alumnae teammates and our NHL Alumnae Oldtimers, thank you for the incredible barnstorming years throughout North America.

To Dave "Tiger" Williams. I now know what having a big brother means. You've made every day of our friendship spectacular. You and Brenda will always be two of my favourite people.

I lost my two Trio Grande linemates prior to this book being published. To Mike Bossy and Clark Gillies, I couldn't have asked for two better people to share that success with. I want to thank them both for being such gigantic parts of Islander magic and hockey history. I'll always treasure their friendship. I miss and love you both.

Big shout out to Waxy Gregoire for getting the ball rolling and convincing me that there was a story to be told, and Dave Bidini for introducing me to the folks that made it all happen.

And finally, I'd like to thank my team at McClelland & Stewart: Stephen Brunt, Joe Lee, and Scott Sellers. You were exceptional and patient with this rookie writer.

© Jen Worley Photography

In 2017 **BRYAN TROTTIER** was voted one of the "100 Greatest NHL Players" in history. He was born in Val Marie, Saskatchewan, and went on to win seven Stanley Cups (four with the New York Islanders, two with the Pittsburgh Penguins, and one as an assistant coach with the Colorado Avalanche). He lives in Pittsburgh, Pennsylvania.

STEPHEN BRUNT is an award-winning writer and broadcaster for Sportsnet, and the co-host of *The FAN Drive Time* with Ben Ennis on Fan 590. He is the author of national bestsellers *Burke's Law* with Brian Burke, *Gretzky's Tears*, *Searching for Bobby Orr*, and *All the Way* with Jordin Tootoo. He lives in Hamilton, Ontario, and in Winterhouse Brook, Newfoundland.

A NOTE ABOUT THE TYPE

All Roads Home is set in Monotype Dante, a modern font family designed by Giovanni Mardersteig in the late 1940s. Based on the classic book faces of Bembo and Centaur, Dante features an italic, which harmonizes extremely well with its roman partner. The digital version of Dante was issued in 1993, in three weights and including a set of titling capitals.